Dear Reader:

The book you are about to read is the latest bestseller from the St. Martin's True Crime Library, the imprint *The New York Times* calls "the leader in true crime!" Each month, we offer you a fascinating account of the latest, most sensational crime that has captured the national attention. St. Martin's is the publisher of bestselling true crime author and crime journalist Kieran Crowley, who explores the dark, deadly links between a prominent Manhattan surgeon and the disappearance of his wife fifteen years earlier in THE SURGEON'S WIFE. Suzy Spencer's BREAKING POINT guides readers through the tortuous twists and turns in the case of Andrea Yates, the Houston mother who drowned her five young children in the family's bathtub. In Edgar Award-nominated DARK DREAMS, legendary FBI profiler Roy Hazelwood and bestselling crime author Stephen G. Michaud shine light on the inner workings of America's most violent and depraved murderers. In the book you now hold, NEVER LEAVE ME, veteran true crime author John Glatt follows the shocking story of a successful man who murdered his wife in a passionate fit of jealousy after she returned home from being with another man.

St. Martin's True Crime Library gives you the stories behind the headlines. Our authors take you right to the scene of the crime and into the minds of the most notorious murderers to show you what really makes them tick. St. Martin's True Crime Library paperbacks are better than the most terrifying thriller, because it's all true! The next time you want a crackling good read, make sure it's got the St. Martin's True Crime Library logo on the spine—you'll be up all night!

Charles E. Spicer, Jr.
Executive Editor, St. Martin's True Crime Library

St. Martin's True Crime Library Titles
by John Glatt

Playing with Fire

Secrets in the Cellar

Internet Slave Master

The Royal House of Monaco

To Have and To Kill

Forgive Me, Father

The Doctor's Wife

One Deadly Night

Depraved

Cries in the Desert

For I Have Sinned

Evil Twins

Cradle of Death

Blind Passion

Deadly American Beauty

Never Leave Me

Twisted

Available from St. Martin's True Crime Library

NEVER LEAVE ME

AN OBSESSIVE HUSBAND,

AN UNFAITHFUL WIFE,

A BRUTAL MURDER

JOHN GLATT

St. Martin's Paperbacks

NEVER LEAVE ME

Cover photo of house courtesy New Jersey State Police
Photo of Jonathan and Michelle Nyce courtesy Larisa Soos

For information address St. Martin's Press. 175 Fifth Avenue. New York, NY 10010.

ISBN: 978-1-250-09293-9
EAN: 80312-93427-9

St. Martin's Paperbacks edition / June 2006

St. Martin's Paperbacks are published by St. Martin's Press. 175 Fifth Avenue. New York, NY 10010.

P1

To William Szigeti (Uncle Bill)
"A Lord Among Men"

CONTENTS

Contents

ACKNOWLEDGMENTS

This is the tenth true crime book I have written and perhaps the most challenging yet. After almost two years of work and nearly fifty interviews, I hope I can shed some light on the strange case of Dr. Jonathan Nyce.

Before his downfall, Dr. Nyce was a world renowned scientist whose revolutionary asthma drug was lauded by the prestigious *Nature* magazine and *Newsweek* as a landmark medical discovery. On a wild ride in the get-rich 1990s, he founded a multi-million-dollar company to develop his drug, making millions and living the pampered life of an international jet-setter.

But he and his beautiful young Filipino-born wife, Michelle, the mother of his three children, had a terrible secret, which they carefully hid from everybody. And after 9/11 when the biotech bubble burst, Dr. Nyce was forced out of his company and his life started coming apart at the seams.

Always possessive of Michelle, he now became jealous, furious if she ever talked to other men. But ultimately his jealousy turned out to be well-founded when she started a long-term affair with their gardener. And after several un-successful attempts to break-up the passionate affair, Dr. Nyce finally resorted to murder, after Michelle returned home from a date with her lover on a freezing January night.

It is a tragic story but the real victims are the three Nyce children, Alex, Trevor and Samantha, who have lost their mother forever, as well as their father, who is now serving an eight-year jail term for causing Michelle's death.

A trust fund has been set up for the children's future edu-cation, and if any readers wish to contribute they can make checks payable to Nyce Children Educational Trust, A/C #2000009726, Hopewell Valley Community Bank, P.O. Box 999, Pennington, NJ 08534.

First I would like to thank Michelle's family, Teodoro Riviera and Melodia Ragenil, for their generous help. They expressly wanted the world know what a wonderful mother, sister and daughter Michelle was, as unfortunately her true qualities were never allowed to emerge during the trial.

I would also like to thank Dr. Jonathan Nyce and his par-ents, for cooperating with my book, by giving me their points of view. Straight after his sentencing, I sat down with Jonathan Nyce for a tough interview about his life, career and his late wife, Michelle, leaving me no doubt that he still loves her in his own way.

I also met his parents Jonathan Jr. and Emma Nyce at their home in Collegeville, PA, in the house where Jonathan and his three brothers grew up. I know how difficult an or-deal it has been for them, from seeing them attend every day of their son's trial, and my heart goes out to them.

Much gratitude is also owed to Michelle's best friend, Larissa Soos, for her help from the very beginning. Through hours of interviews over many months, she patiently shared her priceless memories of Michelle with me, still trying to understand how it all could have happened.

This book would not have been possible without the in-valuable help of the case's lead Detective Daniel McKeown, of the Hopewell Township Police Department and his sister, Sgt. Karen Ortman of the Mercer County Prosecutor's Office. Detective McKeown helped me piece together the investigator's theory of what happened on that fateful night.

Likewise I am also in debt to Dr. Nyce's tenacious defense attorney Robin Lord and her partner Pat Whelan for their generous help, and for arranging my interview with their client.

On the other side of the courtroom, much gratitude is due to Mercer County Prosecutor Joseph Boccini and his excellent team of Doris Galuchie and Tom Meidt. And I also thank Judge Mathesius for granting me an interview in his chambers after the verdict, where he illuminated certain key decisions he made over the course of the trial.

Extra special thanks must also go to the fabulous team of reporters who covered the trial, and for their generous help. The *Times* of Trenton's Lisa Coryell did a superb job covering the trial, consistently demonstrating all the qualities of a truly great reporter. And also thanks to Scott Frost of the *Trentonian*, also a great newshound, writer and all-around good guy, with whom I shared many lunches with over the course of the trial. Thanks also to *The New York Times'* New Jersey reporter Jonathan Miller, who generously provided many leads for me to follow up, as did John Tredea of the *Hopewell Valley News*, who first took me to Jacobs Creek Road in January 2004.

There are so many others due credit; many who wished to remain anonymous for various reasons. I would like to extend my thanks to: Rajni Ajmera, Kuny Brothers, Sandy Chakavarthi, Chief Michael Chipowski, Roz Clancy, Casey DeBlasio, Tracy Evans, Paul Everton, Barbara Fox of *U.S.1* Newspaper, Eugene Hallman, Samuel Hamme, Beth Hopwood, Joseph Immordino, Melanie Jackson, Gary Jodha, Jean Larini, Rosemarie Levandowski, Professor Brian McMillan, Capt. George Meyer, Dennis Murphy, Detective Jeffrey Noble, Detective Matthew Norton, Regina Reyes, Keris Salmon, Paul Savage, Arthur Schwartz, Detective William Scull, Andy Sjamsu and Dr. Wallace Wooles.

As always I would like to thank my longtime editor at St. Martin's Press, Charles Spicer, and his wonderful team of

Michael Homler and Joseph Cleemann. And much kudos also to my Lion King of a literary agent Peter Miller, of PMA Literary and Film Management.

Thanks also to my darling wife Gail (G.K.) Freund and our parents Jerome and Emily and as always there's Roger Hitts, Daphna Inbar, Danny and Allie Trachtenberg, Cari Pokrassa, Benny Sporano (Jr. and Sr.), Virginia and Mike Randall, Tsarina, Jeff Samuels, QUERTY, Annette Witheridge, Wensley Clarkson, Don MacLeod and Mo Mo.

PROLOGUE

As dawn broke on a brutally cold January morning, PSE&G maintenance workers Richard Archer and Chuckie Black, who had been working all night on a downed electric pole, decided to meet two other colleagues for breakfast. Outside, the temperature was just −10 degrees, as Black drove his 22,000-pound aerial lift truck along the single-lane Jacobs Creek Road in rural New Jersey, and Archer, an aptly named avid hunter in his late thirties, carefully scanned the snow-covered creek and ravines for deer.

Suddenly, out of the corner of his eye, he spotted a dark green Toyota Land Cruiser, lying in the icy creek below. It initially caught his attention because his wife had the same model in silver.

"It was first light," Archer recalled. "The vehicle was running and I could see steam from the exhaust. It was in the water."

Thinking it was probably a deer hunter staking out the creek, he thought little of it and they proceeded to Columbo's for eggs and coffee.

An hour later, as the two returned along Jacobs Creek

Road to complete the job, Archer noticed the Land Cruiser was still there. He asked Black to pull over by the side of the narrow road, so he could investigate further.

As he jumped out of the truck, the icy wind chafed against his face. He ventured through an opening in a white picket fence, looking down into the snow-covered creek below. There he saw the green SUV, lying at the bottom in six inches of icy water—its headlights were not on. He could hear the motor still running, and steam was rising out of the engine, like a ghostly apparition.

He clambered down the steep fifteen-foot drop, carefully negotiating the trees and rocks on the way. There were tire tracks in the fresh snow, and to his surprise, there was a single set of footprints, coming from the passenger side of the vehicle. A few yards to the left was an abandoned campsite, with several upturned green lawn chairs, the remnants of a campfire and a discarded frozen apple in the water.

Then, as he got closer, he saw fresh blood frozen solid in the ice next to the driver's door, and more on the outside of the vehicle. His spine stiffened as he shimmied out onto the land cruiser's running board to look inside.

"It was like something out of a horror movie or a concentration camp," he later described it. "There was a lady slumped over with her eyes open, and her hair stretched out around her. There was no doubt in my mind she was dead.

"I said, 'Chuckie, there's some dead lady in the truck! Get help!' "

About an hour later, Detective Daniel B. McKeown Jr. of Hopewell Township Police Department arrived at the scene to help investigate. His colleagues had secured the scene with red accident tape, but there were already suspicions this was no accident. For one thing, there was minimal damage to the vehicle, despite the terrible head injuries to the dead woman, who was covered in blood.

Prior to his arrival, Detective McKeown, 40, had been briefed that the 1997 Toyota Land Cruiser was registered to a wealthy middle-aged millionaire named Dr. Jonathan Nyce and his beautiful young Filipino-born wife, Michelle, a couple he was well acquainted with. Six months earlier, the FBI had asked him to investigate an alleged $500,000 extortion threat by Michelle's lover. Dr. Nyce claimed at the time that the man had played him explicit audiotapes over the phone of Michelle having sex. The detective had dropped the investigation, finding the doctor's allegations unfounded.

Now as Detective McKeown looked at Michelle's battered body, already frozen solid in the blood-soaked driver's seat, he shook his head in disbelief.

"My initial thought was," he remembered, " 'Hasn't this family been through enough?' "

1

The One That Got Away

Jonathan Nyce was the third consecutive namesake in his family. Always fascinated with his ancestry, he once researched his family tree, going back to the Eighteenth Century, when a female member of the family married a native American Indian.

His grandfather Jonathan Nyce had come from Trappe, Pennsylvania, and was a builder. His father, Jonathan Jr., had been born in 1925, growing up around Collegeville, a rural blue-collar northern suburb of Philadelphia.

The Nyces were a prominent family in the area, and Jonathan Jr.'s Uncle Wesley was a daredevil stunt pilot, with his own touring aerial show. In 1939 he'd bought the Pottstown Limerick Airport for the knock-down price of $50,000 before becoming a test pilot for the American Air Force.

"Uncle Wes tested B49s," said his nephew proudly. "One time he didn't bail out in time, and crashed into a dump. . . . he wasn't hurt though."

Unfortunately, Wesley Nyce's luck didn't hold out. In 1948 the fearless flyer was killed during an aerial display, when his stunt plane failed to come out of a roll.

"It was a tragedy," said Jonathan Jr. "He was killed in front of his family."

Jonathan Jr. also held a pilot's license, but joined the U.S. Navy as a teenager, during the Second World War. Soon after his discharge in November 1945, he met a pretty young girl of Polish descent named Emma Dusea, at a local dance-hall. The two found much in common, sharing a passion for ballroom dancing, and were soon dating.

"We met dancing," said Emma. "And we've been going to dances ever since."

On February 26, 1949, they married in Delphi, Pennsylvania, and settled in Skippack, Pennsylvania, where the mechanically gifted Jonathan Jr. found a job running a hosiery mill.

"We had ninety-six machines," he remembered. "I guess you could say I designed things, and I made special stockings for showgirls."

Before long Emma became pregnant, and on May 26, 1950, Jonathan Wesley Nyce was born in Lansdale, Pennsylvania. Named after the family flying ace, he was the first of four sons Emma would bear Jonathan Jr. Two years later David was born, followed by Michael in 1955, and their youngest son Richard came two years later.

Money was tight in the Nyce household and Jonathan Jr. often had a tough time making ends meet on the scant wages of a stockingmaker. So when Jonathan was four, the family moved to Gettysburg, where his father found a better paying job at another mill, as well as moonlighting for several others for extra money.

Later Jonathan would often tell a fanciful story of how in 1953, his father narrowly missed making a huge fortune.

"My father influenced me because of something he didn't do," Nyce would cryptically explain to *U.S. 1* newspaper in 1999. "He worked around the clock one night to design the machinery to knit the first pair of pantyhose. But because he had a new family, he was unable to capitalize on that discovery, whereas his partner was able to run with it."

According to Jonathan, his father then gave him savvy

business advice, which he had lived by ever since: That if he was ever in a similar position, he should "capitalize" on the opportunity, as there may not be another.

"I honestly think that's one of the things that later drove Jonathan," said his future mentor at East Carolina University, Dr. Wallace R. Wooles. "He wasn't about to make that mistake again."

Today his father, now 80, lays no claim to inventing the first pantyhose-manufacturing machine.

"I don't know," he says wistfully. "I doubt that I invented it."

In 1955, the Nyce family moved again, this time to Norristown, and Jonathan began first grade at St. Patrick's School, where he made his first Catholic communion.

As a child, Jonathan was a loner, preferring his own company to that of the other children in his primary school. He had difficulty adjusting socially, and was a serious, quiet boy, who largely lived in his own make-believe world.

But he had a vivid imagination and loved to write stories and poetry.

"He wrote beautiful poems," said his mother, Emma. "He was very good."

As a young child, Jonathan was fascinated by science, and was always doing experiments of one kind or another. He dreamed of becoming a doctor.

"I guess in our family, pilots and doctors are the main occupations," said his father, as his sons would later be split between both professions.

In 1957, the Nyce family finally settled down in a large ranch-style house on Mill Road in Collegeville, Pennsylvania, where Jonathan Jr. and Emma live to this day.

"We moved here when Jonathan was seven," said his mother. "Our baby [Richard] was just born."

Growing up, Jonathan and his brother Michael both suffered from acute asthma and were prone to attacks at any time. It was a terrible physical handicap for a child, making Jonathan feel vulnerable and insecure.

"It's hard to imagine something worse than not being to breathe," he would later explain.

By the time he was 12 years old, Jonathan was six feet tall, standing head and shoulders above his grade school friends. But he soon put his height to his advantage on the school basketball court, where he discovered a passionate love of the game.

Jonathan played center in grade school and also regularly played pick-up games with his father and three brothers, in their Mill Road back yard.

"We'd play a lot of basketball," said Jonathan Jr. "We had a lot of fun."

When the tousle-haired blonde boy started at Methacton High School, directly behind his home, he was as "skinny as a beanpole."

Jonathan was "little better than average" academically, according to his father, and his favorite subject then was English. The future medical pioneer displayed little obvious aptitude for the sciences at this point.

"He loved to write," said his father. "He was always interested in the medical field and then he got more interested as he got older."

Methacton had a solid reputation as a quality public high school, with a flexible curriculum tailored to each pupil's needs.

Jonathan's gigantic size—he would ultimately reach six feet, four inches—set him aside from the other boys. But beneath his quick wit and geniality lay a sensitive, painfully shy boy, who never truly felt comfortable in social situations.

"He was the biggest guy in the school," remembered Eugene Hallman, who became close friends with him in seventh grade, when they took several classes together. "He wasn't one of the most popular kids in school, but we got along."

Jonathan was soon picked to play for the school's basketball team, the Methacton Warriors, where he proved an effective defensive center guard. He also represented the school at tennis, as well as being active in student government and selling advertising for the student newspaper, *Smoke Signals*.

His best friend at Methacton was Samuel Colville, who also happened to be the school's second tallest boy. According to their classmates, both boys vied for the attentions of a pretty girl named Sue Wessner, who briefly dated both of them. Samuel Hamme, a fellow Methacton student, says Sue was as "outgoing" as Jonathan was "introverted." Soon after the junior prom, where Sue was Jonathan's date, they split up, remaining close platonic friends until they left school.

Jonathan Nyce might have been tall and handsome, but there was also something awkward and ungainly about him. He was nervous around girls, seldom venturing outside the security of his small circle of friends.

"He wasn't what you'd call a ladies' man," said Hamme, who was also on the Warriors basketball team. "He just really wasn't."

He remembers Jonathan as "quiet, reserved, but a nice guy," and difficult to get close to.

"I didn't party with him that much," said Hamme. "He wasn't considered one of the more popular kids."

Eugene Hallman also remembers his friend as "fairly backward," when it came to dating girls.

"He was awkward," said Hallman. "But we were the same in that way."

All through his high school and college years he never had a proper girlfriend after Sue, although he did manage to find a date for the senior prom. And while his friends went out on dates, he preferred to study and pursue his own scientific experiments.

"Jonathan was always interested in medicine as a teenager," remembered his father. "He always did a lot of experiments."

One day when he was seventeen, his parents came home to discover an "awful" smell, coming from the kitchen.

"He had a raccoon in a pot on the stove in Clorox," said his father. "He decided he'd cook it and take the meat off because he wanted to see its skeleton."

His mother explained that Jonathan had obtained the raccoon carcass from a furrier, to study its anatomy.

"But that was nothing out of the ordinary," she explained. "He was just learning."

Jonathan and Eugene Hallman co-founded Methacton's Explorers troop, an offshoot of the Boy Scouts. They recruited several other boys into the group, selecting criminology as their specialty.

Twice a month the Explorers would meet at Jonathan's house in Mill Road, where his mother would serve refreshments.

"Jonathan wanted to become an attorney," said Hallman. "We would study cases the police were looking at. And there were some [case histories] the police would put together that we would all read and go through."

The Explorers troop also went on field trips, visiting several Pennsylvania State Police barracks, where they attended seminars, occasionally going out on calls with the troopers.

"We would watch how they handled some of the cases," said Hallman. "But we were really interested in the lawyers' side of it. Not so much the police stuff."

Jonathan's father also played a role in the Explorers troop, organizing several weekend canoeing trips for them down the Delaware River.

Both boys were also in the same advanced Chemistry and Algebra classes, where Nyce was a straight "A" student. And they often socialized after school and on weekends, when Hallman got to know the Nyce family.

Every Sunday, Jonathan and his family attended the Visitation of the Blessed Virgin Mary Church on North Trooper Road, Norristown. They were devout Catholics, always dressing up in their best clothes for Mass.

And according to his parents, Jonathan and his brothers were all well-behaved, never touching drugs or drink like some of the other children.

"We never had any problems with any of the kids," said Emma Nyce. "Jonathan was just there for everybody."

In his senior year, Jonathan Nyce played basketball for

the Warriors against Ridley High School at the University of Pennsylvania's legendary 9,000-seat Palestra sports arena.

"He's a guy who understood the game," said fellow teammate Hamme. "He was a coachable guy who would do what was expected of him. He wouldn't throw himself around, [and] played good defense."

Eugene Hallman was at the game as a spectator and remembers the stadium full to capacity, as several other high schools were competing that day in regional play-offs. Unfortunately the Methacton Warriors were soundly beaten by Ridley, and it was the last game Jonathan Nyce would ever play for them.

In 1968, at the age of 18, Jonathan Nyce became the first member of his family to attend college, when he was accepted at Philadelphia's Temple University. His parents couldn't afford the fees, so he put himself through college, doing a variety of jobs in local hospitals, and even taking a part-time job in a shoe store.

He still lived at home. Every morning his father would take him to Norristown station to catch the train to Philadelphia, and then collect him from the station at night.

"Jonathan was working on being a doctor," said Jonathan Jr. "He'd come home really late at night and make his own dinner."

He soon put his talent for dissecting animals to good use in the university's biology laboratories. But it took him eight years to obtain his undergraduate Bachelor of Science degree at Temple, by which time he had decided to concentrate on medical research.

In the early 1970s, Jonathan Nyce started dating an orthodox Jewish girl named Sylvia. Soon after they met, he proposed and they married, settling down in an apartment near his parents. But there would be problems with their religious differences.

"Sylvia was nice and she was very good," said Emma

Nyce. "She was well-educated, which we weren't, and she let us know that, more or less."

As Sylvia only ate kosher food and did not observe Christmas or other Catholic holidays, there were problems when she came to visit his family in Collegeville.

"I would always go out of my way to make the things that they liked," explained Emma Nyce. "But she was always worried about what we had for dinner, because she didn't eat certain things and all."

At Temple the young enterprising student was doing well working for his Ph.D. He had started selling freelance medical articles to newspapers and magazines. In May 1977 *Philadelphia* magazine carried a seven-page feature article by Jonathan Nyce entitled "Message From a Small Chromosome."

The well-written piece focused on the discovery of the Philadelphia chromosome, a genetic defect found only in patients suffering from a rare form of cancer called chronic granulocytic leukemia (CGL). The chromosome was discovered in 1960 at the University of Pennsylvania, and Nyce interviewed several of his Temple professors. But the article also revealed Nyce's keen sense of medical history, and perhaps how he already saw his place in it.

"Today," wrote Nyce, "solemn portraits of the University of Pennsylvania's past medical greats line the wide, polished corridors and lavish staircases of the old medical school. Between classes a procession of students and faculty traverse the great stretches of hall, and small groups collect beneath one or other of the gilt edge frames to exchange notes or discuss a difficult lecture problem."

And perhaps the highly imaginative young medical student saw a portrait of himself one day adorning the university's wall of honor.

In 1978, Jonathan Nyce was awarded a master's degree in molecular biology. Five years later he received a Ph.D. in biology from the prestigious Fels Research Institute at Temple University's School of Medicine, for a thesis on preventing colon cancer in mice.

Fels Professor of Microbiology Arthur Schwartz, who knew Nyce as a young graduate, remembers him as "an original thinker," although not an academic stand-out from the other students.

"He worked fairly hard," said Dr. Schwartz. "I think he had a bent towards maybe trying to do practical things."

But soon after getting his masters, Nyce's marriage broke up after seven years, following an unsuccessful attempt at counseling.

"I think it was mostly the religion," said his mother. "She was Jewish and he was Catholic, and there were a lot of things he wasn't allowed to do. He couldn't celebrate Christmas or anything like that. And it just got to be real difficult."

After the divorce, Jonathan Nyce, now 30 years old, moved to the West Coast to continue his medical studies. He did post-graduate work at the Childrens Hospital of Los Angeles, before joining the Kenneth Norris Cancer Center.

"Well, he kept in touch for a while when he could," said his mother. "But he was so interested in helping these poor children with the cancer."

His parents only visited him once during his seven years in Los Angeles, but he regularly returned to Collegeville for Christmas. On one occasion he and his parents met up in Aruba for an island-hopping vacation, where he taught his father to scuba dive.

The year-round Californian climate was good for his asthma, which he no longer suffered from.

While he was on the West Coast, Jonathan became something of a laid-back California beach bum, enthusiastically taking up water sports and excelling in surfing and scuba diving. He bought an inflatable dinghy, spending much of his leisure time on the water fishing.

"He loved the ocean," said his father. "He had a little boat and he went out a lot."

He also began dating a California girl named Linda Koewy, who was divorced and had a young daughter. Emma Nyce says she preferred Linda to her son's ex-wife, Sylvia, but they had problems and soon broke up.

"He wanted to have children," said his mother, "and she didn't want to have any more."

It was in Los Angeles that Nyce got his real medical training, treating young leukemia patients. He began working on inventing a drug that would help fight leukemia in children who had a resistance to the normally prescribed drugs.

"What I worked on was direct resistant forms of childhood cancer," he explained. "And this was very difficult work, because I was dealing with children that were all dying."

Nyce wanted to discover why they were dying and why their cancer did not respond to normal drugs. Finally, after watching many young patients die, he found that in a certain percentage of these drug-resistant children, there was an enzyme that was increased a thousand times.

"I found one little girl who had an abdominal mass that was actually one-third the weight of her body," he said. "It was a horrible case, but she was the little girl that I first found this up regulation of this enzyme in her tumor."

Over the next few months, he invented a new drug to treat child cancer patients that would be triggered by the enzyme. In order to get funds for further research to develop his drug, he gave four separate presentations to interested venture capitalists.

"I went to them and I said, 'I have a drug that is completely non-toxic . . . but it's activated to a very toxic intermediate, which kills the tumor.'

"I was very excited, but they were doing calculations which indicated that the small number of patients [that could be treated] would not be a substantial return on their investment."

In August 1987, he returned to the East Coast to be closer to his parents. After turning down a position at the St. Jude's

Children's Research Hospital in Memphis, Tennessee, he accepted an assistant professorship at East Carolina University (ECU) in Greenville, North Carolina.

"It was closer to us," explained his mother. "He wanted to come back East."

At 37 years old, Jonathan Nyce seemed at last to be on track for a successful career in medicine. He was a hard worker and ambitious, with a burning desire to become one of the medical greats he had so admired, and have his portrait hanging over the staircase at Temple University.

Over the next twelve years in North Carolina, he would achieve international recognition, and find his great dream of medical immortality within his grasp.

2

Changing the World

Founded in 1907, East Carolina University began life as a modest teacher training school, but has since become one of the nation's most prestigious research universities. Specializing in health care and the performing arts, its website proudly describes it as "a hotbed of discovery."

In 1987, Dr. Wallace Wooles, the head of Pharmacology at ECU's prestigious Brody School of Medicine, interviewed Jonathan Nyce for an assistant professorship, hiring him on the spot.

"I thought he'd fit in just fine," said Dr. Wooles, who is now retired.

In his early days at ECU, Jonathan Nyce stood out from the rest of the faculty. Dr. Wooles describes him as "a typical California beach boy," who initially came to work in Hawaiian shirts, shorts and sandals.

"But he soon fell in with us," explained Dr. Wooles. "He very quickly adapted to our way of doing things."

Dr. Brian McMillan, who shared a laboratory with Nyce in the Department of Pharmacology, liked him from the beginning.

"I would describe him as a gentle giant," said Dr. McMillan. "He was quite affable and pleasant to be around. Quick to smile and laugh."

Now approaching middle age, Nyce was starting to lose his hair, and had put on weight during his time in Los Angeles, giving him the appearance of a teddy bear. Although he was popular with his new faculty colleagues, he was considered something of an enigma. He made no close friends, rarely socializing outside the obligatory round of ECU Christmas parties and other functions he was expected to attend.

"Jonathan was just as his name implies," said Dr. Wooles. "He was a nice guy. He was polite, very courteous and very solicitous."

Jonathan Jr. and Emma Nyce were delighted to have their son within easy driving distance of Collegeville.

"We would often drive down to see him," said his father. "And maybe he'd come up here. He liked it there."

In his first few months at ECU, Nyce specialized in genetics, refining the drug he had developed in Los Angeles to control cancer cells.

In June 1988, he was awarded a $400,000 grant for cancer research, followed a couple of months later by his promotion to a full professorship.

Professor Jonathan Nyce was an exceptionally hard worker, who impressed superiors and co-workers alike with his single-minded dedication and "outside-the-box" thinking.

"The hours didn't mean anything to Jonathan," said Dr. Wooles. "He'd stay until the work was done, or he'd come in if he had a good idea and work on it. He was as smart as a whip and always wanted to learn."

Dr. Wooles encouraged his staff to attend each other's weekly seminars, so they could broaden their scientific outlook.

"I used to make all the new people attend the lectures," he explained, "so they could hear how their colleagues were teaching. Jonathan was not a pharmacologist by training, but he'd ask all the pertinent questions and listen."

One day Jonathan Nyce attended a presentation on asthma and blood pressure, and the role of adenosine receptors in triggering asthmatic attacks. The one-time chronic asthma sufferer had an epiphany, immediately transferring his research from cancer to asthma.

"At ECU he started with leukemia and the drug that he invented," said his future friend and attorney, Robin Lord. "But the potential patients were very small."

None of the drug companies he approached at this time were interested in a drug that could only treat the small percentage of children, who were resistant to traditional methods.

"And so [he] learned that the same drug did wonders for asthma patients," said Lord. "The drug companies loved that because the potential patients out there was large."

Asthma kills an estimated 5,000 Americans every year and many more worldwide, and Nyce viewed it as his chance to succeed in business.

So Professor Jonathan Nyce joined ECU's Allergy and Asthma Section, teaming up with department head Dr. W. James Metzger. Together they concentrated their efforts on adenosine, a chemical messenger found in high levels in the lung fluid of asthmatics. The two doctors realized the vital role adenosines play in the disease by triggering muscle constriction in the lungs, leading to an asthma attack. So they decided the solution would be to reduce the lungs' sensitivity to adenosine by tampering with the cell receptors, binding them together.

In late 1988, an attractive young woman named Sherry Leonard applied for the vacant position of Professor Nyce's laboratory research technician. He interviewed her and offered her the job, and over the next fifteen years the two would form a close professional relationship.

"He hired Sherry not long after he came here," said Brian McMillan. "She's quiet but she has an evil sense of humor."

The faculty still laugh about the time Professor Nyce went to Burlington, North Carolina, to make a presentation, taking his umbrella, as rain was in the forecast. Then, after the presentation, a couple of professors invited him to join them for dinner.

"As they went outside it started to rain," said Dr. McMillan. "So he popped open the umbrella, which Sherry had filled with the little dots from the three-hole puncher. Although he wasn't happy at the time, when he got back here he was laughing about it."

Over the next five years Professor Nyce passionately devoted himself to asthma research. Before long he had successfully synthesized human and rat adenosine receptors. At the same time, his partner Dr. Metzger was also making breakthroughs in asthma research with rabbits.

The two doctors also created a single strand of DNA they sprayed into the lungs of eight asthmatic rabbits. It caused the number of adenosine receptors to fall back to normal, preventing asthma attacks for twelve hours without any side effects. It was a major achievement, and proof they were on the right track for an asthma cure.

But after Nyce asked several colleagues to test the adenosine receptors in their laboratories, there would be terrible repercussions. For later, when Nyce secretly filed patents for his asthma drug, three of his colleagues in the Allergy and Asthma Department were livid, officially accusing him of misconduct, believing they should have had a stake in the patents.

There was so much acrimony and so many heated arguments in the department that Professor Nyce actually barricaded himself in his laboratory.

"When things blew up in his laboratory he went and closed his door," explained Dr. McMillan. "I asked him, 'Why is your laboratory door locked?' He goes, 'I don't want to deal with it.' "

But he would never bad-mouth his enemies on the faculty, appearing almost meek and non-confrontational.

"He never said nasty things about them," said Dr. McMillan. "He just complained they wanted everything he had, but never used four-letter words or anything. He'd really never say anything bad about anybody."

McMillan admired Nyce for "having the pins" to run with his research, taking it to the next level. He advised him to unlock his door, walk up to his accusers and stare them in the eyes, telling them, "Top of the morning."

"He said to me, 'You're right,' " remembered Dr. McMillan. "And he opened his door and left it open."

As head of the Pharmacology Department it was up to Dr. Wallace Wooles to arbitrate the misconduct accusations now officially lodged against his protégé. He soon determined they had no merit, drafting out a partnership between Nyce and ECU for the patent, with both sharing in any future profits from the drug.

"Jonathan just kept his ears open," said Dr. Wooles. "We had one [professor] who had been working on adenosine for twenty-odd years, and he just felt anything with adenosine should be his. And then there were others that did some work with Jonathan, and they claimed he never said anything about using this data for a patent. But the data was as much Jonathan's as anybody else's."

Approaching his fortieth birthday, Jonathan Nyce had everything going for him professionally, but remained a complete failure in his personal life. There was much speculation among his ECU colleagues about why such an athletic, handsome man apparently had such little interest in women.

"I never noticed that he dated around," said Dr. Wooles. "But I think there were a lot of women that wished he had."

In 1989, Professor Nyce decided it was time to settle down with a wife and children. But finding the right life partner presented a problem, as he always liked to be in complete control of all facets of his life.

Perhaps he felt American and European women too intimidating and liberated for his taste, after his unsuccessful first marriage. But then he met a Filipino girl in the hospital cafeteria, and soon asked her out on a date.

"Actually she was engaged to someone else, or she told

me she was," Nyce would later remember. "So we didn't end up dating."

But a few weeks later he ran into her again and she showed him a lonely hearts section in *The Manila Times*, with a picture of a beautiful 19-year-old Filipino girl named Mechily Riviera, who was advertising for an American pen-pal.

"She said this was someone she thought I would be very compatible with," he said.

Underneath her photograph was a brief listing of the kind of man she was looking for, as well as a thumbnail profile of her.

Nyce was captivated, carrying around Mechily's advertisement for a couple of days before summoning up the courage to reply.

First he wrote her a short letter, shaving more than ten years off his age, and sending an old photograph of himself, taken when he was in his mid-twenties.

A few weeks later she replied, and he began a weekly correspondence with the beautiful teenager, half his age and almost eight-and-a-half thousand miles away. The always secretive Jonathan Nyce told no one about this, embarrassed to face his colleagues' probable reaction if they knew he was now courting and planned to wed what they would see as a mail-order bride.

3

Michelle

Mechily Riviera was born on November 18, 1969, one year after Jonathan Nyce first walked into Temple University. The fourth of seven children born to Teodoro and Trefisa Riviera, Michelle grew up in the tiny village of Depensa Capunitan, just outside the Manila Bay port of Orion, a three-hour ferry ride from Manila.

A carpenter by trade, Teodoro had lived in Manila before moving to Orion, which is in the Bataan Province and has a population of 44,000. It was a tough life for the Riviera family, and Teodoro always struggled to make ends meet and feed his large family.

Even as a young child, Mechily, or Michelle, as she later Americanized her name to, always stood out for her exceptional beauty and perfect olive porcelain features. A highly intelligent girl, she soon set her sights on studying hard at school, hoping to make a better life for herself.

"Michelle was an honor student," said her father proudly. "In high school she always came first in examinations and was academically ahead of the other girls."

With younger brothers, Robbie and Nelson, and sisters

Margie and Melodia, Michelle helped with the housework and bringing up the younger children.

"Michelle was the one that cared for us and babysat me when I was very young," remembered her kid sister Melodia, seven years younger. "She was very responsible and a very loving person."

At the age of 16, Michelle moved to Quezon City, enrolling in the National College of Business Administration. But after just one semester she was forced to drop out, as her father could no longer afford the fees.

"It was very expensive," said her father. "I told her she would have to wait until we had money to continue her classes."

But Michelle was restless, finding it hard to settle back to her tough life in Depensa Capunitan. So she found a job on the former Subic Bay U.S. Naval Base, near Olongapo City. Living with her aunt, Michelle found a job in a dress store, also working on improving her English.

Before the Subic Bay base closed in the early 1990s, it had been notorious for decades as a den of prostitution, with an estimated 17,000 hospitality girls catering to off-duty U.S. servicemen in hundreds of sleazy red-light bars.

There is no suggestion that Michelle was ever involved in prostitution, but later she wanted to hide the fact that she'd ever lived in Olongapo City. It was during the several years she spent there that she had her first glimpse of the affluent American lifestyle, and decided she wanted to live in the States someday.

At 18, she joined one of Manila's many "pen-pal" agencies, which guaranteed to find their clients new male friends in the United States. She already had passable school English, which was good enough to write letters with the help of an English dictionary.

"She was looking for a pen-pal," said Larissa Soos, who was also born in the Philippines before moving to America, where she later became Michelle's best friend and confidante. "It was a big thing to be able to come [to America] and work, especially if you came from a small village like she did. It's not that she was so ambitious, but everybody wanted to come."

When Michelle received her first letter from Jonathan Nyce in the summer of 1989, she was thrilled. Not only did he describe himself as a wealthy successful scientific professor, but she also loved his photograph, showing a tall, young, handsome blonde Adonis.

She immediately replied, telling him about her life and her dreams, and sending another photograph of herself. Over the next few months they began a romantic relationship through a weekly exchange of cards, letters and frequent phone calls.

On October 8, 1989, Jonathan sent her a flirtatious postcard from Columbia, South Carolina, clearly revealing his romantic intentions.

> Dear Michelle,
> I'm off traveling to another medical meeting, and thinking of *you*, not medicine. I can't wait to see you! My room here is right on the ocean. Maybe I should jump in and swim to you today! Remember, dear Michelle, that you are in my thoughts and in my heart.
> Love Jonathan.

Slowly the always-secretive assistant professor began to bare his soul to Michelle, revealing his loneliness and how he wanted a family.

"We had very in-depth communication through letters," Nyce would later explain.

And over the next few months he and Michelle developed a close relationship, regularly talking on the phone.

"It was not like he saw her picture in a catalogue and said, 'OK I want this one,'" explained Larissa Soos. "There was no money exchanged, and it was a long-term thing. There had to be a relationship."

In late May 1990, Jonathan Nyce stunned Michelle: he announced he had bought a ticket to make the 8,400-mile journey to the Philippines to marry her. He asked her to meet him at 10:00 p.m. on the night of his arrival, in the lobby of the Las Palmas Hotel in Manila.

"The reason that I was able to go," he said, "was, I had to attend a joint meeting of the American and Japanese Cancer Societies, that was in Hawaii. And afterwards I was invited to give a lecture at the National Cancer Center in Tokyo. And the Philippines was in between."

Michelle broke the news to her father, explaining that she had "an understanding" with a young American professor. But Teodoro Riviera wanted to know more about his prospective son-in-law before allowing his beautiful daughter to marry a complete stranger.

"Michelle said that Jonathan will come to the Philippines," said Riviera. "I asked for what purpose and she said, 'He wants to marry me.' They had never met except a picture and letters."

So Riviera consulted a friend, who advised him to make sure his daughter's American suitor had a Legal Capacity to Contract Marriage certificate, required by the Philippine government before a U.S. citizen can wed a Filipino national.

"I was very worried," admitted Riviera. "This is the first time they would meet, and I told her to get Jonathan to bring the 'Capacity to Marry,' so we can be sure that he's not married already."

When Michelle relayed this to Jonathan Nyce, he calmly assured her he would take care of everything through the American Embassy.

In early June 1990, Teodoro Riviera chaperoned his beautiful 20-year-old daughter by ferry to Manila, wanting to be there when she met her future American husband for the first time. During the three-hour journey Michelle was apprehensive, wondering if she was making a big mistake. But her father reassured her, saying she could always call the whole thing off if she didn't like Jonathan Nyce in person.

Finally they arrived at the hotel and walked into the

foyer and up to reception, asking if Jonathan Nyce had checked in yet.

"She was very nervous," said her father. "Especially when Michelle saw the log book with Jonathan's name in it."

Then the desk clerk phoned up to the room, informing Nyce that he had a visitor. Jonathan said he'd be right down.

A few minutes later, Michelle got her first look at the smiling, middle-aged American breathlessly rushing out of the elevator toward her. Her initial thought was that there had to be some mistake. The stout red-faced giant with receding blond hair, and obviously twice her age, bore little resemblance to the youthful photographs he had sent her.

Years later Michelle would tell Larissa Soos how shocked she was when she'd first set eyes on Jonathan Nyce.

"When he first wrote to Michelle," said Soos, "he had attached a very flattering picture of himself when he was young. He didn't look anything like that anymore."

For the next two days Jonathan, Michelle and her father stayed at the hotel, filling out the necessary paperwork for the American Service Branch of the U.S. Embassy in Manila. And Jonathan and Michelle spent their first nights together, sleeping in his hotel suite, while her father was in another room across the hall.

"She was the most beautiful woman I ever met," Nyce later remembered. "And when I saw her in person she was everything and more that I had come to expect from her writing. At that time I think she could tell that I was falling in love with her."

Later Nyce would claim that it had been Michelle who had proposed to him, and not the other way around.

"I think she was in love as well," explained Teodoro Riviera. "She was also very strong-minded. I was studying Jonathan because I worried, but Michelle was decided. They already had an understanding through the letters."

Two days after Nyce arrived in Manila, Riviera gave his

consent to the marriage, after seeing Nyce's Certificate of Legal Capacity to Contract Marriage. Then the three of them headed back across Manila Bay to Depensa Capunitan, to apply for a marriage license at the local civil registrar at the Orion municipal building.

When Jonathan Nyce arrived at the Riviera family home, his future mother-in-law, Trefisa, and Michelle's six brothers and sisters were waiting to welcome him into their family. Overcome by emotion, Jonathan hugged and kissed his new Filipino family, who greeted him like a conquering hero.

A sense of family had always been important to Jonathan Nyce. He was genuinely delighted to meet his future in-laws, making every effort to get to know them and win their acceptance.

He immediately gave Riviera some American dollars to have a wedding dress made for Michelle, and matching bridesmaids' dresses for her sisters.

"We all liked Jonathan," said Melodia, who was just 12-years old when she first met him. "We knew he really loved my sister."

But even as the happy bridegroom showered his bride with presents, she began to get cold feet about marrying a virtual stranger from halfway around the world.

"Jonathan was like he'd hit the jackpot or something," said Larissa Soos. "Whereas Michelle was scared and wondering what she had got herself into, and if she was doing the right thing. I know for a fact that the first time she met him she wanted to do it, but she also wasn't sure. But she had to follow her heart."

On June 11, 1990, exactly one week after they first met, Jonathan Nyce married Michelle in a civil ceremony conducted by Judge Antonio C. Quintos, at the office of the local civil registrar in Orion. They were surrounded by Michelle's family, who had come from all over Bataan Province for the great occasion. Michelle's father officially gave his consent on the wedding certificate, and her friends Lolita Guzman, Elizabeth Lopez, Manuel Santos Jr. and Antonio Mariano were listed as witnesses.

"We were married by the chief justice in Orion," the bridegroom later recalled. "Her father, who was the dentist in the area, was the best man, and the mayor was a witness. And they were enemies, so it was very interesting."

Michelle looked stunning, wearing a figure-hugging white brocade wedding dress, white gloves and a double string of pearls. Her long silky black hair was tied back with a white floral headdress. The groom wore a baggy black suit, a white tie and brown sandals, a lock of blonde hair falling over his forehead like a kiss curl.

Prior to the ceremony, Nyce, now 41 years old, had surreptitiously altered his birth certificate, shaving a full eight years off his age. It was a poorly done job. Whiteout was still visible under the retyped number "8," which he'd placed over the "0," changing his date of birth from 1950 to 1958. So his official Filipino wedding certificate stated that he was born on May 26, 1958, and was just 32 years old. Amazingly, Jonathan Nyce would keep up the pretext of being eight years younger than he really was for the first ten years of the marriage, until Michelle accidentally found out the truth.

In one wedding photograph, as they take their vows, Nyce looks victorious, while Michelle has the frightened look of a cornered animal. In another one after the ceremony, they are both smiling, as the bride holds the marriage certificate towards the camera.

Jonathan and Michelle certainly looked an odd couple, the six-foot, four-inch bridegroom towering over his diminutive five-foot, two-inch bride, who didn't even reach up to his shoulder.

After the ceremony they had a reception on the beach, where the bride and groom were toasted with 7Up.

The newlyweds spent the first week of their marriage ensconced in a local hotel room, getting to know each other. They spent long romantic days on the beach followed by candlelit dinners with Michelle's family, before the honeymooners retired for the night. Jonathan was the perfect gentleman, generous, kind and considerate. The Riviera family all liked him, and Michelle truly believed her dreams had come true and she had found her American knight in shining armor.

Before he returned to the United States, Nyce set up a bank account for Michelle, also giving her father a sum of money. For Michelle would have to remain in Depensa Capunitan to apply for an American visa before she could join her new husband in North Carolina, where they planned to set up home.

After Jonathan and Michelle said a tearful goodbye at the Manila airport, he flew home, resuming his life at ECU as if nothing had happened. He never told a soul he had got married, including his parents.

He explained his absence to colleagues, by claiming that he had attended a cancer conference in Hawaii, never mentioning his side trip to the Philippines.

But it didn't go unnoticed that the strangely distant professor had a new gleam in his eye and a spring in his step. Some remarked that they had never seen him so happy.

4

A New Life

After Jonathan Nyce returned to the United States, he and Michelle corresponded daily, enthusiastically planning for their new life together in North Carolina. Nyce began taking care of Michelle and her family, opening a bank account for them and mailing monthly checks to help them have a better life. Later he said he had taken an evening job to earn extra money to finance his philanthropy.

But the weeks grew into months, and by that winter, Michelle's visa had still not been granted by the U.S. Immigration Service. Jonathan was getting more and more frustrated that Michelle had not yet joined him.

Since his marriage he had began to cultivate a big brotherly relationship with Michelle's 12-year-old sister Melodia, offering her advice and guidance. He would also use the letters to gain snippets of information on Michelle, attempting to exert some control over her life from thousands of miles away.

"Hi, little sister! How are you?" he wrote Melodia on December 17, 1990. "Are you getting ready for Christmas? Or has Christmas already happened?"

Then he told the little girl how she would see snow for the first time if she were to come to America to go to school or visit them.

"Maybe I'll throw a snow ball at you!" he wrote jokingly. "Maybe I'll put some cold snow down your back."

After urging Melodia not to allow Michelle to ride motorcycles—"It's *too dangerous*"—he apologized for telling Michelle about her little sister's secret crush on a guy in a photograph she'd sent him.

"I heard that you're mad at me . . . It was just too cute . . . and I had to let your sister tease you a little bit. Forgive me."

He then told Melodia how both he and Michelle were "very upset" that the U.S. government was taking so long to approve her visa.

"Ouch! Our separation hurts!" he wrote. "Gosh, I miss your sister *so* much. I wish she were here already. It's taking so long for the U.S. Government to approve Michelle's visa. We're both very upset about it. We want to be together as soon as possible."

Then, after asking if she'd been "a good girl?" he urged Melodia to study hard at school and make Michelle her role model.

"Take good care honey," he wrote. "If you follow in your sister's footsteps you'll do very well."

Three months later, Michelle's visa had still not come through. Jonathan Nyce was becoming increasingly anxious. Like a lovesick adolescent he was now telephoning Michelle daily, as well as sending her floods of romantic cards and letters.

"I LOVE YOU," he wrote in giant three-inch letters in blue and red ink on one card, which had the legend of the dogwood, the tree used to crucify Jesus Christ.

"Because of your regret and pity for My suffering," read the front of the card, "never again shall the dogwood tree grow large enough to be used as a cross."

A few days later on March 6, 1991, Jonathan sent Michelle a postcard while attending a Chapel Hill, North

Carolina medical conference called "Cancer Treatment in the 21st Century."

> Hi Honey!
> How is my favorite darling wife today? (My only wife, of course! Oh, Didn't I tell you about my six other wives? I'm an Arab sheik with a harem! Just kidding. I only have eyes for you, my darling!)
> Sure wish we were together right now. I really need to have you by my side. I love you with all my heart, Michelle.
>
> > Love Jonathan.

Then, in a postscript, he asks what she meant writing that she had eaten so much at the festival, that her pants no longer fit. "Oh No!" he wrote.

In late March, Michelle's visa had finally come through and Jonathan Nyce booked her a one-way plane ticket to California, where he planned to meet her for a short vacation, before bringing her back to Greenville.

"Hey pretty girl," he wrote her, after getting off the telephone with his travel agent. "She said you must call her a week in advance of your flight so she can print up your ticket."

He also told her he was wiring the Manila airport departure tax of 1620 pesos ($28 U.S.) to her immediately, and that he loved her very much.

Three days later he sent Michelle a suggestive postcard, after apparently having shared a sexy telephone call with her the night before.

"I'm *too* excited about you finally coming here," he wrote breathlessly. "Also, you were very sexy in the things you said and that kept me awake (daydreaming) too. Ummmmm."

He joked that his friends had had to invite him out to a movie to calm him down, although he doubted that was possible.

"All I can think about is you (and your sexy, red bathing suit—although in my daydreams you're not always wearing it!)," he wrote flirtatiously. "I love you Michelle, and am looking forward very much to beginning our life together. Take care. Love. Me."

But even though she was now free to come to America, Jonathan felt Michelle was dragging her feet.

"What's keeping you?" he wrote her on April 1. "I miss you and want you here."

He told her that his family was "dying to meet [her]," and were really excited about his marriage.

But the truth was that he had still not told his parents or anyone else about Michelle and getting married, let alone prepared them for her imminent arrival.

Finally, on April 19, 1991, Michelle said goodbye to her parents and family and flew to California, where Jonathan Nyce joined her for a brief romantic reunion.

But before he'd left Greenville he'd prepared the groundwork for her sudden arrival as his wife. Apparently believing it would be unseemly for an ECU professor to marry a Filipino mail-order bride, Nyce had concocted an elaborate cover story to explain how they had met. While they were vacationing in California, he carefully coached Michelle in it. She was to tell everyone that they had met in Hawaii, while he'd been attending a medical conference. He had literally tripped over her foot while scuba diving during a break, and it had been love at first sight.

But later he would claim it had been Michelle who had invented the cover story, in case his colleagues mistook her for a prostitute.

"I don't know why exactly she should have been that concerned," he explained. "But she had this feeling that my friends in North Carolina would think that since she had worked in Olongapo at the American bases, that she might have prostitution in her background. Which she did not."

Then they flew back to Greenville, where he proudly introduced his young bride to his colleagues as if there was nothing out of the ordinary.

"We were all dumbfounded when he came back married," said his Pharmacology Department head, Dr. Wallace Wooles. "He said he met her on the beach in Hawaii at a meeting."

Dr. Brian McMillan was also surprised when his friend first introduced him to Michelle, and was somewhat suspicious of their story.

"He just went off to the South Pacific," said Dr. McMillan, "and came back with Michelle."

Before long, the 21-year-old Filipino beauty had become a subject of much speculation among some members of the faculty, who quietly deliberated whether she was a mail-order bride.

The sole person at ECU who may have known the truth was Jonathan Nyce's technician Sherry Leonard. They worked together so closely, she might have known if he had really attended a cancer conference in Hawaii. But ever-protective, she would always deny having any knowledge of how they couple had met, saying she was never "terribly curious" about it anyway.

"He really didn't give me the details," she would later explain. "He said he was corresponding with somebody and mentioned meeting them in Hawaii on a scuba diving trip."

Jonathan's elderly parents also had no idea he was married when he first took Michelle home to Collegeville to meet them.

"We didn't know about Jonathan and Michelle until he brought her back here," said his father. "That was the first time we heard anything."

But after they got over their shock of having a new daughter-in-law, they tried to make her welcome in the family.

"He was so happy when he got married," said Emma Nyce. "He said, 'Now I'm family. I'm family.'"

His parents immediately liked the beautiful young Filipino, and had no qualms about how they had first met.

"It's his choice and he liked her, and that was all that mattered," said his mother. "She was very nice. We had no problems with her."

Nyce says his parents accepted his new wife into their family immediately.

"My parents treated her just like a daughter," he said. "Because her parents were far away, they paid extra attention to her."

Back at ECU there was much discussion as to what the brilliant professor in his early forties could possibly have in common with the stunningly beautiful but unworldly Filipino girl, barely out of her teens.

Dr. Wallace Wooles said he was puzzled by his protégé's unexpected choice of wife.

"She was not the kind of girl that I thought Jonathan would pick out," he said. "He was far older than she was, and she was a more outgoing and happy person. But apparently in the beginning she made Jonathan very happy."

Before Michelle had arrived, Jonathan Nyce had rented an off-campus apartment in Greenville for them to live in. Within a few months Michelle became pregnant, and Jonathan was delighted at the prospect of at last becoming a father, something he'd always dreamed about.

"It was idyllic," Nyce would later explain, calling his early life with Michelle the happiest time of his life. "I couldn't imagine myself being happier or more blessed."

On January 29, 1992, Michelle gave birth to a baby boy they named Alex, whom Jonathan helped deliver, even cutting the umbilical cord.

"The bond was incredible," he remembered, "to be with my wife when she was delivering [him]."

Alex was a beautiful, healthy baby, and his proud father delighted in showing off Michelle and his new son to the other ECU professors and their families at their annual retreat or the regular round of faculty social events.

Jonathan was delighted to have a son, and doted over the little boy, spending as much time as he could playing with him. Michelle, now 22, was also happy to be a mother. She immediately sent her parents photographs of their new grandson, together with a postcard, captioned, "Having a Ball Along Coastal Carolina."

"The baby is fine," she wrote. "I can't wait to visit you there Mom & Dad to show you my baby Alex."

In May, Nyce took his wife and son to San Diego, for their first family vacation. They visited SeaWorld, where they saw Shamu the whale, who splashed his tail in the water, soaking the crowd. Little Alex began crying and was inconsolable, until his father finally managed to pacify him.

"He just loved that little boy," said Emma Nyce. "Alex wasn't even seven months old and he had him swimming."

Back in Greenville, Michelle had soon won over the faculty members and their wives, who liked her happy-go-lucky attitude to life. She had a thick Filipino accent, but worked hard improving her language skills and taking the edge off it.

"She got on with everyone and was fine at gatherings, so I'd talk with her," remembered Dr. McMillan. "They were kind of like Mutt and Jeff. He was like six-foot-four, and I don't think she was over five foot."

Whenever out in public, Michelle rarely left Jonathan's side, appearing highly dependent on him.

"In public she would hang on his arm," remembered Sherry Leonard, who often saw them socially. "He would jokingly say that Michelle was trying to make him fat and unattractive, so that other women wouldn't look at him."

But Nyce was also very possessive of his beautiful young wife, preferring she not become too involved in campus life, or too friendly with other male faculty members.

"Jonathan was very protective of her," said Dr. Wooles, who hosted the faculty's annual Christmas party at his house. "He was very solicitous of her and they would come to all the parties."

Ironically, Michelle would later tell friends that when they were first married, Jonathan had encouraged her to dress sexily in short, thigh-hugging skirts.

In early 1993, Michelle become pregnant again. On November 8, she gave birth to another son they named Trevor. Once again Jonathan Nyce was the proud, devoted father, spending as much time with his family as he could.

He was now working long days with Dr. James Metzger, perfecting his asthma drug, but he still found time to see Michelle and his sons whenever he could.

"Between our apartment complex, which was quite huge, and the medical center, there was a duck pond," Nyce later reminisced. "Michelle would often give me a call on the phone and we would meet at the duck pond . . . and eat lunch. The kids would feed the ducks. It was great. I just couldn't imagine myself being a happier man."

In the fall of 1993, the Nyces attended a birthday party at ECU, where Jonathan introduced Michelle to a colleague named Shekar Chakarthi and his wife, Sandy. The two young women started talking, finding much in common as stay-at-home moms with young children. They began going out on play dates together with their children.

"There was this place called Explorer Town, where we used to take our kids," said Sandy. "It was an indoor play place, and we'd sit there and have lunch while the kids played."

Michelle encouraged Sandy to join the Polks Athletic Club gym, where she'd recently started daily work-out sessions. Michelle had always been in excellent shape, and now became fanatical about keeping fit.

Every morning, after Jonathan left for work, she would take Alex and baby Trevor to the gym, depositing them in the creche while she did a strenuous work-out on free-weights and machines. Before long she had developed a close-knit circle of friends at the gym and started having a social life.

"We were work-out partners for several years," remembered Kuny Brothers, who became her best friend. "We weight-trained and we'd get together every day on a basis."

Michelle and Kuny soon bonded, often discussing their

husbands and children during their daily work-outs. Like everyone else, Kuny and Sandy heard the apocryphal story of how Michelle had first met Jonathan.

"She told me that he was on a medical conference in Hawaii and they met on the beach," remembered Brothers. "I guess that she was ashamed to be a mail-order bride."

Soon after they met, Michelle introduced her new friend to Jonathan when they went out to dinner.

"He was very pleasant and so calm," Kuny remembered. "He was protective, but it was the age difference, I guess."

Kuny also noticed how Michelle's exotic beauty turned a lot of men's heads, and was surprised when Michelle told her how Jonathan encouraged her to wear short skirts.

"But then longer into the marriage he did not like those things," she said. "I always thought he was kind of odd. He was distant. I guess not the typical masculine man."

During this period Sandy Chakarthi was a frequent visitor to the Nyce apartment. Despite the age difference, and Jonathan being far more reserved than his outgoing wife, she thought that they were a happy couple—"Although when I think back, I did notice that if we walked [across] the room, his eyes would follow us," she said. "I thought it was just because he liked to watch her, as she was very pretty. But maybe I was wrong."

5

EpiGenesis

In spring 1995, Professor Jonathan Nyce took a leave of absence from ECU, setting up a company he would christen EpiGenesis Pharmaceuticals. After years of hard research, Nyce, now using the prefix "Doctor" (although holding a doctorate of Biology, he was not an MD), proudly claimed that his revolutionary asthma drug, tentatively named "EPI-2010," had already passed "rigorous" early trials with rabbits, "with no adverse affects."

One early article about the fledgling company in an ECU publication called *Edge* created a lot of buzz in the North Carolina medical establishment.

"Teamwork leads Dr. Jonathan Nyce and Dr. James Metzger to a new treatment for asthma," read the caption for the article, entitled "Breathing Easier." It was accompanied by a posed picture of Nyce with arms folded, standing opposite his research partner Dr. W. James Metzger.

The article told how Dr. Nyce and his team of researchers at the ECU school of medicine had discovered a drug that appeared to prevent asthma attacks. Dr. Metzger was quoted as saying he believed EPI-2010 would help almost all asthmatics, however serious their condition.

It went on to explain that the drug was being developed in partnership with ECU, under a licensing agreement with EpiGenesis, a university spin-off company, which retained the drug patent as well as an equity interest in the new company.

"Some large pharmaceutical companies have expressed interest in cooperating with EpiGenesis on developing and marketing the drug," claimed Dr. Nyce.

He boasted his new company already had a five-year, five-million-dollar venture capital agreement with a yet unnamed investment banking firm, as well as "peer-reviewed awards" from the National Institutes of Health and the North Carolina Biotechnology Center.

"Nyce hopes the federal Food and Drug Administration will allow clinical trials to begin [soon]," ended the article. "It will take at least four to five more years to get the drug to market."

Years later Jonathan Nyce would look back at the mid-1990s as the time he believed he could change the world.

"My work was going very well," he explained. "I was discovering a whole plethora of new drugs . . . for a number of diseases. So well in fact that I was able to spin out a company called EpiGenesis Pharmaceuticals, which began to take off."

As EpiGenesis looked set to become a successful and profitable company, there was increasing acrimony directed towards its founder. Spending more and more time with venture capitalists and presenting medical papers, Dr. Nyce was now rarely in the ECU laboratory. He loved all the attention and was generally a good spokesman for his company, although he was not above embellishing the truth when he felt it necessary.

One day in the middle of an EpiGenesis presentation, he had an uncontrollable fit of coughing. Struggling for breath he turned it to his advantage, telling the meeting that approximately 7,000 people die from the disease every year.

"His company was attracting money," explained Dr. Wooles, now advising Nyce on business strategy. "He got the patents assigned to him, which was a pretty big deal. I think there were people at the University that wanted these patents to be sold so they could collect royalties."

Wooles explained how the agreement between ECU and EpiGenesis was based on a standard agreed formula where both sides split the stock shares. There were certain payments due to the university at different milestones during the company's growth.

"And it was kind of funny," said Dr. Wooles. "I told Jonathan that, when there's money involved, strange things happen."

In late 1995, Nyce attended a biotechnology roundtable meeting at the North Carolina Biotechnology Center, where he struck up a conversation with an ex–Johnson & Johnson executive named Dennis Burns, who specialized in biotech licensing.

"We hit it off," said Nyce, who immediately offered Burns the newly created part-time position of EpiGenesis Interim President, having already appointed himself Chairman and Chief Scientific Officer.

And when EpiGenesis Pharmaceuticals began to take off, Jonathan and Michelle Nyce's life slowly changed as all the venture capital beginning to come into the company raised their standard of living.

When he finally received his patents for EPI-2010, Nyce celebrated by telling Michelle she could either buy an expensive new car or send a large sum of money to her family back in the Philippines.

According to Michelle's father, Teodora Riviera, she decided to use the money to help her family buy land and start a duck farm, to help them become self-sufficient.

"We bought two thousand ducks and started the farm," said Riviera. "They were soon laying eggs and it was a living for the family."

Jonathan Nyce also claims he paid for Michelle's older sisters to go to nursing school, as well as building a children's playground in nearby Balanga City. Later when he became a wealthy man, Nyce would contend he'd built a school, and six houses for Michelle's parents and siblings, as well as supporting Michelle's extended family.

He would also maintain that when he first met the Rivieras, they were in such dire poverty that one of Michelle's sisters had starved to death.

Michelle's youngest sister, Melodia Ragenil, says that is a figment of her brother-in-law's fertile imagination.

"He lied," said Melodia. "Nobody has starved to death in my family. My sister planned the duck farm and Jonathan never cared about that."

In late 1995, Michelle began lessons at a Greenville driving school, where she soon made friends with another student named Rajni Ajmera.

"She loved to talk to people," said Rajni.

Soon after they met, Michelle introduced Rajni to her husband.

"He was so good and really cared about her," she remembered. "And they obviously loved each other. She said Jonathan was a very good man and helped her with everything."

Unlike Rajni, who was a full-time working mother, Michelle was a stay-at-home mom who spent her days going to the gym and looking after her two young boys.

"She did not work," said Rajni. "She just wanted to stay home and be a housewife."

Occasionally when she visited Michelle's apartment to take their children swimming in a nearby park, she would see Jonathan at home, puttering around in the kitchen or calling prospective investors.

Sandy Chakarthi said the early success of EpiGenesis made Dr. Nyce something of a star at ECU, with some colleagues trying to get a stake in his business.

"I know some people wanted to get in on the investment," she explained. "At one point we were asked, but we didn't want to do it."

Jonathan Nyce's parents also regularly visited their son and his new family in Greenville. They got on well with Michelle, although Emma Nyce soon noticed a change in her daughter-in-law.

"When they first got married we went down there," said Emma. "She wanted to go shopping, and I'd take her out. The only thing I can say is, one time I brought her some material and she said it wasn't good enough. I said, 'Well, that's all I can afford.'"

That December, Nyce brought Michelle and their two young boys to Dr. Wooles' annual Christmas party, where there was some tension among some of the other professors.

"All the faculty and technicians were invited," explained Dr. Wooles. "Jonathan got along swimmingly with everybody, except the three people who were bent out of shape as they thought part of the patent belonged to them."

In February 1996, the North Carolina Biotechnology Center published a newsletter applauding Dr. Nyce's breakthrough research. It forecast he might soon become a major player in the $4 billion worldwide asthma drug market.

"A startup company has spun out of East Carolina University to tackle some old diseases with an innovative new weapon: epigenetics," read the glowing article, hailing Nyce as a pioneer in his field. "Based on technologies developed by Dr. Jonathan Nyce . . . EpiGenesis Pharmaceuticals Inc. is developing a new class of proprietary therapeutics aimed at a variety of diseases, including cancer and asthma."

Nyce explained Epigenetics was a new idea to treat disease, by manipulating genetics to rectify aberrant genes.

"We're looking at disease in a different way," he told the newsletter. "We're asking, how can we intervene . . . ?"

He boasted his new company had already widened its horizons, now offering EpiGenRx, a medication for asthma, and EpiCyte, as a treatment for leukemia.

"Jonathan was a great scientist with good ideas and on the cutting edge," explained Dr. Wooles. "But he was probably the worst manager in the world, with no sense of management or business."

After hiring Dennis Burns to attract venture capital and run the company on a day-to-day basis, Dr. Nyce refused to let him do his job.

"For some reason he would not relinquish control," said Dr. Wooles. "Jonathan would not let him make decisions. He had to make them all."

Dr. Jonathan Nyce's obsessive need for control would be his downfall in the years to come, but at the moment many were seduced by his charismatic and passionate "mad scientist" persona.

On February 20, 1997, EpiGenesis Pharmaceuticals took a quantum leap forward, when the highly influential British scientific journal *Nature* published Dr. Nyce's paper, making him an instant spokesman for global asthma research. Entitled, "DNA antisense therapy for asthma in an animal model," the exciting results promised to revolutionize the whole way asthma was treated.

In the past, treatments had solely attacked the symptoms of asthma, using steroids to temporarily ease constricted bronchial tubes. But now Nyce and his co-author Dr. W. James Metzger intimated that their research on "antisense molecules" could prevent the protein-producing gene that caused asthma.

The implications were huge, and after *Nature* published the paper, the big venture capital money soon started rolling into EpiGenesis. Even before the article appeared, a group of investment bankers had raised $300,000 in a private offering. And this consortium was now concentrating on a secondary offering of twice that amount, as well as a multi-million-dollar foreign one.

In May, the financial floodgates really came down when

Newsweek magazine carried a cover story entitled, "Yearning to Breathe Free: With New Drugs and Devices, Asthmatics Avoid Attacks."

The article, by Sharon Begley, highlighted a host of exciting new drugs coming on the market that could drastically improve the quality of life for millions of asthma sufferers.

"Back in the dark ages of asthma care—like five or so years ago—" began the article, " 'managing' one's asthma meant scrambling for a puff of bronchodilator as breathing suddenly became as arduous as sucking peanut butter through a straw."

Millions of people all over the world would read the article, singling out Dr. Nyce for his pioneering work in asthma treatment.

"Jonathan Nyce of East Carolina University," wrote Begley, "has created a molecule that strikes at the very core of asthma: the hyperreactivity of the airways."

It quoted the EpiGenesis founder, saying his EPI-2010 drug "could be the first once-a-day asthma medication to treat the underlying cause of the disease."

On March 8, 1997—two weeks after the *Nature* article was published—Jonathan Nyce received a standing ovation during the ECU Founders Day speech, celebrating the ninetieth anniversary of the university. The speech, entitled, "ECU and the 21st Century," was delivered by ECU Chancellor, the late Richard R. Eakin, who lauded Dr. Nyce for his work.

"Jonathan Nyce, a member of our medical school faculty, is succeeding at research that could truly revolutionize the treatment of asthma," he told the students. "Just last month the journal *Nature*, one of the world's leading medical publications, recognized the significance of the work of Dr. Nyce and his colleagues."

In the wake of the *Nature* and *Newsweek* articles, many leading pharmaceutical companies, such as Merck and Glaxo Wellcome, began to take note, and actively courted EpiGenesis.

Things were moving so fast that in April, Dr. Nyce

opened a new office in Durham, North Carolina, hiring his first full-time employee.

Vance Parker was appointed EpiGenesis' vice-president of operations, working out of Durham with three part-timers, including Nyce's long-time technician Sherry Leonard. In the nine years since Leonard had begun working for Nyce, they had forged a close professional brother/sister relationship, spending long hours together in the laboratory.

Now less than a year away from human trials, Jonathan Nyce publicly declared he was searching for a big drug company to finance his expensive tests, in return for a licensing agreement.

By late April, EpiGenesis had been approached by no fewer than twenty-five companies, and was in serious discussions with four of them.

"We didn't have to get in the door," Vance Parker told *Business North Carolina* in July. "Our door was open and they made an entrance."

6

The Big Time

By the summer of 1997, EpiGenesis started to take off in a big way, and Michelle was feeling neglected. The demands of his fast-expanding company meant Jonathan Nyce was often out of town, talking to prospective investors or giving speeches to scientific organizations. He was spending less and less time with his wife and children.

Michelle was pregnant again, but never let up on her strenuous daily work-out program, telling friends it kept her sane.

"When she was pregnant with her third child we couldn't even tell," remembered Sandy Chakarthi, who saw Michelle almost every day. "She was so tight that we used to joke that there wasn't any baby in there."

With two young children and another on the way, the 28-year-old Filipino national was now applying for American citizenship. After six years in North Carolina she was feeling lonely and insecure. But she never complained, always appearing happy and positive. Over long lunches at Explorer Town with Sandy and Kuny, Michelle was always playfully upbeat.

"We loved to giggle," said Sandy. "And she'd talk about her baby and her belly and we'd make jokes about it. It was just a fun time in the middle of the day."

The only person who suspected anything was wrong with Michelle was her husband's faithful research assistant Sherry Leonard. Her female intuition told her that Michelle was slightly hostile towards her. She began to worry that her boss's wife might think she and Jonathan had become romantically involved, when nothing could be further from the truth.

"She never made direct comments to me to indicate that she was jealous of my relationship with Jonathan," said Leonard. "But you could sense it to a degree."

By late 1997, Dr. Jonathan Nyce's dream of helming a multi-million-dollar company, and helping mankind by discovering cures to asthma and cancer, seemed within his grasp.

"Greenville-based EpiGenesis Pharmaceuticals Inc. has enjoyed its fifteen minutes of fame since the February 20 issue of *Nature* appeared," wrote *Business North Carolina* magazine in July. "Companies like Merck and Glaxo Wellcome have been calling almost daily. Founder Jonathan Nyce attended a conference where the moderator showed a slide of a major new discovery: 'Our *Nature* paper,' he boasts."

In October, EpiGenesis received a $100,000 Phase 1 Small Business Innovation Research grant from the National Institutes of Health to continue tests on its EPI-2010 drug. It was a major step forward for the company, now officially based in Durham.

Later, in a display of false modesty, the doctor would tell a business writer that Institute reviewers had made "embarrassingly nice comments" about him.

On October 27, EpiGenesis issued its first-ever press release, with Dr. Nyce explaining how the $100,000 grant would speed his plans to file an Investigational New Drug application with the U.S. Food and Drug Administration.

"It also validates our unique use of antisense oligonucleotides," he intoned, "to selectively manipulate gene expression in pulmonary diseases such as asthma."

Distributed over the Internet by the New York–based *PR Newswire*, EpiGenesis was described as "a privately-held research and development company . . . engaged in the discovery and development of proprietary pharmaceuticals, based upon their ability to selectively alter gene expression in disease states."

Now back at ECU, Jonathan Nyce found that he was a big fish in a small pool. The once shy and reserved biologist was now talking big about his grandiose plans for the future.

"He talked about it often and seemed driven," said Kuny Brothers, who attended several dinner parties at the Nyces' apartment over this period. "He seemed really excited."

Holding court, Dr. Nyce—looking every inch the CEO with expensive made-to-measure suits and a growing collection of brightly colored designer ties—would boast about his new jet-setting lifestyle, with frequent trips to Europe and Japan.

"He said he taught himself Japanese and German on his own to help his business," said Brothers. "He was traveling to these places to obtain millions of dollars to invest in this company. And he told us Merck was looking to purchase it."

As he waxed to friends on his ambitious plans for the future, Michelle would look on admiringly, cracking the odd joke. And although she always seemed warm and affectionate around her husband, friends began to notice a growing detachment.

On March 22, 1998, Michelle gave birth to a daughter, Samantha, to complete the family. Soon after leaving the hospital, Jonathan Nyce proudly took Michelle, their two boys and new baby to the EpiGenesis office, so his staff could see his family.

"They looked so happy," said Dr. Wooles. "Like a perfectly contented couple. And they certainly enjoyed the children as they came along."

Years later, Jonathan Nyce would fondly reminisce about those halcyon days in North Carolina.

"We were just the happiest couple you could imagine," he remembered. "And everyone was jealous of us because we were so happy."

But some wondered if the Nyces tried a little too hard to create the perception of the perfect family.

"Whenever I saw them they were both smiling," said Doctor Brian McMillan. "But you never know. Some people smile on the outside and bleed on the inside."

In February 1998, Muzinich & Co. Inc., a private New York–based institutional asset manager, pumped $5 million into EpiGenesis, half in immediate cash and the rest to be exercised in warrants the following year. But the venture capitalists believed that the company had outgrown its small Durham office and limited laboratory space at ECU, insisting it now move into a bigger space.

"Well, the money was coming in and things were expanding," said Dr. McMillan. "[Jonathan] told me that when word got out that he was looking for space, cities all across America wrote to him, saying, 'Come and look what we've got.' "

And before long Dr. Nyce was wooed to Princeton, New Jersey, with an attractive low tax package, all fully negotiated by his major new investor Muzinich.

In June, Dr. Nyce closed his small Durham office, announcing EpiGenesis would be relocating to New Jersey. He now sought an additional $6 million in venture capital, to hire up to twenty new employees, so he could advance to the next stage of Phase 1 human trials.

"We love North Carolina . . . and we would really love to stay here," Dr. Nyce told the Raleigh/Durham–based *Triangle Business Journal*. "We're all very upset at the prospect of having to move to the Northeast . . ."

Nyce told the paper that unfortunately North Carolina was "too small," offering "too few opportunities" for his growing company.

Desperate to keep EpiGenesis in the town, the Greater Durham Chamber of Commerce countered by offering Nyce a large new space to become available in 1999. But after going through the motions of inspecting it, the EpiGenesis CEO was unimpressed.

"The time-frame is a bit off," he explained. "If we don't move into new space rapidly, we'll lose valuable time with EPI-2010. I think we'll have to pull the trigger fairly rapidly."

7

New Jersey

In the fall of 1998, EpiGenesis Pharmaceuticals moved to a brand new 5,100-square-foot shell-space facility in Cranbury, off Exit 8A of the New Jersey Turnpike. CEO Jonathan Nyce was ecstatic, optimistically forecasting that the turnpike corridor between New York and Maryland would soon become "Carbonyl Valley," the pharmaceutical equivalent of the West Coast's Silicon Valley.

Several of the original EpiGenesis team moved to New Jersey, including loyal research technician Sherry Leonard. And Dr. W. James Metzger, who had helped him start EpiGenesis and would tragically die of cancer two years later, was appointed to the board of directors.

Other members of the board included representatives of EpiGenesis investors Glaxo Wellcome and Muzinich & Co., who now wanted to play a bigger role in company policy and protect their investment.

"We started a company up there," Nyce later explained. "Things [were] going very well."

One of Dr. Nyce's first New Jersey hires in July 1998 was Amanda Gillum, whom he appointed his vice-president of operations. Gillum was introduced to Nyce by his lead investor, Muzinich, and had a Ph.D. in Biochemistry from MIT, as well as a post-doctorate at Stanford. She had lived in nearby Pennington for twenty years and had two teenage daughters.

Gillum remembers it as an exciting time. "When the group first moved up," she said, "[there was] a lot of cohesiveness, enthusiasm, optimism."

But from the start Gillum wondered if Jonathan Nyce's "big ego" might be a problem, and the staff he had brought from ECU might be too blindly supportive of him.

"I did have a sense that some of the people he brought with him didn't tend to challenge him," said Gillum. "They respected him from his professor days. I wasn't close enough to how the money was burned up."

His new VP of operations saw Nyce daily, when he wasn't off on his frequent trips abroad. She always found him "moderately approachable," but felt he put up "barriers."

"He was very creative and had good scientific ideas," she said. "[But] he didn't want to be challenged. He was generally softly spoken, but I can't recall him ever losing his temper and raising his voice."

Jonathan moved Michelle and their three young children into a rented townhouse on Sayre Drive in Princeton Landing, New Jersey, by the Ivy League university campus. Michelle was left to make it into a home, as her husband ratcheted up his workload, spending even more time away on international business trips.

Michelle had been devastated at having to leave her life and friends in Greenville to move to a strange town where she knew no one. In the weeks before the move she had had tearful lunches with Sandy and Kuny, promising to always keep in touch.

During the first few months in New Jersey, Michelle became even more depressed, questioning if she had made a huge mistake ever leaving the Philippines. When she first moved to New Jersey, she often called up her old friends for a chat, frequently breaking down in tears.

"She would call me crying," said Kuny Brothers, "and say she hated that they moved and she'd never find another friend. She'd ask me to please come visit."

Michelle's eldest son, Alex, was now 7 and Trevor was 5. When they went to school she would take her toddler Samantha to a nearby gym, while she pumped iron and used the machines. It was perhaps the only time she ever felt totally happy and at peace during those early days.

Soon after the Nyces arrived on Sayre Drive, they became good friends with their next-door neighbors, Andy and Cynthia Sjamsu, who had also just moved in.

"Jonathan and Michelle were in their garden, playing with their kids," remembered Andy. "And she just walked over and started talking to us. They're nice people."

Over the next few months they got to know the Nyces well, often socializing together. As usual they told the Sjamsus that they had met on a romantic Hawaiian beach and it had been love at first sight.

"We'd see a lot more of Michelle than him," said Andy. "She was doing the suburban thing and was a stay-at-home mom. The boys were just starting baseball and soccer, and Samantha was a baby in diapers at the time. Michelle had her hands full."

But Sjamsu thought them an oddly matched couple, both age-wise and physically. He also noticed how Michelle always wanted to go out partying, while her soft-spoken husband preferred a quiet night at home with the kids.

"Michelle was so young," he said. "I thought it a little peculiar, because she always wanted to go out more than he did."

One day over dinner, Andy Sjamsu, an engineer by trade, asked Jonathan what he did, spending so much time away from home.

Remembered Sjamsu: "He told me about EpiGenesis and I said, 'You've got my attention.' He said they'd just raised a new round of funding from boutique banks, and he was busy doing the conference circuit and being a guest speaker.

"He was traveling a lot. At least one week a month and

going to Europe, Sweden and Japan. But it was nothing out of the ordinary for a biotech CEO."

Sjamsu also observed Jonathan's discomfort in social situations, and his lack of people skills.

"Jonathan was not exactly a social mover," he said. "He was more geeky than anything else, and a pretty quiet guy."

That first Christmas in New Jersey, Amanda Gillum organized an EpiGenesis Christmas party at her home. Jonathan and Michelle Nyce and their three children attended, as did the rest of the company staff.

"If you met Jonathan," said one member of the management team, "you'd say, 'Jeez . . . what an intelligent, nice, personable man who founded this company.' With his beautiful wife and kids, on the surface, at least, it was the all-American success story."

As Nyce and his staff toasted EpiGenesis' future with champagne, they believed the company was destined for biotech greatness, and everybody would soon be millionaires.

On March 17, 1999, the prestigious *U.S. 1* business newspaper featured Jonathan Nyce and EpiGenesis in an extensive, wide-ranging cover article. The article effectively introduced the company to the prosperous New Jersey business community.

"CEO Jonathan Nyce of EpiGenesis Hopes to Be a Player in the $9 Billion Asthma Market," read the headline, alongside a large front-page photograph of a boyish-looking Nyce with his arms folded, behind him a family snapshot of him and Michelle.

In the article, entitled "For Asthma, A Genetic Kill Switch," Nyce told *U.S. 1* the only "drawback" to his successful business was his "frequent separations" from his family.

"My driving force," he explained, "is that I want to help sick people."

The reporter initially sent to interview Jonathan Nyce had been so charmed by the CEO that the resulting article was almost too fawning. *U.S. 1* senior editor Barbara Fox ended up re-interviewing Nyce by phone, toning the piece down to make it more objective.

Jonathan Nyce now claimed to be 44 years old, although he was actually five years older. He also repeated his apocryphal story of how his father had designed the first pantyhose machine, but hadn't made a dime. This, he explained, was the driving force behind him founding EpiGenesis, coupled with the fact that he had once been a chronic asthma sufferer himself.

Nyce boasted that apart from his own investment in the company, he had personally raised $11 million in two private placements. He said he was "heartened" by all the money and the scientific validation he'd received so far.

He confidently predicted EpiGenesis' imminent expansion, saying he was already headhunting a company president and full-time chief financial officer. He also planned to triple the number of current employees and hire seven Ph.D.s and two technical staff, on top of the six scientists already working there.

He ambitiously described the company's database of genes and innovative technology as "cash cows," although refusing to be more specific.

"It will be very significant," he assured the business paper. "Our work has not gone unnoticed."

Explaining his "baby" EPI-2010, Dr. Nyce said his drug could be administered with an aerosol, instead of a pill or a shot.

"The lung is kind enough to repackage it for us and distribute it," he explained.

U.S. 1 predicted a bright future for Dr. Nyce and his company, citing how twelve other companies were also working on new genetic methods of treating asthma.

"If imitation is the sincerest form of flattery," Fox wrote, "then the scientists at EpiGenesis Pharmaceuticals must be blushing from all the attention. What gives [them] the edge and Nyce his confidence of success, is that his company has been the only one with the proven ability to selectively attack a particular 'villain' gene in the respiratory system—to knock out the target gene."

But already, Jonathan Nyce's colleagues inside EpiGenesis began to suspect that he was a compulsive liar and had lost respect for him as a leader. And over time he began to become more and more tangled up in his untruths.

One colleague, who wished to remain anonymous, said Nyce had been caught several times in "bald-faced" lies, but would never back down from his original fabrications. Many were suspicious of his story of tripping over Michelle on a Hawaiian beach. If he had bought her family a duck farm, as he always told them, could her parents have afforded to send her on a Hawaiian vacation?

Some of his major business decisions simply appeared to defy logic, and many wondered how he could afford to live like a millionaire when he was cash-poor, with most of his wealth tied up in company stocks. While EpiGenesis was riding the biotech wave, his faults didn't appear too dangerous, but that would change soon enough when the company started to unravel.

That Easter, Kuny Brothers took her three children to New Jersey to visit Michelle. During their brief stay, Michelle and Jonathan were the perfect hosts.

Early every morning Jonathan left for work and then returned in the evening, where he would often cook them a meal. Kuny spent the days with her old friend, who appeared upbeat.

"They were very hospitable," remembered Brothers. "One night they took us out to a Japanese restaurant. He talked about his work and the multiple millions of dollars the Japanese were going to give him."

Over sushi, Nyce told them how he often had to eat "disgusting" dishes, in order to charm his Japanese hosts and not seem bad-mannered.

"For instance," said Kuny, "he said he had to eat a uterus sushi in order to get the deal going. He said he was disgusted, but did it anyway, as they were going to invest in his company."

With millions of dollars of new venture capital pouring into his company—including a $15 million licensing arrangement with Italy's Chiesi Farmaceutici, Jonathan Nyce now lived the high life, reflecting his new position as a captain of industry. Later he would claim that his business deals with multi-national pharmaceutical companies had netted EpiGenesis $65 million. But though he paid himself a salary, he was only a millionaire on paper, as his drug was still being tested and had yet to make a cent.

Nevertheless he and Michelle began shopping for a new million-dollar home in New Jersey's ultra-exclusive Hopewell Township, and he bought himself an Audi 280i sports car and Michelle a green Toyota Land Cruiser.

He also gave Michelle a generous allowance to buy anything she wanted, although she would send much of it back to the Philippines every month to her family.

"We were doing very well," Dr. Nyce later explained. "[But] the fortunate part of our relationship became the unfortunate part. Michelle saw all these numbers rolling in ... she was becoming an American citizen and somehow she developed the idea that as an American citizen she could pretty much have whatever she wanted."

Samuel Jones [not his real name], a member of the EpiGenesis management team, was hired in early 2000 to oversee the clinical development program. By this time Dr. Nyce had completed his Phase 1 study, using two dozen patients who were not asthma sufferers, to test for possible side effects. Now they were ready to move on to Phase 2, to be carried out in England, this time testing mild asthma sufferers.

Jones had first met Nyce in North Carolina, where they'd attended the same professional meetings, getting to know each other. One day Nyce told him he was relocating his company to New Jersey, offering him an executive job managing his drug testing.

"Jonathan's expertise was not in the clinical process and how to manage trials," he explained. "He needed to find somebody to do that."

When he started working full-time at EpiGenesis, Jones was most impressed with his new boss.

"Jonathan's a very intelligent guy, sincere," said Jones, "[but] he seemed to know his limitations."

V.P. of Operations Amanda Gillum believes Nyce spent too much of his time traveling the world, raising venture capital, instead of staying in New Jersey to concentrate on vital scientific research.

"I could see that as the company was growing, the business development was taking more of his time," she said. "You can't do it all yourself."

Part of the problem appeared to be Nyce's inability to delegate, and his insistence on doing everything himself. And no one in the company would stand up and tell him he was wrong.

"It was his baby," said Gillum. "People might have hesitated to challenge him."

Jones also agreed that many of the problems facing EpiGenesis lay with its founder.

"You have very bright people who found a company," he explained. "The skills that make them an excellent researcher are not the ones that make them an excellent businessman. Jonathan wasn't unique in that regard."

But as EpiGenesis moved into the next century, there was only clear blue sky on the horizon, and no hint of the trouble to come.

8

The Billion-Dollar Player

In early 2000, Jonathan and Michelle Nyce bought their $880,000 dream house, in the exclusive Princeton suburb of Titusville, Hopewell Township. Perched on the top of a hill at the end of a cul-de-sac, 1 Keithwood Court looked down on its neighbors and was surrounded by more than three acres of land.

When the Nyces first saw the brand-new, 5,600-square-foot, twenty-one-room colonial with sweeping views, they made an offer on the spot. Jonathan Nyce soon secured a $625,000 mortgage, and within a couple of months they had moved in, falling easily into a millionaires' lifestyle.

"We had never owned a house," said Nyce. "We'd lived in apartments for our entire time together. So for the first time I was earning enough that I could consider buying a house, and also my board was giving me bonuses for signing these big deals."

Hopewell Township, which dates back to 1695, surrounds Hopewell Borough and is a rural 60-square-mile area of lush rolling hills, parks, forests and historic landmarks. An old Presbyterian church still has a cemetery stone wall that the

British troops used to practice jumping over with their horses before the Revolutionary War.

Titusville is a village west of the Delaware River in the southwestern part of Hopewell Township. It was named in the early Nineteenth Century after a merchant named Joseph Titus, who owned the land on which the village was built and developed it into a thriving area.

By the 1850s it had a population of three hundred, boasting several large stores and hotels, two churches, a harness shop, a blacksmith and a schoolhouse. There were also many gentleman dairy farmers up till the Second World War, as well as acre upon acre of cornfields, which are now sprawling shopping malls.

Keithwood Court was built on the site of an old dairy farm, and is just a short drive from Princeton and not far from Trenton, the New Jersey state capital.

"Room to grow and lots of space to enjoy," boasted a Realtor brochure for the house; "the perfect combination for active lifestyles."

A flexible floor plan gave the Nyces formal and informal first-floor areas, with a spectacular gourmet kitchen, containing state-of-the-art custom cabinetry, top-of-the-line stainless-steel appliances, granite countertops and a generous breakfast room. It also boasted "an exceptional library/office suite, a bright conservatory and a striking family room with a towering floor to ceiling stone gas fireplace."

On the second floor were five spacious bedrooms, including Jonathan and Michelle's 16' × 18' master bedroom. Additionally there were three full bathrooms and a laundry area, as well as a massive family room and a first-floor office for Jonathan.

There was also a huge basement, running the entire length of the house, which could be accessed from the kitchen, as well as an attached three-car garage.

"It was Michelle's house," said Nyce. "I bought it for Michelle and it was the one she picked out. I actually had picked out a house closer to Princeton Junior School, where the kids were going at the time, for about half the price, but Michelle fell in love with this development and this house.

"And I loved her and trusted her and I let her go ahead and outfit the house the way she wanted to."

Michelle Nyce spared no expense, selecting only the best custom-made fittings for the interior of her new home. On one shopping spree she surprised her sales staff by casually picking out thousands of dollars' worth of *the* most expensive bathroom and kitchen fittings, by just pointing, never once asking the price of anything.

"She had to get the best of everything," said her mother-in-law, Emma Nyce. "She got a beautiful chandelier, but it wasn't good enough. So Jonathan finally got her the diamond one she wanted, and put it up. He said to me, 'She's never satisfied.' "

Michelle also embarked on a two-year search to find a five-tier water fountain, which was eventually placed in the middle of a circle driveway by the front door, alongside six thousand freshly planted tulips.

Somehow Jonathan never seemed to be able to say no to his beautiful wife.

"She got what she wanted," said his mother. "He just . . . kept saying, 'She's the mother of my children and I love her.' "

Nyce's outlay for the new house were massive. In addition to paying monthly installments on his $625,000 mortgage, the annual taxes alone were more than $25,000.

Keithwood Court was mainly compromised of successful businessmen and their wives, who were always trying to outdo each other materially.

"It's not a super-close neighborhood," said one neighbor, Mary Gregg (not her real name). "It's the kind of neighborhood where the women try to get in your house and see all your stuff." Soon after the Nyces moved in, a procession of their new neighbors came by to introduce themselves—and peek around to see what they owned.

Michelle was down-to-earth, a refreshing balm in stuck-up Keithwood Court, refusing to put on any airs.

"[It's] full of stuffy, wealthy women, and Michelle was not one of them," said Gregg. "She didn't care about keeping up appearances."

Within weeks of moving in, Michelle had ordered the diamond chandelier and a grand piano for the living room. But the massive home—far too big for the family—would always remain sparsely furnished, with many rooms empty.

"He lived very high," said Nyce's old ECU mentor Dr. Wallace Wooles, who was still in close touch with Jonathan, as a scientific advisor to EpiGenesis. "But his wealth was mainly on paper."

Dr. Wooles said Nyce might have been drawing a good salary, but was living off "venture capital comfort money," as EpiGenesis had never actually made any profits.

"So mostly his wealth consisted of all the stock that he had, and the potential," he said. "When he left here, he started getting a bigger home, big sports cars. That wasn't the Jonathan that we knew."

Dr. Wooles blames Michelle for encouraging Jonathan to live well beyond their means.

"Michelle was a very ambitious woman," he said. "She wanted the better things. And I think the age difference between them was just too much for Jonathan to handle."

In early April 2000, on the fifth anniversary of his founding EpiGenesis, Jonathan Nyce signed a massive $100 million deal, with Japan's biggest over-the-counter drug company, Taisho. The two companies would become partners in marketing Nyce's EPI-2010 in Asia. It was a wide-ranging agreement which made EpiGenesis a major international player, and had the potential to make Jonathan Nyce wealthy beyond his dreams.

"EpiGenesis is a pioneer," declared Taisho's executive vice-president Akira Ohira, in an April 7 press release. "We are extremely pleased to collaborate."

And Dr. Nyce, the proud EpiGenesis Chairman and CEO, said how "very pleased" he was to be signing an agreement with Taisho, describing the Tokyo-based company as "an exceptional partner."

In the weeks leading up to the deal, Nyce had been assiduously courting the huge Japanese company. To celebrate signing the agreement, he held a lavish, fully-catered Japanese-themed party at his new home.

"It was an important time with Japan," said his mother, who babysat her grandchildren upstairs during the party. "They had a sushi bar and there was a harpist playing before the band came on later. What a wonderful party."

Soon after signing the deal, EpiGenesis moved into a large new 20,000-square-foot facility at the Cedar Brook Corporate Center in Princeton, now needed to accommodate the growing company.

"I immediately started pushing for fifty employees, fifty-two employees," Nyce would later explain. "These were heady times."

Dr. Brian McMillan says Nyce told him his long-term plan was to eventually sell off EpiGenesis to a major international drug company, such as Taisho or Merck, while he still had a large stake in it.

"His big hope was that it kept expanding and moving into critical trials," said Dr. McMillan. "It would solve the headache of him constantly having to find money."

Soon after they moved into 1 Keithwood Court, Michelle flew back to the Philippines to visit her family. It had been her first visit since her marriage nine years earlier, and she returned, the prodigal daughter.

Michelle had wanted to bring her three children to meet their grandparents, aunts and uncles and cousins, but Jonathan had demurred. "He refused to allow Michelle to bring the children to meet us," said her father. According to Teodoro, Jonathan had seized their passports and locked them away, fearing the children could be targeted for kidnapping.

Eight-year-old Alex Nyce was now enrolled in Timberlane Middle School in nearby Pennington, while his 6-year-old brother Trevor went to Bear Tavern Elementary School in Titusville.

When Michelle returned to New Jersey from the Philippines she seemed different, as if she had found a new emotional independence from her husband. She began sending her family large sums of money on a regular basis, to pay for education and housing.

"She sent me about 400,000 pesos [$7,150 U.S.] so I could build my house," said her father. "And she sent my son 500,000 pesos [$9,000 U.S.] so he could build a house. Michelle helped us build six houses [as well as] a playground with a slide."

Riviera says his son-in-law was far less generous, once sending 30,000 pesos ($536 U.S.) for his grandson's tuition, and also paying for a minor operation when another grandson swallowed a coin.

With little to do every day now that Samantha was in kindergarten and the boys at school, Michelle started spending more and more time at a local gym, working out. She would often take powdered energy drinks to get her through her grueling schedule, keeping her perfect body in top condition.

"She was moving into the direction of eternal youth," Nyce would later say. "That's what she was driving toward."

And, always insecure about their age difference, Nyce became increasingly concerned about his beautiful young wife meeting men in the gym. So he spent thousands of dollars building a well-equipped gymnasium with all the latest machines on the ground-floor sun room of their new house.

"I know for a fact that that's why she had a gym in her house," said Larissa Soos. "Jonathan did not want her to go to a local gym, because there are so many people there, and guys. She's beautiful, she's twenty years younger than him. He felt vulnerable."

Once again Michelle covered up for Jonathan, telling friends the gym was part of a new business she planned to start as a personal trainer. But it would be more than a year before she did anything further about becoming officially certified.

On October 30, 2000, EpiGenesis began its first human trials for EPI-2010. Using a randomized, double-blind study, the Phase 1 tests were designed to assess the effects and side-effects of the drug.

"This is extremely important," explained Dr. Nyce, in a press release. "We feel strongly that we are on the threshold of major progress against asthma—a disease with a death rate that has rocketed more than 60 percent here in the U.S. in less than a decade."

That Christmas, Michelle Nyce attended a poetry evening at Bear Tavern Elementary School, where 7-year-old Trevor was reading. During a break she struck up a conversation with another mother named Roz Clancy, whose son Joseph was in Trevor's class.

"I always become friendly with my son's friends' parents," she said, "because I want to know who they are. Luckily [Michelle] just happened to be the sweetest, kindest person."

Over the next few months Roz Clancy and Michelle often saw each other at school functions. They began to socialize, getting to know each other around their children's little league and soccer schedules.

"She was a very charming, genuine person. Nothing artificial," said Clancy, who ran a modeling agency in Trenton. "It's funny because she always wanted to meet me at her house. It was like, Why not my house? But it had to be there."

Nevertheless, Clancy was most impressed with the Nyce home, especially Michelle's private gym.

"The inside of their home was immaculate," she said breathlessly. "Exquisite furniture."

Soon after they met, Michelle introduced her to Jonathan, who she felt was "strange," and the polar opposite to her gregarious, outgoing friend.

"I got to know him from a distance," she said. "He was quiet and I couldn't read him. He was different."

Whenever Roz and her husband were at a school function with the Nyces, Jonathan seemed preoccupied, like he was somewhere else. Roz thought him "cold" and socially inept.

"It was hard for him to carry a conversation," she said. "He didn't open himself up and he didn't feel comfortable around me."

That Christmas, Jonathan took Michelle to his annual family celebration at his parents' house in Collegeville, Pennsylvania. Once again Michelle felt uncomfortable with her in-laws, telling friends they disapproved of her. She was convinced they believed Jonathan had married beneath himself.

In summer 2001, Kuny Brothers visited again, finding Michelle totally immersed in her new affluent lifestyle.

"It was a big change," said Kuny. "They moved from a small rental here to a multi-million-dollar home. I thought maybe money went to her head. She seemed to be really into Jonathan's work. But she always wanted everyone to see the good side. I don't think she wanted anyone to know their dirty laundry."

After they moved to Keithwood Court, Sherry Leonard noticed that Michelle would visit her husband at EpiGenesis less and less often, even detecting a slight tension between them.

"Sometimes he would voice frustration regarding her spending habits," she said, "and occasionally her irresponsibility with making sure the kids got to appointments on time."

But EpiGenesis V.P. Amanda Gillum thought the Nyces still seemed a very devoted couple, whenever she saw Michelle and the children at the laboratory or dropped off work at their home.

"They seemed fine," she said. "Quite affectionate. He was devoted and attentive to them."

EpiGenesis executive Anthony Sandrasagra, who spent

two years at the company, thought his CEO was a devoted family man.

"He'd go into his office [where] he'd have the picture of his wife and kids," said Sandrasagra. "And he spoke very positively of his family."

Whenever Michelle visited EpiGenesis with her children, she would take them to play in a little park next door. Then Jonathan would come out to meet them, and they'd all go to lunch.

"She was obviously very young compared to Jonathan," said Sandrasagra. "She seemed like a very nice person."

Later, Jonathan Nyce would pinpoint this as the time when his marriage began to spiral downwards, blaming it on his success going to Michelle's head.

"We moved into an expensive neighborhood," he later told police. "As we settled, Michelle began to unravel psychologically."

From early childhood Jonathan Nyce had been passive-aggressive, learning never to show his real feelings. He always kept the world at a distance, using his natural shyness as a carefully constructed protective wall around him.

But occasionally on international business trips and after a few drinks, Nyce did let down his guard and talk about his marriage.

"We traveled the world together," said Samuel Jones. "But the things he said in that regard should stay there. They are private conversations and I think I should leave it at that.

"Jonathan wanted very much to give outsiders the perception that he's a very successful businessman [with] a very happy home life. So if there were problems, he wouldn't be the kind of person to share that."

And Michelle too never mentioned any problems she might have been having with Jonathan, always portraying him as the perfect husband and her soul mate.

But in late 2001, after Michelle sent Kuny Brothers' son a birthday present, she broke off all contact with her North Carolina friends, as if they'd never existed.

9

The Seeds of Destruction

In July 2001, Alex and Trevor Nyce were winding up a week-long golf camp in Pennington when Michelle brought along their 3-year-old sister Samantha. Also at the range that day was another Filipino-born woman named Larissa Soos, with her 6-month-old son.

"Oh, you have such a cute baby," Michelle told Larissa, who thanked her and then asked if she was Filipino too.

"She said yes," remembered Larissa, "and we just started talking."

Soos explained that she and her husband, John, and their three young children were moving to Hopewell Township in a couple of months' time, and they exchanged phone numbers.

"It was just a five- or ten-minute thing," Larissa said. "But it was just luck that we happened to be in the same spot at the same time."

When Larissa moved in September, she called Michelle Nyce, inviting her children to Keithwood Court for a play date. The two young mothers soon discovered much in common. Both came from the same rural area of the Philippines, were the middle children of large families, and both had married successful men and moved to America.

"We were both not the type of people to sit down and wait for things to happen," said Soos, who was five years older than Michelle. "If we want to do something, we go for it. I always felt like my family were poor but I guess if you compare it to [Michelle's] they were well off."

Soon after they met, Michelle invited Larissa to work out in her personal gym, and the two women began training together. Michelle told Larissa she was studying to be a personal trainer, and began whipping her friend into shape.

She explained how her husband, Jonathan, had built her an expensive gym, as he refused to allow her to join a public one.

"There were guys there, so she had her own gym," said Larissa. "And she got bored working out by herself, so she would invite friends to come over. And she's pretty tough on people working out with her, I can tell you from experience."

On other occasions Michelle would visit Larissa's home, as all their children got on well together. While the kids played, the two young women opened up to each other about their lives. Once again Michelle told the fabricated story of meeting Jonathan on the beach in Hawaii.

The first time Larissa met Jonathan was at his 2001 Halloween party at Keithwood Court. But they hardly talked then, and it would be more than a year before they became friends.

"I didn't really get to know him right away," said Soos. "Because at that time he was at EpiGenesis, and he got home about eight o'clock every night and he traveled."

As with millions of other Americans, everything changed for Jonathan Nyce when the World Trade Center and the Pentagon were attacked on September 11, 2001. Up to that time, there had been plenty of venture capitalists, only too willing to invest in biotech start-up companies or the proliferating dotcoms. But in the wake of 9/11, the cash well began to dry up, fast leading to an industry-wide recession.

"Just before 9/11 we had actually signed preliminary documents with one of the major pharmaceutical companies for eight hundred million dollars," said Nyce. "And we thought that was going to propel us into the upper ranks of the pharmaceutical companies."

The first week of September, EpiGenesis had staged an ambitious cross-country roadshow, hoping to raise new venture capital funds. And then Al Quaida hit.

"We call it the nuclear winter," said Samuel Jones. "[After September 11] markets shut down for two or three years. After that the investor climate became very cold."

The company roadshow soon ground to a halt and the money-men Nyce was so assiduously courting were looking for investments much nearer market than EPI-2010, which was still in its test phase.

Nyce said that in the wake of 9/11 his $800-million deal fell through.

"And that caused huge repercussions," he said. "Our funds became short and the venture capital companies took advantage of that."

U.S. 1 newspaper's senior editor, Barbara Fox, believes that "In ordinary times" Nyce's company and his technology . . . might have succeeded, as clinical trials had already proved one of his therapies "partially successful."

But his company's main problem was having a small investor base, with most of its funding coming from Taisho, apart from a few government grants.

"This was during the dotcom bubble," she explained. "When Internet companies were sucking away money from biotech. And at the moment when Nyce needed to raise some serious money, the web bubble had burst."

For the rest of the year EpiGenesis would limp along, but by early 2002 it would be in deep, deep trouble.

In the fall of 2001, Michelle Nyce decided to landscape the extensive grounds around 1 Keithwood Court. She hired the

Ostrich Nursery in nearby Hightstown to plant $50,000 worth of trees she had personally selected.

A few days later a crew of five gardeners arrived at the house, led by a handsome 31-year-old Puerto Rican named Miguel deJesus, better known by his nickname Enyo.

The gardeners worked hard through the day, planting saplings around the house and other shrubs. After they finished, Enyo knocked on the front door and presented the bill to Michelle Nyce.

"That's how I met her," he would later remember. "My boss had sent me to plant trees."

Although they didn't talk that day, there was a mutual attraction between the rich young mother of three and the rough-and-ready gardener. But it would be another nine months before they would meet again and take it any further.

In the spring of 2002, Jonathan Nyce was forced to start laying off staff in the first round of cuts that would slash the number of his employees to just a dozen. The company's finances were a nightmare, and one business newspaper estimated EpiGenesis had already "burned through" a staggering $40 million of venture capital, with few results.

"The company was running out of money," said Jones. "Taisho and Chiesi were running out of money. Was there pressure building at EpiGenesis? Sure."

As the year drew on, there was tremendous pressure on Jonathan Nyce to keep his company afloat, as he urgently needed a fresh cash injection to pay for his ongoing clinical tests. In desperation, he took out a $200,000 home equity loan against his new house, but this was just a drop in the ocean.

"Funding was tight and we cut heavily into research," said employee Anthony Sandrasagra. "Basically the company was running out of cash and there were discussions ongoing with the current investors."

Publicly EpiGenesis put on a brave face, with a constant

stream of positive press releases aimed at attracting new
venture capital. Trumpeting its early clinical test results for
EPI-2010 as "promising," Dr. Nyce described the latest results as "truly significant," although his drug still had to un-
dergo "more definitive" evaluation, as well as a Phase II
clinical program.

But Sandrasagra said the press release was highly optimistic, as, from the results he'd seen, "it didn't look like the
compound was working better than steroids."

That May, Michelle Nyce's father, Teodoro Riviera, arrived for a six-month stay at Keithwood Court. Her quietly
spoken father soon made himself useful around the house,
cooking Filipino and Chinese dinners and babysitting his
grandchildren.

Although Jonathan Nyce spent so much of the time away
on business, when he was home he got on well with his
father-in-law.

"On the whole we had a good relationship," said Riviera.
"I lived at their house and Jonathan left in the morning and
got back in the evening."

Emma Nyce suspected Riviera had a hidden agenda to
bring over the rest of the family, using the green card he had
just received.

"You've got to read between the lines," she explained.
"But I'll tell you one thing—her father was her maid. He did
the washing, the cleaning, the dishes and everything."

Larissa Soos arranged for Riviera to work for her father-
in-law's company, installing radon gas fans. During his extended stay he thought his daughter and son-in-law were
getting on fine.

"Everything seemed to be OK," he said. "They got on
well because he was working."

If there was tension in the house, nobody on the outside
saw it.

Larissa Soos, who became "sisters" with Michelle that
summer, had hardly spoken to Jonathan when they'd first
met at his Halloween party, but when she did she liked him.

"I didn't really meet him right away," she remembered.

"When I finally did I didn't know how to deal with him. But then he opened up and started smiling and making jokes. And after a while I really felt that he was a nice guy."

She was also impressed by Nyce's obvious rapport with children, and how well he got on with her kids. Soon after they met him he organized a fossil hunt for the children, as part of a birthday party. Billed as a "scientific party" for his two boys, he had hidden items like shark teeth and fossils in the garden. The highlight of the party was a model hot air balloon that he released into the sky.

"He went out with the kids to search for the fossils," she said. "That was great fun."

When Larissa and her husband, John, went out for dinner and movies with them, the Nyces always appeared very close and affectionate with each other. Jonathan was very courteous, gallantly moving a chair so his wife could sit down, or opening the door for her.

"She would sit on his lap sometimes," said Larissa. "They would be all over each other and they would kiss each other in front of us. My husband was like, 'Look at them.' "

Although Nyce had always been wary of Michelle's friends, he thoroughly approved of Larissa and encouraged the friendship.

"I really liked people like Larissa Soos and her husband, John," he later told police, "who were a good influence on Michelle."

During their regular workout sessions, which were followed by lunch, the two women often discussed intimate details of their lives. Michelle never said a bad word about her husband

"We did speak about the sexual subject," said Larissa. "She said she liked sex with her husband."

About this time, Jonathan and Michelle Nyce were at a family birthday party for his brother Michael. At one point Michelle was talking to her mother-in-law when Jonathan's birthday came up in casual conversation. Emma Nyce happened to remark that her eldest son had been born in 1950, and Michelle said she must be mistaken—that would make him 52, and her husband was only 44 years old.

But Emma insisted she was right and should know her son's age better than anyone.

It was a terrible shock for Michelle to discover her husband and the father of her children had lied about his age from the very beginning, even on their wedding certificate. From then on, her attitude towards him changed from love into resentment.

Now, little by little, she would try to get out of the marriage, but found herself trapped, as Jonathan controlled all the finances. But that would soon change.

10

Enyo

In July 2002, Michelle ordered more trees for her front garden from the Ostrich Nursery. And once again Miguel deJesus and his team arrived to plant them. They worked in the garden all day and at about 5:00 p.m., before they left, Enyo walked up to the front door to question Michelle Nyce about the bill.

"I wanted to ask if the balance was paid or not," said Enyo. "I talked to Michelle in front of her house. It was our first conversation."

Michelle wanted him to get rid of some extra dirt they had dug up, but then she suddenly requested his cell phone number.

"I asked her why," he would later remember. "She said she would like to be my friend, [so] I gave it."

Then Michelle gave him hers, asking him to call her when he was ready to leave. And a few minutes later he telephoned her from his Ostrich truck, parked outside in the street.

"She said, 'I want to talk to you,'" he remembered. "'I want to be your friend.'"

Michelle said she was busy and promised to phone him

back in a few minutes. Fifteen minutes later she called, saying she wanted to get to know him better.

Over the next few months, Michelle and deJesus talked on the phone regularly, having long conversations and starting a friendship. Although he had been born in Puerto Rico, he told her he was from Guatemala and that his name was Alexander Castaneda, but everyone called him Enyo.

She would never know that he used at least three different names, including Sergio Martinez and Miguel deJesus, which was his real name. He also employed no fewer than three different Social Security numbers and various addresses.

Although he was something of a ladies' man, Enyo was not particularly handsome. He was short and stocky, with a gray streak running through the top of his closely cropped brown hair.

DeJesus had lived in America for fourteen years, working for the Ostrich Nursery for the last five, where he ran a crew of five gardeners. He had a common-law wife of nine years named Patricia Abad, and they had two young daughters together.

But he was also a deadbeat dad, with a warrant out for his arrest for non-payment of child support. A few years earlier he had fathered an illegitimate daughter, after a one-night stand with a female colleague at the L'Oréal Perfume company. In order to evade the police warrant, he had adopted the alias Alexander Castaneda, the name Michelle knew him by.

Scarcely out of her teens when she'd married Jonathan, and having three children in rapid succession, Michelle felt she had missed out on her youth. She had never dated or gone to clubs like most American teenagers, so she now decided to make up for what she had missed.

She felt comfortable with the charming gardener, looking forward to his calls, which were coming in daily. She even bought herself a pay-as-you-go cell phone, so Jonathan wouldn't find out.

For the first few months the relationship remained platonic, but Michelle felt very attracted to Enyo. She bought him expensive presents, like a watch, a coat, some jewelry and chocolates. And, according to Enyo, she ardently pursued him.

"We were talking more and more on the phone," Enyo would later testify. "Then we started meeting in several restaurants for lunch, or after work for a drink. For the first six months there was no sex in the relationship. We were friends at that point."

By September, they were meeting so frequently that Enyo's wife, Patricia, began to suspect her husband was being unfaithful. One day she checked all the incoming calls on his cell phone, discovering five she could not account for.

"He was going out a lot," she explained. "[I] thought he was having an affair."

When Patricia dialed the number to investigate further, a female voice answered, saying, "Hi, honey."

Furious that her suspicions appeared to be true, Patricia snapped back angrily, "I'm not your honey . . . I'm your honey's wife." The woman then hung up.

Patricia called straight back, this time getting an answering machine.

"This is Michelle," said the female voice in a distinct accent. "Leave a message."

"This is Patricia," replied Abad. "I have a family, and stay out of our lives!"

She then re-checked Enyo's cell phone, discovering several text messages signed "M. Nyce." One of them read, "I miss you, call me."

That night she confronted Enyo, accusing him of cheating on her.

"[He was] nervous," she said, "and denied all knowledge of M. Nyce."

So from then on Patricia regularly checked his phone, discovering he was still placing calls and texting the woman.

Then, in a second attempt to persuade Michelle to leave her man alone, Patricia left a message on Michelle's cell phone, asking her to phone to discuss the situation. But Michelle never returned the call.

A couple of weeks later, when Patricia had taken Enyo's

cell phone to work, Michelle called. The two women then had a thirty-minute conversation, during which she asked Michelle point blank if she and Enyo were having an affair. Michelle denied the accusation, saying they were "just friends."

During the conversation Patricia asked how they had met in the first place, and Michelle said he had seen her at a swimming pool, asking some friends to get her number.

"He was shocked by my beauty," Patricia claimed Michelle told her, before asking her for some personal details, like her and her children's ages, and where she worked.

Abad said the conversation ended with Michelle complimenting her, saying she seemed like a "nice person," and even hoping they would meet in person one day.

In October, Michelle severed all ties with her old North Carolina friends, refusing to return their calls. Kuny Brothers spent months leaving messages on her answer phone, eventually resorting to telephoning Jonathan at EpiGenesis and e-mailing him, asking him to have Michelle get in touch. When there was still no reply, Kuny wondered if he was deliberately trying to separate Michelle from her old friends.

"We lost contact," she said. "And I still don't know why. We never had an argument. That's why I said it's not in her personality not to call me back. She's up to something."

On January 15, 2003, Brothers was on the computer with her niece looking at obituaries, when she had a strange premonition that something terrible had happened to Michelle.

"I said to my niece, '[Jonathan's] done something,' " she remembers. "He's the type of personality that would snap. It was scary, but I knew something happened because she wouldn't return my calls."

So Kuny asked their mutual friend Sandy Chakarthi, who had recently moved to New Jersey, to check up on Michelle and make sure she was all right.

"So I went and knocked on the door," said Sandy, "and she opened it and invited me in."

But immediately Sandy recognized a change in her friend, and felt like a stranger.

"She was very standoffish," she remembered. "She looked the same, but she was different. She seemed uncomfortable."

Sandy noticed when Michelle wrote down her phone number, she wrote it on a piece of paper at the back of her address book.

"And she refused to give out her home number," said Sandy, "and gave me her cell instead."

Michelle then took Sandy on a tour of her luxurious new home, making a special point of showing her the gym with all its expensive equipment.

"I didn't want to see the house," said Sandy. "I wanted to see her."

When she asked about Jonathan, Michelle was evasive.

"She said he was working a lot," recalled Sandy. "But she didn't say how she was getting along with him. I could tell that she was nervous about me being there."

That would be the last time Sandy would ever see her friend. Over the next year she called her cell phone and left numerous messages, but Michelle never returned the call.

"I even went over a couple of times and knocked on her door," she said. "But there was no answer."

That October, Michelle Nyce consummated her affair with Enyo in a seedy motel room off Route 1. After months of anticipation they discovered an easy sexual rapport, which Michelle had rarely enjoyed with her middle-aged husband.

"We came to a point where we both decided to have a sexual relationship," Enyo later testified. "We were both kissing each other."

For the next six months the lovers met once a week in either the afternoon or evening, having sex in motel rooms all over Lawrenceville, New Jersey. Once, according to Enyo, Michelle even brought him back to 1 Keithwood Court, where they made love while her father was in the house.

During their time together Michelle would discuss Jonathan and her three children, often showing him pictures of them. According to him, Michelle said she had grown bored in her marriage, but was reluctant to leave because of the children.

Later Michelle would tell police that three months into their sexual relationship, Enyo suddenly started asking questions about her husband's finances, while they were sitting in Mercer County Park.

"How much does your house cost?" Michelle said he asked her, adding that he also wished to borrow $3,000 for his family to buy property in Guatemala.

"No," Michelle said she told him, "I don't have that kind of money."

Michelle Nyce was now leading a double life, and her husband was too busy keeping his company afloat to notice. But to all her friends she appeared the perfect wife and mother, telling no one about her secret romance.

"She never mentioned anything about the affair," Larissa Soos later explained. "I had no clue."

Always more social and gregarious than her insecure husband, Michelle had also started throwing expensive parties for their friends and their three children. It was not unusual for her to invite a dozen of her children's friends and their parents out to an expensive meal to celebrate one of the kids' birthdays.

"Michelle always wanted to go out," said her mother-in-law, Emma Nyce. "They'd go to these big places where the kids would be catered to. It would cost them several thousand dollars for a little birthday party for a six-year-old."

And Jonathan Nyce had recently taken out two mortgages, totaling $825,000, paying off his initial one of $625,000. Although he was mortgaged to the hilt, he was still living well beyond his means.

Concerned about her son's finances, Emma advised him

to have the parties at home to save money, as well as making other cutbacks.

"I said, 'Jonathan, come on. Why don't you have them like we did? It's so much nicer.' "

He agreed, even building a skateboard ramp in his basement, proving a big hit at Alex's next birthday party.

"The kids loved it," said Emma. "They said it was the best party they had ever been to."

In late 2002, a new consortium of investors began negotiating a deal to rescue EpiGenesis, which was now sinking in red ink. Despite Jonathan Nyce's optimistic claims in a December press release that recent results from clinical trials were "intriguing," his company was sinking fast.

A group of high-powered venture capitalists led by David Ramsay, a partner at Care Capital LLC, started talks to save the company. As Nyce was no longer in control, having traded ownership for capital, he was soon in a very vulnerable position and fighting for survival.

"If you capitalize too soon you end up losing control," explained his friend Dr. Brian McMillan. And that's what happened with Jonathan."

There was another round of savage cuts in October, slashing the EpiGenesis staff to the bare bones. One day Samuel Jones was told he no longer had a job. With the writing on the wall, Jonathan Nyce seemed to be breaking under the pressure.

According to friends, when he drank he would boast about his achievements, and all the millions of dollars he had raised.

"It became clear as the new [venture capital] money came in that Jonathan would not be retained as CEO," explained Samuel Jones. "The well had been poisoned. It's on those terms we left, and we haven't spoken since. I put my hand out. He wouldn't even shake my hand to say good luck. I didn't understand what that was about."

But clearly the idealistic pharmacologist was out of step with the cut-throat world of big business in the new millennium.

"He is more of a scientist and a discoverer," explained David Ramsay, the man who would ultimately wrestle Epi-Genesis away from him.

11

You're Fired

n February 2003, Michelle Nyce flew to the Philippines to visit her family, with Jonathan planning to join her the following week. Once again he refused to allow his three children to come along and meet the Filipino side of their family, saying it was too dangerous, and that they might be kidnapped. So his parents agreed to move into 1 Keithwood Court to babysit Alex, Trevor and Samantha while their parents were away.

A few days before Michelle left, Enyo again asked if he could borrow money. This time she agreed, handing him a thousand dollars out of travelers' checks that her husband had given her to take to her family.

"Well, my husband gave me travelers' checks for spending money," she would later tell police. "The one thousand dollars was to give my brothers and sisters back home . . . and Alexander paid me back soon after I returned."

It was Jonathan's first trip to the Philippines since his marriage thirteen years earlier, and Michelle's family welcomed him back to Depensa Capunitan, throwing a family party to celebrate. At the beginning, everything was fine, but before long it became obvious Jonathan and Michelle were constantly fighting.

Throughout his stay, Jonathan—now under extreme pressure from the new board at EpiGenesis—seemed irritable and bad tempered. He was also drinking heavily.

"He always drank," said Nyce's brother-in-law, Sonny Ragenil.

The highlight of their Philippine vacation was when Nyce took all Michelle's nephews and nieces for a trip to Boracay Island, on the northwestern tip of Panay. Described in the travel brochures as "the finest beach in the world," the four kilometers of sugary white sand is renowned for its scuba diving.

One day during lunch Nyce decided their hunky tour guide was paying too much attention to Michelle, and started screaming at her in front of everyone.

"Jonathan got mad at my sister," said Melodia, who witnessed the outburst, saying it made everyone highly uncomfortable. "He was so angry. They were fighting in front of my nephews, just because my sister talked to the tour guide."

Melodia's husband, Sonny, said Nyce constantly argued with Michelle while they were in the Philippines.

"He was very jealous of everybody," said Sonny. "He was mad at Michelle and they were fighting."

The Riviera family was also in financial trouble. Their duck farm had gone bankrupt.

"It was very, very sad," said Teodoro Riviera. "One year the ducks were not laying eggs anymore and we have no money to replace them."

Later Nyce would describe the conditions of "extreme poverty" he claimed to have witnessed the Riviera family living in when he had first met them.

"It's hard for anyone here to believe the circumstances in which the Rivieras were living," he said. "Michelle's family had constructed shacks out on the water on stilts. It was a community of squatters."

He claims that he'd built Michelle's family six houses and a school inland, so they would not be "washed away" by a typhoon or tsunami. The main purpose of their visit was to see what improvements had been made.

But the Riviera family strenuously deny Nyce's claims that they ever lived in squalor and were starving, accusing him of inventing the story to gain sympathy and make himself look good. And they claim it was always Michelle who sent money over to help them.

Before their departure, according to Nyce, he called a family meeting on the beach to explain how his finances were "stretched fairly tight," and that, although he was making a "big salary," his future was uncertain.

"I said, 'Look, we're all in this together,' " he said. " 'My job is coming up for new financing and it is possible there could be changes.' "

When he returned to the States, he claims, he sent them a freeze-dried "emergency food shipment," costing about $6,000.

"There were twenty-seven kids there, so they were ecstatic to receive this food," he explained. "Now they could eat."

During his two-week stay in the Philippines, Jonathan Nyce kept in daily touch with EpiGenesis, but the news was not good. As the new board of venture capitalists moved in to take over his company, he felt his control slipping away.

"The company was restructured," explained Sherry Leonard, who had by this time been Nyce's assistant for fifteen years. "Someone needed to take the blame for past failures, and it was Jonathan."

On Friday, March 28, 2003, EpiGenesis founder and CEO Jonathan Nyce was summoned into the boardroom and summarily fired. All parties involved signed a confidentiality statement agreeing never to reveal details of his financial severance package. But later Nyce told friends, "I was irritated by the way my being let go was handled. I was unhappy the way things ended, but I had two years of full salary, and very good benefits."

Joanne Leonard (no relation to Sherry), who joined Epi-Genesis in October 2002 as chief financial officer, explained that Nyce was "no longer useful" to the company, becoming expendable after its focus changed with the new board.

Six months later she told *U.S. 1*'s Barbara Fox that potential new investors were unimpressed with early-stage drugs like EPI-2010. Therefore the company had halted any further development of Nyce's platform technology. And distancing itself even further from its founder, the new team announced plans to develop a completely new asthma drug.

"Now, with new financing [and] a new management team," enthused Joanne Leonard, "new board members and new scientific advisors, we are excited about the new direction of the company."

A year later, Jonathan Nyce would attempt to put a positive spin on his dismissal, saying it was common place in the cut-throat world of big business.

"I was trying to do a final round of financing for my company," he explained. "EpiGenesis was in clinical trials with two drugs . . . and I needed about eighteen million dollars to move forward with these drugs. So I hooked up with a big group who, immediately on signing the deal, fired me. It is not unusual. They replace CEOs all the time."

The Thursday before he was fired, Jonathan Nyce organized a lavish, no-expense-spared fifth birthday party for his daughter Samantha. The morning of the catered children's party, a large truck pulled up in front of 1 Keithwood Court, and several workers began inflating a huge thirty-foot plastic castle in the garden.

"It was the kind you rent for a carnival," said Andy Sjamsu. "The hire company had to drive it in, waiting around until the end to take it away again."

The party was held in the Nyces' double garage, and all Samantha's school friends were there. Nyce had laid on pony rides for the children and gift baskets, and everybody loved bouncing up and down on the inflatable castle.

Although under great stress at work, Jonathan Nyce was the perfect host that day, organizing the children's games and making sure everything went off perfectly.

"They were extremely good parents," said Sjamsu, who took digital photographs, printing them on the spot and handing them out to the guests.

12

Setting a Trap

In the days after he lost EpiGenesis, Jonathan Nyce fell into a deep depression, retiring to his office for hours at a time. He refused to discuss what had happened with anyone, reading voraciously to escape his problems.

"It was heartbreaking," said his mother. "I think he was too hurt to even talk about it."

Michelle's best friend, Larissa Soos, only found out weeks later, when she saw Jonathan sitting by himself in the kitchen one morning. She asked Michelle why he was home early and offered to leave, but was told not to worry, as from now on he would be working from home.

"We never thought that he'd lost his job," said Larissa. "They told me he sold his shares at EpiGenesis and was getting two years' worth of pay. That's when I started seeing more of him."

In an effort to put a positive spin on his situation, Nyce announced he was taking a sabbatical, to concentrate on his writing and developing a new cancer drug.

"I was being paid from EpiGenesis for two years," he later explained. "Full salary. Full benefits. So I was going to use the first year to do something I always wanted to do, which was to write."

Working on his computer in his first-floor office, Nyce began writing a children's book, entitling it *Dr. Nyce's Poems for Children and the Parents Who Love Them*. He dedicated it to Michelle and his children.

"The first six poems were about my kids," he explained. "And then I had a second section where I had a poem I had written recently for Michelle."

Nyce used his three children as characters and even hired an illustrator. There was one picture of him rocking Samantha to sleep and another of Trevor, staring at the stars. But when his eldest son Alex complained he was not in the book, Nyce promised to put him in the next one.

"It was like a love letter to my family," said Nyce. "And that made me feel good."

The first poem was based on a true story about how his sons Alex and Trevor had once used a piece of deer hide to fashion him a shoe for Father's Day, because they couldn't afford a present.

> *Son one and son 2 made dad a new shoe*
> *They didn't have quite enough stuff to make 2*
> *But what would dad do with only one shoe?*
> *Said Son 2 to son 1 and son 1 to son 2*
> *But their dad was happy to get such a prize*
> *He sat himself down to try it for size*
> *"It fits just so perfectly well," he exclaimed.*
> *"That I think I shall never wear 2 shoes again."*
> *He hopped up and down. He hopped left and right.*
> *He hopped so fast he gave mom a fright.*
> *He hopped all the day until it was night.*
> *Then he hopped into bed and turned off the light.*
>
> *He dreamed all night long of son 1 and son 2*
> *His heart filled with joy for the gift of the shoe*
> *For gifts from the heart mean so very much more*
> *Than anything anyone could buy in the store.*

"He wrote a beautiful children's book," said Emma Nyce. "It was supposed to be the first in a series."

He also worked on developing a new company he called Prism Pharmaceuticals. This one would utilize a drug he'd invented as a professor at ECU, to prevent lung cancer in smokers.

"[It] was my pride and joy," he explained. "I decided, after my experience with EpiGenesis, that I would develop this drug through the N.I.H."

Now that Jonathan was at home all day, it became harder for Michelle to slip out and meet her lover, Enyo, as easily as before. She began to resent Jonathan spending all day at home on his computer, urging him to find a job, as they were running out of money.

"I remember her coming into my office one day when I was working," Nyce would later claim. "And just wiping my desk clean [with her hand], everything on the floor. And that evening I asked if I could take her to see a psychiatrist, because her attitude was not appropriate."

But she was still regularly meeting her lover, whom she had affectionately nicknamed "Honey," at seedy motels for sex, telling Jonathan she was going shopping or meeting friends for dinner. And when she enrolled for night classes at Mercer County Community College to become a physical fitness instructor, she told Jonathan the course began a month earlier than it actually did.

In late May 2003, Jonathan Nyce telephoned his former assistant Sherry Leonard, inviting her to lunch to celebrate his fifty-third birthday. Two weeks earlier Taisho had officially severed all ties with EpiGenesis, finally shelving his EPI-2010 asthma drug due to disappointing test results.

They met in a Japanese restaurant in Cranbury, New Jersey, and Leonard was delighted to see him in such good spirits. He said he was now over EpiGenesis, enthusiastically telling her about his children's poetry book.

"He was very excited about it," she remembered. "He had

just recently met with an illustrator [and] he had talked with various people about writing a foreword. It sounded like it was going well."

As they left the restaurant, Sherry asked him to say hello to Michelle. But Nyce suddenly stopped in his tracks, telling her it would not be a good idea. Then, to her horror, he said Michelle had once accused him of having a long-term affair with Sherry.

"My reaction was shock," she said, "and [I] commented that that would be gross . . . somewhat incestuous. I always thought of Jonathan as a family member, something like a brother. He was taken aback that I had voiced such a disdain at the idea."

A couple of weeks later, Michelle's father, Teodoro Riviera, arrived from the Philippines, moving into 1 Keithwood Court for a second extended stay. He found that Michelle and Jonathan's relationship had changed beyond recognition in the six months since he had left.

"When I arrived he has no more job and they are always fighting," Riviera explained. "Jonathan is always staying in the house and he's jealous of my daughter."

On Thursday, June 26, Michelle slipped away in the morning to go to the seaside with Enyo. After going shopping they had lunch, before checking into a tiny hotel for two hours of sex.

"After the hotel," Michelle later told police, "we went for a walk on the beach and then came home."

That morning, Enyo's wife Patricia Abad had suspected he was up to something when he left for work. So she called the Ostrich Nursery, and a supervisor told her he had not come in to work that day.

"I'm very jealous," said Patricia. "[He] never came home so I went to [Michelle's] house."

When she arrived at Keithwood Court and rang the doorbell, Teodoro Riviera answered.

"An old man said she wasn't home," said Abad. "I asked for her husband, but he wasn't home either."

The following day Patricia called Michelle on her cell for

an explanation, but she hung up as soon as she recognized Patricia's voice. Then Patricia searched Enyo's room, finding a sexy silk thong in one of his pockets, as well as some suggestive text messages on his cell phone.

On Saturday she confronted Enyo, accusing him of cheating on her, and showed him the thong. Furious, he told her he was leaving, and packed up his belongings, moving in with friends.

To celebrate the July Fourth holiday, Jonathan Nyce had arranged a week-long vacation with his parents, three brothers and their families, to the Outer Banks of North Carolina. But at the last minute, Michelle announced she had a physical training examination the following Sunday, and had to remain behind to study.

"I begged her to come with us anyway," said Nyce. "But she said no, she had to take this exam."

He eventually drove his three children to the house he had rented for everyone, while Michelle stayed at home with her father.

On Friday, July 4, Michelle invited Enyo to spend the afternoon at her house.

"We had sex one time in her home," Enyo would later tell police. "She said her husband was away [and] her father was there."

Three days later, Michelle and her father caught the bus to North Carolina to join the family vacation, but there was tension in the air.

"We treated [her father] like he was one of ours," said Emma Nyce. "One night we had pork and asked Michelle what we were going to give her dad, as he can't eat it. She said, 'He can eat peanut butter. Don't worry about him.'"

Jonathan Nyce would later claim he had first become suspicious of his wife while he was still at EpiGenesis. One day Michelle had telephoned, saying she was at Larissa Soos' house. But when Larissa called for Michelle a few minutes later, saying she wasn't with her, he knew something was wrong.

"Ten minutes later I got a call from Mercer County College," Nyce said. "They said, 'Michelle's classes are going to begin in two weeks.' I said, 'what do you mean? They've already been going on for two weeks.' So she had been telling me that she had been going to night classes."

After they returned from North Carolina, he began checking the dialed numbers on her cell phone, soon noticing one particular number showing up repeatedly. So he did a reverse telephone number search on his computer, coming up with the name "Alexander Castaneda," but no address to go with it.

He then signed up an Internet detective agency to search Alexander Castaneda. "I paid seventy-five dollars for name, address and cell phone number," Nyce later told detectives. "I needed confirmation because there were so many cell phone numbers on my wife's cell phone bill."

On Thursday, July 10, the agency reported Alexander Castaneda lived at the Windsor Castle Apartments in Cranbury. Now certain Michelle was cheating on him, he jumped into his Audi sports car, driving straight to Castaneda's address.

He arrived, crying uncontrollably, and parked outside the tatty apartment block to wait for his rival. But when nobody appeared, he panicked, reaching out in desperation to Sherry Leonard, and calling her at EpiGenesis on his cell phone.

"[He] was crying," Sherry later remembered. "He said Michelle had been having an affair."

Nyce was hysterical, begging Leonard to meet him immediately. She said it was impossible, as she had an early morning business meeting. Sobbing, he told her how he was in his car outside Michelle's boyfriend's home, unsure of whether to "beat up this guy" or kill himself.

Sherry had never heard him so desperate and believed he truly might be suicidal.

"I was very alarmed," she said. "I told him that no good was going to come out of beating up this man, and I asked him where the children were.

She then tried to calm him down, telling him that revenge was wrong and nothing good would come from it. She urged him to leave immediately, as his children needed him at home. Eventually Nyce agreed she was right, promising to go straight home.

Police believe that at this point Jonathan Nyce hatched a deviously elaborate plot to get Michelle to confess to the affair and break it off forever. After calling Sherry Leonard, they think he drove to a Shell gas station on nearby Route 1, Lawrenceville, where Michelle and Enyo sometimes met.

Then, police think, at 9:48 a.m. he called his own cell phone from the Shell station's public pay phone and then hung up. Two minutes later he placed a second call to his cell.

Then having laid the bait, he drove back to Keithwood Court, waiting for Michelle to return home from taking the children to school. As soon as she walked in, he told her he'd just received a telephone call from a man who had played him audio tapes of her having sex.

"I confronted her with the fact that somebody is taping her on her cell phone," Nyce later told detectives. "And it's real sexual stuff."

Michelle was shaken, and initially lied, claiming she'd taken a job on a phone sex line. But Nyce did not believe her and demanded the truth.

"Come on," he told her, "just be a wife and tell me what's going on."

She claimed she had only had sex twice, and been drunk on both occasions. But Nyce pressed for more details.

"Finally, I got her to admit that it's an ongoing affair," he said. "She admitted to everything eventually."

Later, Jonathan Nyce told police that Michelle had ended the affair that afternoon. He had been with her at 2:00 p.m. when she'd telephoned Enyo to tell him.

But it would be another two weeks before Nyce implemented the second part of his plan, police believe—to put Enyo in jail, so Michelle could never see him again.

* * *

Two days later, Jonathan Nyce locked himself in his office and wrote a poem, attempting to put his anguish into words.

Michelle:

Your stainless steel heart,
Like a knife, rips open my soul
To bleed, unattended, dying.
With another man's semen
Still warm within your belly,
You call me on the telephone
And tell me not to worry.
When, oh when, will my dying end?

He then put it away in a desk drawer near a bookcase, where he kept a .380 Pietro Beretta Gardone pistol and three magazines with ten rounds of ammunition.

13

Sex, Lies and Videotapes

On Wednesday, July 23, a furious Jonathan Nyce left a message on Enyo's cell phone.

"I want you to keep away from my wife," he demanded. "If you put your hands on my wife, you're going to be a dead man."

Two hours later, Enyo, who had recently reconciled with Patricia Abad, returned the call, asking if he was looking for him. But when Nyce said he wanted Alex Castaneda, Enyo hung up, saying he had the wrong person.

Shaken by Nyce's threat, he immediately called Michelle on her cell phone, saying they had to stop seeing each other.

"I said, 'He already knows,'" Enyo would later testify. "'We have to stop. This is a big problem and I don't want to do it. This is not right. It is not good.'"

According to the gardener, Michelle was "so sad," she kept calling him, saying she needed to see him so they could talk.

The next day Jonathan Nyce went to the FBI's West Trenton field office, meeting with Special Agent John Mulligan. He told the agent an extraordinary story of how he was being shaken down by his wife's boyfriend for half a million dollars in exchange for a tape of her having sex.

He claimed he had been pulling into the parking lot at Hopewell library when he received two calls in quick succession on his cell phone from a man he later found out was Alexander Castaneda, also known as Enyo.

In the first one, he said, Enyo had played a brief portion of a videotape of his wife, Michelle, having sex with him, before hanging up. He was sure it was his wife, he said, because he'd recognized her distinctive accent. A few minutes later there was a second call from the same man. This time he demanded $500,000 for the sex tapes before disconnecting.

Nyce had even brought in his cell phone bill for July 10, clearly showing the two calls two minutes apart.

Agent Mulligan decided Nyce's allegations were outside the jurisdiction of the FBI, and drove to Hopewell Township Police Department, handing the case over to Detective Daniel McKeown Jr.

A few minutes after he had briefed Detective McKeown, Jonathan Nyce telephoned, inviting him to Keithwood Court to interview him and his wife.

Later that day when McKeown arrived, an emotional Jonathan Nyce answered the door.

"I could see that he was upset," remembered McKeown, a genial man with the intimidating build of a pro-football quarterback. "Then he brought Michelle down the stairs."

When the detective asked to interview them separately in the living room, Nyce left them together. The detective was surprised when Michelle readily admitted to an affair, saying she had ended it that very day.

"She was very distant," he remembered. "Just very matter-of-fact. She showed absolutely no emotion. I had the impression of a woman who was in a loveless marriage."

Throughout their interview Michelle avoided eye-contact with Detective McKeown, answering "Yes" or "No," unless he probed further.

She had last seen Enyo a month earlier, she said, when they had gone to the seaside together. She had recently ended the affair, after the gardener became too interested in her husband's financial affairs, asking how much the house was worth. But she admitted lending him $1,000 in February, which he'd paid back when she returned from the Philippines.

When Detective McKeown asked Michelle if she knew about the $500,000 blackmail attempt against her husband to purchase explicit sex tapes she was in, Michelle denied any knowledge of it.

She was then asked who might possibly make such a call to her husband, and for what reason.

"No, I don't know who would do this," she replied. "But I guess they would want us to get a divorce, sell the house and liquidate it."

Asked if she thought they should pay the alleged extortionist, Michelle replied, "I don't think we should pay it, but my husband does. He is the one that usually makes the big decisions and I just follow along."

Finally he asked if she wanted a divorce.

"No," replied Michelle, "he wants to stay together for the kids."

Detective McKeown then interviewed Jonathan Nyce, who repeated his story of Enyo's two telephone calls. The detective was immediately suspicious that something was wrong with his sensational allegation.

"Well, the first thing that raised a red flag," he explained later, "was that he had waited so long to contact anybody. Why all of a sudden is this a threat for the family? Are you going to wait two weeks? I don't think so."

He was also suspicious that the caller had never given any instructions of how the money was to be paid.

"The first call is 'We have the tapes,'" said Detective McKeown. "The second is, 'We want five hundred thousand dollars, goodbye.' Then they never hear from him again."

But he gave Nyce the benefit of the doubt, spending the next few days checking out his story.

First he went to the Shell gas station and looked at all the surveillance tapes for July 10.

"I watched the tapes," he said. "I especially looked for any vehicles that matched Enyo's Nissan Maxima or the Ostrich Nursery van. I didn't see anything."

Back at Hopewell Township Police Department, when he ran the name "Miguel deJesus" through the police computer, he discovered he had an alias of Sergio Martinez, who had a warrant out for his arrest for non-payment of child support.

Several days later, McKeown drove to the Ostrich Nursery and asked about Enyo, saying he was part of a routine investigation. But eventually, after a tip-off, Officer James Geary of East Windsor police tracked down Enyo to an apartment in Cranbury, New Jersey, and he was then brought to the Hopewell Police Department, to see if he had any further outstanding warrants.

By sheer coincidence, as police escorted Enyo into the police station, Jonathan Nyce happened to be in the lobby, signing a harassment complaint against him. It was the first time the two men had ever seen each other face-to-face, and a loud argument ensued.

"There was a verbal confrontation," remembered McKeown. "Enyo made threats to Mr. Nyce."

On July 25, Jonathan Nyce officially swore out a civil harassment complaint against Miguel deJesus. He claimed that Enyo had telephoned him twice, threatening, "I'm going to fuck her up!"

And so the hapless gardener was ordered to appear before Hopewell Township Municipal Court Judge Bonnie Johnson on August 21, to answer Nyce's complaint.

After discovering Michelle's betrayal, Jonathan Nyce started seeing a psychiatrist. He was prescribed the strong antidepressant lorazepam, making his behavior even more unpredictable and erratic. He drove to his elderly parents' house in Collegeville, breaking down in tears on the living room couch, as he told them of Michelle's betrayal. Then he made them promise never to reveal to her that they knew.

"He said she had a boyfriend," said Emma Nyce. "We

couldn't believe it, and he was very upset. We told him to have her followed, but he wouldn't do that. He said, 'No, she's my wife. I can't hurt my wife.' "

Shortly thereafter, in a bizarre display of controlling behavior, he started lavishing Michelle with expensive gifts, at the same time, closing their joint bank account, denying her access to his money.

"I put her on an allowance," he explained. "I wanted to teach her finances. But she hated that and was mad at me."

Now, forced to survive on a $300 monthly allowance, Michelle told her family she would no longer be able to support them in the Philippines, and blamed Jonathan.

"She told me that she wanted to get a divorce," said her sister Melodia. "That Jonathan's possessive and controlling and they are always arguing."

With no money coming in to support their lavish lifestyle, unpaid electricity and gas bills began to mount up, but this did not stop Nyce from leasing a $52,000 top-of-the-line red Hummer H2. A few weeks later he listed his 2001 Audi TT, with its leather interior with "baseball glove" stitching, for sale in the Trenton *Times'* classified section for $30,000.

According to his parents, Michelle had wanted the Hummer and their son just could not refuse her.

"She said she wanted it for protection," said Emma Nyce. "It was all for her. And I said under my breath . . . 'It looks like a fire trap to me.' "

But Michelle never used the Hummer, telling friends she couldn't afford the $46 it cost for a tank of gas.

The last week of July, Nyce took Michelle to Charleston, West Virginia, for a second honeymoon. He was determined to "fix" their marriage, deciding that maybe they needed a "change of pace."

Before leaving he went to a urologist, who prescribed him Viagra, as he wanted to prove he was more than a match for Enyo in bed.

"I was trying to get back into that thing," he would later explain. "She had complained, during her manic phase, that she could have sex three times a night . . . and that my limit was two. So to actually help to get up to the three [I] got some Viagra and I was able to go three or four myself."

And during the Charleston trip, he attempted to inject some new excitement into their sex life.

"I would take her to hotels on the spur of the moment, like the Hyatt," he said. "We basically had sex all night."

When they returned to New Jersey, Michelle Nyce finally sought financial independence, no longer wanting to be reliant on Jonathan. As Samantha was 5 and about to begin kindergarten, Michelle would soon have a lot more free time.

She soon found a part-time job as a beauty advisor at the Chanel Cosmetics counter at Macy's, in the Quaker Bridge Mall in nearby Lawrenceville. She worked an average of twenty-five hours a week at just $9.25 an hour, wearing a black uniform with a brass nametag pinned to it.

With Jonathan now at home all day she felt completely smothered, and working in the mall was like a breath of fresh air.

"She told me she had a job at Macy's," said Larissa Soos. "For the longest time she had been a stay-at-home mom, and she would drive the kids all the time. Now she was starting to figure, 'Let me find a job.' "

Larissa thought it was a great idea and encouraged her, but her husband was most unhappy.

"Their roles were reversed," explained Larissa. "He was staying at home and taking care of the kids, and she was out at night working.

"At one point he really wanted to make her stop working at Macy's, because he wanted her home with him. I think they argued about that quite a bit."

Soon after she started at Macy's, Michelle met an attractive, vivacious 21-year-old Filipino girl named Amy Sumayang, who was also a Chanel trainee.

The two became friends and confidantes. Amy had just found out she was pregnant, by a married man who had abandoned her. Michelle told her about Enyo, whom she was still in daily contact with, and how Jonathan had discovered the affair.

Michelle said she and Jonathan had been fighting for the last five years, and argued daily, often in front of their children. But the fights were verbal and so far he had never been violent. Michelle said she had often asked Jonathan for a divorce, but couldn't afford an attorney.

She also told Amy she believed Jonathan had once had an affair, as she'd discovered a condom in his suitcase on his return from a business trip to Japan.

Amy advised her to work on her marriage and not risk losing her children in a bitter divorce.

Since early July, Jonathan Nyce had kept in close contact with Detective McKeown, regularly updating him by telephone or fax with new information about the threats posed by Enyo. He had also hired an attorney named Lee Engleman to represent him in Hopewell Township Municipal Court.

On August 19, Nyce sent Detective McKeown such an outlandish fax, he immediately closed down the investigation, deciding the whole extortion allegation was a figment of Jonathan Nyce's imagination.

"My wife has stated to you that Mr. Castaneda encouraged her to kill me," began the fax, marked "urgent." "When she told him he was crazy for suggesting that, he said then he would do something himself, although he wouldn't tell her for fear of frightening her."

McKeown read the fax in disbelief, as Michelle had never suggested Enyo wanted her to harm her husband. But the final paragraph was even more bizarre, alleging a sinister incident outside their house the night before.

"A truck sat in front of my house and its occupants watched my wife through a kitchen window," read the fax. "It was dark and I was outside, putting some equipment in a tool shed. I approached the truck from the rear left, trying to get a license number, but he saw me and drove off rapidly."

When McKeown telephoned Nyce, asking why he hadn't called the police, he agreed that he should have, saying he hadn't had his cell phone with him.

An hour later, the detective officially closed the case after his month-long investigation, writing in his report that the extortion allegations were "unfounded."

Two days later in Hopewell Township Municipal Court, Jonathan Nyce came face-to-face with Enyo again. This time Miguel deJesus had hired an attorney named Gary Jodha to represent him in the civil action.

"The real issue for me," Nyce told Municipal Court Judge Bonnie Goldman, "is, I want him to stay away from my wife and her place of business. That's the critical thing for me."

Then the judge, Nyce and Jodha began discussing the restraining order, asking whether Enyo should even be allowed inside the Quaker Bridge Mall.

When Judge Goldman asked which part of the mall Enyo should avoid, Jonathan Nyce turned towards Enyo, bristling with anger.

"Just stay away from my wife!" he threatened in a chilling voice. "That's all I ask. If he sees my wife, he turns the other way."

Finally Judge Goldman ordered a mutual restraining order, preventing all parties from having any further contact for two years. If they complied, it would be dismissed without prejudice. But she warned deJesus that if he violated the order, he would be charged with harassment, facing a possible 6 months in jail and up to $500 in fines.

"[If he] sees wife [he's] to turn the other way!" wrote Judge Goldman on the court order.

A natural workaholic, Jonathan Nyce now found he had too much time on his hands. When he wasn't writing his books or working on his various other projects, he started remaking furniture and even tried to invent a new comfortable type of footwear, somewhat reminiscent of his poem of his sons fashioning a shoe out of deer hide.

He had recently bought himself a new electric scroll saw and had started teaching his eldest son, Alex, how to use it. One day he went down to his basement with a pair of his size 12 Brahma boots and a pair of moccasins. Using the saw he cut the soles off the boots and the moccasins, gluing the boot soles onto the bottoms of the moccasins.

Presumably he thought it would make a more comfortable pair of hybrid shoes for the upcoming winter.

14

Quagmire

Over the next few months the Nyce marriage went from bad to worse. Jonathan Nyce began writing a new book he called "*Quagmire*," which might well have described the mental anguish he was sinking into.

In direct contrast, Michelle seemed more upbeat and optimistic than ever before. Her job at Macy's was going well, as she discovered a natural talent behind the Chanel counter as a saleswoman.

"She liked it," said Larissa Soos. "She was making friends. She was doing well. She liked to be out."

She also looked to a long-term career with Chanel, faxing her Pennsylvania-based supervisor Gina this tongue-in-cheek note, punning her name: "Thanks for your 'Nice' comments about my work. I am enjoying my job and look forward to a potential future with Chanel."

But Jonathan Nyce was not so happy about the job, disliking the seismic change in the dynamic of their relationship. For the first time ever, Michelle was no longer financially dependent on him, and he felt all the control he'd once exerted over her slipping away.

Initially he pressured her to quit Macy's, but Michelle refused, saying she was finally doing something for herself.

"She married young," said Larissa Soos. "She had kids right away and she never finished college. Now she had found a job she liked and was good at. She was making money on her own and meeting other people. It was her time."

Eventually Jonathan resigned himself to Michelle's new career, even admitting she was a first-class saleswoman.

"She's really good," he later told police. "From the beginning she had the most sales per hour."

Then he tried to regain some measure of control by announcing he would start his own perfume company, to be run by him, Michelle and Larissa Soos. He christened the company "Sampaguita," after the national flower of the Philippines, which signifies innocence.

"As a scientist I was already putting together scents," he said. "Michelle was very good at what she did at Chanel, so I suggested to her that she start her own business and I would help her. Maybe I was trying to tell my wife that despite what she had done before, I had forgiven her. Now that we were back together, I still thought of her as innocent."

The plan was for him to get a sample of the Sampaguita flower, buy the necessary oils and chemically duplicate its fragrance. He began drafting a business and marketing plan, portraying his new fragrance as the innocent alternative to all the raunchy sexual images used to sell perfume that he so disapproved of.

"It was *the* big idea," said Soos. "He was going to start a business for her. And he told us he knows how to make perfume, so he and Michelle were going to work together. I guess he figured that because Michelle was doing well selling Chanel, she should sell her own."

Larissa and Michelle enthusiastically started researching possible names for the perfume, while Nyce started experimenting on mixing the right fragrance.

"He was going to make fifty types of scent," said Larissa.

"And me and Michelle were supposed to be this target group of women to do blind tests."

Jonathan was now busy working in his office for hours at a time, only coming out to take the children to school or take care of them at night, when Michelle worked her Macy's shift.

"He was always on the computer," said Larissa. "He was always surfing the Internet."

Most mornings Larissa would arrive at Keithwood Court to work out with Michelle, now a certified personal trainer, and see Jonathan moping around the house.

"He'd say, 'Hi,' to me or 'Goodbye, I have to work now. Have a good workout,' and he'd go upstairs into his office."

Larissa also observed a change in their relationship, now that they were both home all day. Michelle had started complaining about Jonathan's possessiveness, and that he always wanted to know where she was.

It became a running gag that whenever they were out and her cell phone rang, it would be Jonathan calling to check up on her.

"And she would hand it to me," said Larissa, "just so he could make sure she was with me. It got a lot worse when she started working at Macy's."

But Larissa knew nothing about her affair with Enyo, as Michelle had merely told her that she had reported a stalker to Hopewell police.

"That's about what she told me," said Larissa. "She never mentioned anything about extortion or anything about an affair."

In September, things became even worse when Nyce put the Keithwood Court house up for sale at $1.6 million, announcing that he wanted to move the family to Pennsylvania, to be nearer his aged parents. This was a bitter blow to Michelle, who loved her new life in New Jersey and did not want to move to the rural backwoods of Collegeville to be with her in-laws.

Their frequent fights now became more and more heated,

and Teodoro Riviera observed several instances of his son-in-law's violent behavior, sometimes in front of their children.

"Once he bashed the table with his fists while we were eating," said Riviera. "Michelle got up and went to her room because Jonathan was fighting and angry."

On another occasion he went into their master bedroom, noticing a gaping hole by the side of the door. When he asked his daughter what had caused it, she said Jonathan had punched it out with his fist in a temper tantrum. Michelle told him she had threatened to call the police if he was ever violent again.

"I told her, 'It's good that he doesn't bash you,'" said her father. "'It's only a wall.' I think Jonathan didn't hit Michelle because I was there."

Later Nyce would accuse Michelle of deliberately picking fights with him.

"Things were getting progressively bad," he said. "I told her on many occasions . . . it looks [like], 'Honey, you're picking a fight, just so you can go out and do what you want.'"

Often, after a bitter argument, Nyce would tearfully go into his children's rooms, complaining about their mother. He would accuse her of being mentally ill, asking them to be patient with her.

"He was a big baby," said Larissa. "He would be in tears. He would try and get sympathy from the kids."

One night Michelle came home from Macy's and went up to her father's room, saying she was fed up with all the arguments and wanted out of the marriage.

"She told me," said Riviera, "'I am very tired. I have a problem.'

"I said, 'What's your problem?'

"She said, 'I do not want to stay with Jonathan anymore.'

"I asked why. She said, 'Because we are always fighting. He's *so* jealous of me.'

"So I said, 'If you have no interest in Jonathan, why don't you file a divorce?'

"She said, 'It's very hard, as I have no money to pay the lawyers.' "

At the beginning of October, Michelle's friend Roz Clancy offered her a well-paid assignment as a model in a five-minute TV commercial for a homecare company. Since they had met a year earlier, Clancy, who runs a model casting agency in Trenton, had promised to find her work as a model.

Now one of her clients needed a Filipino model to play a granddaughter in the advertising campaign for a new homecare program for the elderly.

"I told her I'd picked her," said Clancy, "and she was overjoyed."

Roz then set up a meeting with her client, who loved Michelle and immediately booked her for the project. But just two days before the scheduled photo shoot, Michelle called Clancy in tears.

"I can't do it," she said.

"Why?" asked Clancy. "Have you chickened out?"

"Roz, you know me," said Michelle. "I'd love to, but Jonathan won't let me."

Clancy was livid. She had a photographer and wardrobe already booked, as well as a studio. She even offered to personally talk to Jonathan, but Michelle said it would not help.

Finally Michelle suggested she use Larissa Soos, who stepped in at the last minute and did the advertisement.

"I asked my husband," said Larissa. "He said, " 'OK, sure.' It was a low-budget type of thing. They ended up filming it in my house."

A few days later an excited Michelle called the agent, asking if she could guess why she was so happy. Roz immediately speculated that Michelle was pregnant, but she said no. Jonathan had relented and given her permission to do the next modeling job that came up.

"I said, 'I'm sorry,' " said Clancy. " 'I've booked people already.' "

At the end of September, Sherry Leonard called her old boss to see how he was doing, and left a message. She hadn't spoken to him since July, when he'd called contemplating suicide. She also had a job interview and needed a reference.

When Nyce called her back a few days later, he expressed concern about Michelle's state of mind, even talking about "committing her." He complained she now thought she was "the head of the household" and the main "bread winner," with her job at Macy's. He also grumbled that Michelle had bought a Hummer, which they couldn't afford, and certainly didn't need.

"I said they had hard decisions to make," Sherry later told police, "and he needed to decide what was the best for him and his family and his marriage."

Jonathan Nyce was now drowning in a sea of red ink. There were unopened piles of unpaid bills mounting on the desk in his office, and his creditors were calling every day, demanding he settle his debts. He was even being sued by their dentist, Dr. Frederick Babinowich, for a $1,113 unpaid bill. The dentist would win a $1,633 settlement a few months later.

"He did not want to get on the phone because his creditors wanted money," said Michelle's father. "He has no more money and he would not pick up the phone."

15

Collision Course

Less than a month after Hopewell Township Municipal Court ordered Michelle Nyce to stay away from Enyo, they were back in each other's arms. According to him, it was Michelle who was the pursuer, and he had not wanted to rekindle the relationship after reconciling with Patricia Abad.

Later he would testify that one day she had called him on his cell phone, saying she needed to talk.

"She sounded so sad," he said. "I said we shouldn't do this anymore, and she started to cry."

After several more calls, Enyo finally agreed to meet Michelle outside a Pizza Hut on Route 33 in Hamilton, New Jersey, where they spent fifteen minutes talking in his car.

"That day we just talked and that was it," he said. "She was crying and very sad. I said, 'We should stop this. I don't want to keep doing it.'"

Two days later Michelle called his cell phone and they talked every day, until the following week when they arranged another meeting.

"She said, 'I want to see you one last time,'" said Enyo.

"I said, 'I'm working. I can't be on the phone with you all day. I can't see you every time you want. I've got to do my work.'"

When Michelle started crying on the phone, he agreed to meet her after work, across the street from Applebee's restaurant on Route 33.

Once again, according to Enyo, they talked for about twenty minutes, before going their separate ways. But at the end of September, they met again by Applebee's and then went to a cheap motel for a few hours.

"We had sex again," said Enyo. "A hotel down on Route 130 South."

Over the next three months they met every week at different motels.

"We met six or seven times," said Enyo. "But not all for sex. We were friends."

Often, after finishing a shift at Macy's, Michelle would meet her lover, telling her husband she was going out with her friend Amy Sumayang, whom he strongly disapproved of.

"Amy's a bad influence," said Nyce. "She said Larissa's getting boring and all her friends her own age were getting boring."

Since she'd started working for Chanel, Michelle had begun dressing like a teenager, shopping at trendy fashion stores, like Forever 21 and Victoria's Secret.

Now 34, she was still stunningly beautiful, and a perfect size 2. She started wearing ultra-sexy short skirts and fashionable clothes, more in line with the young MTV crowd than a suburban mother of three.

"She'd come down here dressed like a teenager," said her disapproving mother-in-law. "High boots, tight skirt—I couldn't believe it."

She also started frequenting the fashionable KatManDu night club in Trenton, with her teenage friend Amy, often staying out until the early hours of the morning. She met a new set of younger friends whom her husband considered bad influences, going out dancing with them several times a week.

On one occasion Emma Nyce remembers Michelle returning from a shopping expedition, and proudly displaying what she had bought.

"She came out with a miniskirt about this big," said Emma. "Jonathan said, 'What's that?' And he threw it. He said, 'Take it back. It's not for you.' She was just difficult, and that was it."

Michelle was also flirting with men while she worked at the Chanel counter. One afternoon in November, 29-year-old Paul Everton was walking through Macy's when he spotted the beauty consultant.

"We made eye contact and she called me over," said the handsome trainee corrections officer. "You know that look."

Michelle began telling the Colombian native about Chanel's special cosmetic offers.

"She was flirting," he said. "She never mentioned she was married, and she wasn't wearing a wedding ring. That would have been a red flag to me. She came on to me as single as they come, and said she found me attractive. I guess she liked Spanish men."

They agreed to go out on a date and play pool, with Michelle giving him her cell phone number and telling him to call her.

"I think she was intrigued by my barbell tongue piercing," he said. "She said she had never met anyone with a pierced tongue before."

Over the next two months they often talked on the phone, with Michelle confiding that she was worried about a "possessive, very jealous" ex-boyfriend.

"She told me that an ex-boyfriend instilled fear in her," said Everton. "He played head games, always telling her he knows who she is going to meet. Then she warned me that her ex-boyfriend might come after me and she hoped he didn't have my number. That's why we didn't get together."

That Thanksgiving, Jonathan, Michelle and their children drove to Collegeville for their traditional family gathering. Earlier they had dropped Michelle's father off at Larissa Soos' house so he could play cards with his friends.

But there was tension throughout the day. Later Michelle told friends how everyone had totally ignored her during their four-hour stay, never speaking to her once. Her in-laws had cold-shouldered her, never mentioning that they knew of her affair.

"She's not really close to them," said Larissa. "Once she said, 'I can't believe you're so close to your mother-in-law.' "

On Sunday December 7, Michelle and Larissa attended the annual American-Filipino Association Christmas party at the Hyatt Regency hotel in Princeton. During the meal, they struck up a conversation with a young Filipino woman named Jean Larini, and soon became fast friends. Jean came from the northern side of Manila and was also married to an American.

"That was the beginning of our friendship," said Larini, who closely resembled Michelle with long, luxuriant black hair. "And from then on we started calling almost every day, going out once or twice a week."

Soon after they met, Jean and her husband, Keith, went out for dinner with the Nyces. It was the first time Jean had met Jonathan, and she was surprised by how different they were.

"He was older and pudgy," she said, "and she was young and beautiful."

As usual Jonathan Nyce spent much of the evening holding court with boastful tales of his glory days at EpiGenesis.

"He talked about his brilliance," she remembered. "About when he was in Japan and eating sushi."

Nyce also told them about his ambitious plans for marketing his Sampaguita perfume, recruiting Jean to join Michelle and Larissa as part of his development and marketing team. He told her he had now formulated three fragrances, and was ready to begin testing.

Through December the three friends met regularly for lunch at each other's houses, while their kids were at school.

They'd often discuss their husbands, with Michelle constantly complaining about Jonathan's jealousy and possessiveness.

"One time they went to a party and she was talking to one of Jonathan's friends," said Larini. "Suddenly he came up and grabbed her. He pulled her away from their conversation."

Teodoro Riviera says his son-in-law became incensed whenever Michelle talked to a man.

"He was jealous," he said. "She would say, 'I don't care if a guy looks at me.' But he would still be mad. He would say, 'I don't want anybody looking at my wife.' He didn't want a man to make a play for Michelle."

On another occasion Michelle was at Jean Larini's home, when the conversation turned to divorce.

"I told her my husband had a hard time during his divorce," she remembered. "I'm like, 'In the States women get everything they want.' So she's just listening very carefully and looking at me. And then she said, 'What else?' "

During the Christmas period, Michelle worked as many shifts as she could at Macy's, at one-and-a-half times her normal $9.25 hourly wage. She often worked until midnight during the holiday period, and would then go out to meet Enyo or her other friends, coming home when it was getting light.

"During the holidays she was working every day and the weekends," said Larissa. "As much as she could."

Jonathan Nyce would later tell detectives that whenever Michelle went out late at night he would take a lorazepam, to calm him down so he wouldn't worry. Then he'd go for a walk outside his house, often ending up at the swing-set in his children's playground he had built. Then he'd sit on the swing, contemplating his miserable situation.

"[When] Michelle was having her affair I was absolutely beside myself," he later explained. "When Michelle goes out, and if she's going to be late, which she tells me as she is going out the door, I will take one. Then I don't care."

On Saturday, December 27, Jonathan and Michelle went to a Christmas party at Jean Larini's home in Princeton. It was a great party and Michelle was having a fine time, singing Madonna songs on the Larinis' karaoke machine.

"He wanted to go home early," said Jean. "Michelle was still having fun and she seldom goes out."

When Michelle insisted they stay, Jonathan sulked, going over to the front door and standing there alone. A few minutes later he returned to Michelle, demanding they leave immediately. When she refused again he went back to the door, but Michelle looked sad and embarrassed.

They finally left while the party was still in full swing. But on the drive home they had a big fight, and when they walked in the door Michelle told her father to go to his room.

"I heard them fighting," said Teodoro Riviera, "over Michelle talking to guy friends at the party."

A couple of days later, she and Amy Sumayang went Christmas shopping at the Freehold Mall, where Michelle received a call on her cell phone. A few minutes later she led Amy to the food court, where Enyo was waiting for her. Amy would later tell police the meeting had made her "very uncomfortable."

Looking back, Michelle's friends would wonder if Jonathan Nyce had already begun to follow her, discovering she was seeing Enyo again. For suddenly his whole attitude towards her changed. He began talking of future plans with just his children, without including Michelle.

In early December, Nyce called his sister-in-law Melodia Ragenil in the Philippines, fishing for information on Enyo.

"He said did I know my sister had a boyfriend?" said Melodia. "I said no."

He then asked if she knew "Alex," and Melodia said she'd only heard of him as one of Michelle's friends.

"You know!" Nyce shouted accusingly into the phone before hanging up.

A few days later he gave his father-in-law $300 towards a one-way ticket back to the Philippines, as a Christmas present from him and Michelle. With it he included a handwritten note, thanking him for everything he'd done for his grandchildren.

"Dear Dad," he wrote. "It has been a pleasure having you live with us this past year. You are a good man, and working hard, and I recognize that, and I know that God recognizes it too.

"For your Christmas present, the kids and I and Michelle are contributing $300 toward your airline ticket back to the Philippines."

He explained that he had already given the money to Michelle, who was placing it in her American Express credit card account, and would make the reservation.

"You can give her the remaining amount to cover the cost of your ticket," he wrote. "Be careful as you leave us for your visit home, Dad. We want to see you again real soon. Love, Jon and family."

At the end of December, Sherry Leonard called him, and he sounded positive and happy for the first time in months. He told her of a new business venture on the horizon, saying he couldn't say any more until after March.

"He was more upbeat, more optimistic than he had been in the past," she said. "He said he had gotten some counseling, that he was resigned to his children being the focus of his life, and that his marriage is more of a secondary aspect now. But it seemed OK for him."

Leonard later told detectives she believed her former boss must have discovered Michelle was seeing Enyo again.

"I can only assume," she said, "it was finding out about the affair. I think most of his energy was being focused on the kids and taking care of them."

On New Year's Eve, Jonathan and Michelle threw a lavish party for all their friends. There was no hint that there were any problems between them. They appeared the perfect married couple, as the two dozen guests arrived to find Jonathan mixing punch in the kitchen sink. Unlike the old days, when their parties were fully catered, Michelle had asked her friends to bring food.

When Andy Sjamsu walked in with his wife, Cynthia, he was surprised to find the kitchen faucet was still broken, some months after he had first noticed it was.

"Excuse me," said Sjamsu. "Why don't you mend the faucet? I mean, they lived in a million-dollar home. He always said they couldn't get a plumber."

Jean and Keith Larini also attended the party, bringing along their karaoke machine for entertainment. Jean found Jonathan more relaxed than ever, chatting happily about his new children's book and proudly showing them a copy.

"He was just showing us a book," she said, "about a kid with one shoe."

Michelle's friend Amy, now eight months pregnant, also came with her parents, to Jonathan's disapproval. And Teodoro Riviera was there, quietly staying in the background for much of the time.

As midnight approached, all the guests took turns singing karaoke. Jonathan sang his favorite song, "House of the Rising Sun," while Michelle did the old Madonna hit, "La Isla Bonita."

"That was her song," said Jean. "She sang it really well."

Then later, after toasting in 2004 with Jonathan's punch, Michelle returned to the karaoke machine to perform Gloria Gaynor's stirring hit, "I Will Survive."

"She was bopping around," said Andy Sjamsu.

Like all the other guests, Sjamsu saw nothing out of the ordinary that night with the host and hostess.

"That's what bothers me," he said. "Usually you can tell if something's amiss. But there was nothing I saw."

The Nyces both seemed upbeat and getting on well, enthusiastically making future plans with their friends. They had scheduled a romantic St. Valentine's Day dinner in Philadelphia with the Larinis and the Sooses. And they also planned a summer vacation to Cancún, Mexico, with Larissa and John Soos and all their children.

"We had long-term plans," explained Larissa, "so I didn't think they had a problem, or why would they want to commit to us if they're not getting along?"

On Friday, January 9, Michelle's father returned to the Philippines after spending six months in New Jersey. The night before he left, Michelle came into his room, closing the door to have a father–daughter conversation.

"She told me she wanted to divorce Jonathan and leave the house," he remembered. "But she could not do it because of the kids."

When Riviera asked what she planned to do, Michelle told him she had a plan.

"She said, 'I'm waiting only for the house to be sold,' " said her father. " 'And then I'm going to file a divorce.' "

It would be the last conversation Teodoro Riviera would ever have with his daughter. He left for the Philippines early the next morning.

On Saturday, January 10, the Nyces and Larinis went out for dinner at an expensive restaurant in Philadelphia. Then they drove back to Trenton and went dancing at the KatManDu night club. The club was full of young people and Jean Larini felt out of place, but Michelle was in her element.

"Michelle and I went to the bathroom one time," remembered Jean. "When we finished, Jonathan was waiting outside for us. That was kind of funny."

Then they moved on to another night club, and all danced until it closed.

"[Michelle] was very proud of how I was dancing," Nyce would later boast. "She said I was the hottest guy in the bar. But I knew that wasn't true," he chuckled.

16

"The Suspect Heard a Thud"

On Thursday, January 15, there was a heavy storm and Hopewell Township schools were closed for a snow day. That morning Jonathan Nyce worked on a color layout for his Sampaguita perfume, while his three children played computer games in the living room.

Michelle had her first evening shift of the week at Macy's, and went out a couple of times to go shopping, coming home in the early afternoon. After making the children lunch, Nyce took 5-year-old Samantha out sledding.

"We had a big hill behind our house," he remembered. "And whenever it snowed, I always had one of those rollers for grass, and I would make a nice sledding path for the kids. It was great sledding. Very powdery snow."

He spent most of the day playing with his children, but at one point little Samantha fell off the sled, bursting into tears, and had to go back inside. He then took his two sons, Alex, 12, and 10-year-old Trevor, sledding down the hill for the rest of the afternoon.

At 4:00 p.m. Michelle took a shower, preparing for her shift, which would begin in two hours. While she was in the shower, Nyce dressed the children up warmly to go to Samantha's 4:15 gymnastics class.

"Michelle informed me that she had to work late at Macy's," he would later tell detectives. "After she was going to go [to the Metuchen Mall] with her friend Amy."

When he told her the mall closed at 10:00 p.m., Michelle snapped, "Out!"

During Samantha's one-hour class, at Motion Gymnastics on Route 31 in Pennington, Alex and Trevor played with their computer games. Then Nyce drove a few blocks along Route 31 to T J's Trattoria, where they ate a pizza dinner.

A little before 7:00 p.m. they arrived home to find that the children's much-anticipated *Lord of the Rings* model castle had finally arrived.

"I was working on a project with them," Nyce explained. "We were building one of the castles from the *Lord of the Rings* on the kitchen table. And we did that for a while."

Then Samantha wanted to see a particular movie, and Nyce started readying them all for bed.

"I started herding them towards the bathroom," he said. "Eventually everyone was in bed, all four of us, by 8:00 p.m."

When they were all tucked up in his king-size bed in the master bedroom, Nyce called Michelle's cell phone, but there was no answer. Then he put his phone on speaker, so little Samantha could leave her mom a goodnight message.

They then settled down to watch the new Jim Carrey movie *Bruce Almighty*, on pay-per-view, which Alex wanted to see. Then at about 10:00 p.m. Jonathan turned the light off and they all fell asleep in his bed.

Earlier that evening at 5:30, Michelle Nyce called Enyo on his cell to arrange a rendezvous that night. He was plowing snow when she called, telling her he was busy.

"She said, 'Can I see you tonight?' " said Enyo. "I said, 'I'll call you when I get back.' "

Michelle said she would finish work at 9:30, so Enyo promised to call her at 9:00.

Then Michelle drove to the Quaker Bridge Mall, clocking in at 6:03 p.m. She and Amy had previously arranged to meet at the Chanel counter and go out later to a mall, But Amy was tied up and couldn't call to cancel.

It was a busy Thursday night for Michelle. She was working on her feet all evening long at the Chanel counter, near the front entrance of Macy's. At 8:30 Enyo called and they arranged to meet in an hour at the Applebee's restaurant parking lot on Route 33 in Hamilton.

At 9:15 p.m. Michelle finished her shift, going to the bathroom to put on her makeup. Then she walked out into the freezing night to her Toyota Land Cruiser, parked in the Macy's car lot. On her way out she was pictured by the store's CCTV camera, still wearing her black uniform with her brass Chanel name tag and a thick gold chain around her neck. There is a haunted expression in her piercing eyes, as if she is looking over her shoulder in case she's being followed.

She drove out of the mall along Quaker Bridge Road to Hamilton Township, drawing into the Applebee's, where Enyo was waiting in his 1997 Nissan Maxima. Although she had dressed immaculately for the date, Enyo wore his regular work clothes, a tee-shirt, green jacket, gray sweatpants and his size 9½ Wolverine work boots.

Then they drove in separate vehicles to the nearby Quakerbridge Plaza, on the corner of Youngs Road. At 9:54 p.m. Michelle parked and got into Enyo's Nissan Maxima, as her cell phone started ringing. It was her friend Amy, apologizing for not coming to see her in Macy's as arranged.

Speaking Filipino, Amy asked about her plans for the rest of the evening. Michelle said she was going to Wegmans supermarket in West Windsor, but when Amy suggested they meet up there, Michelle said no.

By the time they finished talking, Enyo was pulling into the car lot, outside the seedy Mount's Motel on Route 1 in Lawrenceville, opposite the Quaker Bridge Mall. The downmarket motel rents rooms by the hour, offering waterbeds and a whirlpool.

"Wait for me," Enyo told Michelle. "I'll go and get a room."

Soon after 10:00 he walked into the motel lobby, booking a room for two hours under the name "Jose Pineda," so there would be no record of him for his wife, Patricia, to find.

"The guy at the counter told me to wait five minutes, because the room wasn't ready yet," he said. "I asked him how much it would be and he asked how long I would stay. I told him we would be here until about midnight."

The room cost $25, plus $5 deposit. Enyo gave the clerk the money and was handed the key to Room 202, and the TV remote control.

Then he went back to the car, collected Michelle, and they went up to the second-floor room. After locking the door, Enyo began undressing Michelle, who was wearing a red Victoria's Secret bra and matching thong. Later he would tell police she was still wearing her wedding ring, as well as an expensive watch worth $1,100.

"We started to have regular sex," he said. "Then oral sex."

And soon after they started having unprotected sex, Jonathan Nyce called her cell phone. Michelle took one look at the caller name, and switched it off. They then continued, with Enyo straddling her over a round table in the room. Eventually when they had finished, Enyo noticed blood on his penis, and asked Michelle about it.

"She said she was supposed to have her menstrual cycle the next day," he later explained.

Then he called a friend named Edgar Mejia, who he'd told his wife, Patricia, he was out with that night. Earlier, on his way to meet Michelle, he'd stopped off at Edgar's house to brief him on the cover story.

"I said, 'If my wife is looking for me,'" recalled Enyo, "'let her know I'm having a drink with you.' I had told her I was going to see Edgar and I wanted to make sure she wasn't looking for me."

He told his friend he was almost done with Michelle, and hung up.

"After sex," he said, "we started talking."

Michelle said she suspected a female neighbor might be following her, and then reporting back to Jonathan. And she showed him a cell phone photograph she'd taken of the woman. Enyo was concerned, asking if the neighbor knew they were seeing each other. Michelle said she did.

Later, as they were taking a shower together, the motel phone rang and Enyo answered. It was the clerk telling them it was midnight and their time was up. While Enyo went down to the front office to get his $5 deposit back, Michelle freshened up to go home, spraying herself with her favorite Chanel 22 perfume, so she wouldn't smell of sex.

"She put perfume on before we left," he remembered. "We left the room and we went back to my car."

He then drove back a different way to the Quakerbridge Plaza, where Michelle had left the Land Cruiser.

"She said she was going home," he said. "She got in her car, rolled down the window and gave me a kiss. Then she drove off."

At about 12:30 a.m. Michelle Nyce steered the Land Cruiser south onto Quaker Bridge Road and from there to I 95, for the thirteen-mile journey home.

Investigators believe that as early as the first week of December, Jonathan Nyce had discovered Michelle had resumed her affair with Enyo. Although he remained calm on the outside, his seething rage had been rising to boiling point ever since.

That night, after putting his children to bed at about 10:00, he had fallen asleep and then woken up a little later.

At about midnight he had tried to call Michelle again. When her answer phone message came on, they think he went downstairs to wait for her to come home. For the next forty-five minutes or so he sat in his dining room with the lights out, looking out at the snow-covered drive, through a big window.

Michelle arrived home at about 12:45 Friday morning, and Nyce watched her pull into the garage. Detectives think he got up and walked to the first-floor entrance to the garage, going down to the short flight of stairs into it. As

Michelle got out of the Land Cruiser, he held the garage door button down for eleven seconds, to close it.

Then the argument began. When Nyce demanded to know where she had been, she told him to fuck off and mind his own business. As she walked past him into the house he smelled the Chanel perfume she had put on in the motel, confirming his worst fears that she had just come from her lover's bed.

Then she came into the house, going upstairs to where their three children were sleeping. The argument continued and detectives are certain the children heard their parents shouting at each other.

Finally Michelle had enough and called him a "fucking freak." She said she was leaving him, and went into the master bedroom. She began to pack a large black suitcase as fast as she could, throwing in sweaters, jeans and some sexy underwear as he raged at her.

When she went to the bathroom to get some toiletries, her six-foot, four-inch husband rushed in after her. They scuffled in there and a wine glass was broken.

Investigators believe she then dragged the heavy suitcase downstairs into the garage in just her stocking feet, as her furious husband followed behind. The only light in the garage came from the interior panel of the Land Cruiser, so it was hard to see anything distinctly.

Then Jonathan Nyce came unhinged, realizing that he was about to lose Michelle once and for all, and could no longer control her. As she got into the Land Cruiser to escape, he yanked her out with such force that he left bruised impressions of his fingers on her left arm. Detectives believe he then picked up a baseball bat from the wall and smashed it full-force across the back of her head, fracturing her skull.

The tiny woman fell to the ground, hitting the back of her head on the Land Cruiser's running board. Bravely fighting for her life, she put her hands up to her face in a reflex action to protect herself. Covered in blood, she managed to get up and tried to run away, sliding in her own blood. But he easily caught her and threw her to the floor.

Grabbing her by the shoulders, Jonathan Nyce fero-

ciously drove her head face-first into the concrete floor again
and again.

Later Nyce admitted he only stopped after hearing a
"thud" that "made me sick."

The medical examiner believes Michelle may have lived
for a further ten minutes before finally choking on her own
blood.

When Jonathan checked her pulse and was certain she
was dead, he panicked.

Covered in blood, Nyce picked up Michelle's lifeless
body, placing it into the driver's seat of the Land Cruiser, before placing her blood-soaked suitcase into the back seat.

Then around 2:15 a.m. he opened the garage door, got
into the passenger's seat and started the engine, reversing
out of the garage. Careful not to attract any attention, he
kept the headlights off, manipulating the accelerator pedal
with a plastic ice scraper.

Although it was just 6 degrees Fahrenheit outside, he was
operating on pure adrenaline, wearing only a tee-shirt, black
pajama trousers and his custom-made moccasins, with the
glued-on heavy work boot soles.

Outside the double garage he stopped, changing into forward gear. Initially he lost control of the vehicle, and it
veered across the drive all over his snow-covered front garden. Detectives believe he then put the driver's seat back as
far as it would go, and may even have sat on his wife's dead
body, to be more in control of the vehicle.

He turned right out of his driveway to the stop sign, and
onto Todd Ridge Road. He soon got used to maneuvering the
accelerator pedal with the ice scraper, using his other hand
to steer. Then he turned right onto Jacobs Creek Road, following the desolate, lonely creek for about half a mile. Investigators think that he may have scouted out the area
earlier, looking for a suitable opening into the creek, for
what he was about to do.

He finally stopped at a white picket fence about a mile
from his home. It was the only opening along the complete

span of the two-and-three-quarter-mile creek. He stopped and turned into it, stopping at the very edge.

Then he relaxed the brake and the Land Cruiser coasted down the fifteen-foot drop, into the frozen creek below. It plowed into an abandoned campsite, hitting several metal chairs and a tree stump once used as a table.

When it had finally ground to a halt, he got out from the passenger's side, leaving Michelle's body lying in a bloody heap, propped up in the driver's seat, the engine still running.

He walked across the creek towards the roadway, leaving a set of deep footprints in the snow, coming from the vehicle. At one point the ice broke beneath him and his foot plunged into the freezing water below.

At about 3:00 a.m. he walked back along Jacobs Creek Road, but police believe he did not come straight home. Eventually when he finally did get back to Keithwood Court, he began to clean up the garage, trying to get rid of all the bloody evidence.

He cleaned up Michelle's blood using white paper towels and hydrogen peroxide, dumping them in white plastic trash bags. He put one bag in a trash can and the other in a flue behind the fireplace in the basement.

At 6:00 a.m. he accidentally set off the burglar alarm in the basement and panicked. Knowing it was only a matter of time before the police came to investigate, he went back upstairs, leaving a trail of Michelle's blood to the second-floor bathroom. He placed his red-stained pajamas in the washing machine and hid a pair of blood-soaked pants behind a couch.

Then he went back to bed with his children, pretending to have slept soundly through the night, when his father telephoned at about 6:30 a.m., after being contacted by the alarm company.

17

Panic

Within minutes of PSE&G maintenance worker Chuckie Black's distress call, the first officers from nearby Hopewell Township Police Department arrived at the scene. At 8:43 a.m., Officer Michael J. Sherman had received a signal eleven from the Hopewell Township police dispatcher, meaning an accident with injuries. Eight minutes later he pulled his black-and-white alongside the PSE&G truck on Jacobs Creek Road, at the same time as his colleague Officer Louis Vastola arrived.

"There were two PSE&G workers on the left side of the truck and two on the right," remembered Officer Sherman. "One worker said, 'You can slow down from running. She's already dead.'"

The two officers walked down into the creek and along the ice, observing a set of footprints from the passenger's side of the vehicle, running back across the creek and up to Jacobs Creek Road. In one of the footprints there was a small hole in the ice. They carefully walked together alongside the footprints, making sure they did not disturb them, in case they might later be evidence.

The dark green Toyota Land Cruiser's engine was still running as Vastola opened the driver's-side door. Inside was Michelle Nyce's horribly battered body, frozen rigid and covered in blood. By the side of it was a bloody white pillow.

Vastola checked her pulse and screamed: "No pulse! She's dead!"

Officer Sherman walked to the back of the Land Cruiser to inspect it. He noticed there was blood on the left running board, on both the passenger and back doors, and blood smeared inside, on both front seats and the steering wheel.

"I observed an Asian female slumped over, sitting in the driver's seat," said Sherman. "Her torso was slumped into the passenger's seat."

They also noted how the driver's seat was pushed as far back as it would go, meaning Michelle's shoeless feet could not possibly have reached the pedals. Sherman then notified the Mercer County Prosecutor's Office that it was a suspicious death, and began securing the scene with red evidence tape to preserve it.

Within minutes Hopewell Township Police Chief Michael Chipowsky arrived at the scene, and he too realized this was not an ordinary traffic accident.

"There were footprints leading away from the vehicle," said Chief Chipowsky, who had been in charge of the thirty-six-member rural police department for nine years. "The injuries to the victim appeared much more severe than would have occurred in a car accident, with a kind of minor damage to the car. So it just looked out of place and was starting not to add up."

By this time the Toyota's number plates had been run through the computer, with the name of Dr. Jonathan Nyce coming up as the owner.

"It was a local resident," said the chief, "and there was the possibility of foul play, so we called the New Jersey State Police Major Crime Unit. We're not geared up for this sort of thing."

There had only been one murder in living memory in the sprawling 64-square-mile Hopewell Township, and that was a domestic murder/suicide. In 1993, 64-year-old Arthur Daniels of Crusher Road had killed his estranged wife, Betty Jean, 57, with a shotgun. Then he turned the gun on himself.

Four years earlier Hopewell was tangentially involved in one of the seventeen murders committed by the notorious serial killer Joel Rifkin.

In what has become known locally as "The Hopewell Head," a young woman's severed head was discovered at a Hopewell golf course.

"That had the neighborhood in a tizzy for a while," explained Chief Chipowsky. "But generally it's just very quiet."

As soon as Dr. Nyce's name came off the computer, Chief Chipowsky ordered Officer Sherman and Sergeant Michael Cseremsak, who had just arrived at the scene, to go to 1 Keithwood Court and interview him.

They arrived at 9:13 a.m., having learned the Nyces' burglar alarm had gone off three hours earlier.

"I was looking to see if there was anything out of the ordinary," said Sergeant Cseremsak. "I saw an open garage door and a vehicle in it."

Cseremsak, who was not in uniform, then walked around the house, where there was a large flagpole with a Stars and Stripes blowing in the wind. He also observed a set of footprints, realizing they belonged to Officer Lincoln Karnoff, who had been called out earlier to check the burglar alarm, but had found nothing suspicious.

The two officers walked across the snow-covered driveway to a side entrance and knocked on the door.

Trevor and Samantha Nyce answered and Cseremsak asked for their father.

"They said neither parent were there," he remembered. "Their mother had left because she starts work early before they get up. The father was dropping off the other boy at school. They said he'd be home in a little while and said he drives a Hummer H2."

They then went back to the warmth of their police car to wait for him. A few minutes later Dr. Jonathan Nyce drove up in his red Hummer and stopped alongside them. The officers introduced themselves and after confirming he owned the Toyota Land Cruiser, they asked to go inside and talk.

Nyce agreed and they followed his Hummer up the driveway to the front door. But on the way Cseremsak noticed Nyce closing the single garage door with a remote control as he drove past it. The officer wondered if there was something inside Nyce didn't want them to see.

Nyce brought them into the foyer, asking why they had come as he took off his overcoat.

"He was disheveled," Cseremsak would later testify. "His hair was messy. His clothing was messy. His button-fly jeans had one or two buttons undone."

Then he brought them into the large dining room and as they sat around the table, they could hear his two youngest children watching a cartoon in another room.

Cseremsak explained that the Nyces' Toyota SUV had been involved in a crash and asked who was driving it. Nyce said it was his wife Michelle, immediately wanting to know her condition and what hospital she was in.

"I didn't tell him she was deceased," said the officer, "as I didn't know it was his wife."

The softly spoken doctor told them that last night Michelle had been working the 6-to-10 p.m. shift at Macy's, and was then going out with a friend. He said she'd told him she'd be home by 1:00, pointing out that that usually meant 2:00, adding it was not unusual, and sometimes she stayed out all night.

Cseremsak was suspicious of Jonathan Nyce and thought his behavior odd. For one thing, his mood seemed inconsistent with his wife being in an accident. And why had he surreptitiously closed the garage door, as if he had something to hide? So he went out to his police car, radioing his supervisor, Lieutenant Francis Fechter, for further instructions.

Fechter informed him that they believed the body in the vehicle was that of Michelle Nyce, telling him to advise Nyce of his rights and then tell him the news. Then Cseremsak went back into the dining room and took Sherman outside, asking him to turn on the police car's video camera with its powerful long-range microphone. He wanted an audio record, as he did not have a Miranda rights form in the car.

After advising Nyce of his rights and asking if he wanted an attorney present, which he didn't, Cseremsak told him that the dead woman in the vehicle was his wife Michelle. Nyce displayed little reaction to the terrible news.

"Minimal," was how the officer would later describe it to a jury.

"He didn't seem to get upset. We went over her plans and routines and then he talked of her extra-marital affairs."

Nyce calmly spoke of the nights Michelle never came home, and when Cseremsak asked if she was seeing anybody, he was only too willing to talk.

"He said she had been having an affair with a gardener and had broken it off," said the officer. "But he believed she was seeing him again."

Then 5-year-old Samantha came in, sat on her father's lap and began drawing a picture. To Cseremsak's astonishment, Jonathan Nyce continued discussing Michelle's infidelities right there in front of her.

"He said in the past the boyfriend had attempted to extort money," he remembered. "And at some point he'd threatened the life of the family. As his daughter was on his lap, I didn't press him, but he just continued to talk about it."

Nyce said he believed Michelle had been cheating, and was very worried she was back with this man.

Officer Cseremsak then asked if he could look at the basement and take photographs with a disposable camera, as the burglar alarm had been activated. Nyce agreed and accompanied him into the basement, before showing him the master bedroom, kitchen, bathroom and laundry room.

In the foyer on their way out, Nyce said he was concerned about how to tell his children their mother was dead, and if they should go to school or not.

"We were talking about his children getting counseling," said the officer, "when he broke down and began to cry."

Then Nyce asked if he could call Michelle's best friend, Larissa Soos, and after giving him a business card, Cseremsak left, taking the drawing Samantha had given him.

While Jonathan Nyce was talking to the police officers, Larissa Soos had telephoned. That morning she had arranged for Michelle and Jean Larini to come to her house at 10:00 for a scrapbook picture workshop.

"Michelle's always running late," said Larissa. "So I thought I'd call and remind her."

Larissa asked Jonathan how he was doing.

"Not so good," replied Jonathan.

"Oh, are you sick?" she asked.

"No," he said. "Michelle's been in a car accident."

Larissa was so shocked to hear this, she asked him what he meant.

She could hear some voices in the background, as Nyce asked her if she had been with Michelle the previous night. When Larissa said no, he asked if she had Amy's cell phone number. Larissa said she didn't, but suggested it might be stored on Michelle's phone.

"He was so calm," said Larissa. "I can hear the police in the background and he just says, 'I'll call you back later.'"

Then he hung up, leaving Larissa to wonder what could have happened to her best friend.

"I was just shocked, shaking," she said. "Then I was waiting for him to call me back with more details."

For the next hour Larissa waited for his call, which finally came at 10:30.

"He was crying," she remembered. "He told me that she was dead. That they had found her car on Jacobs Creek Road in the water. I was like, 'What do you mean, she's dead? Have you seen her? Maybe she's in the hospital?'

"He just said she was dead and he didn't know a lot about the accident. I was crying and he was crying. Then he said he was going to meet with detectives that afternoon for an interview."

After about fifteen minutes, Nyce said he'd call later when he knew more.

Then Jean called to say she was running late. Without telling her about Michelle, Larissa asked her to come over as soon as possible.

A few minutes later Jean arrived at the Sooses' house, carrying snacks and a cake for the workshop. Larissa opened the door and Jean asked where Michelle was and if she was late.

"Michelle's dead," sobbed Larissa.

In shock, Jean dropped all the food as the two friends hugged each other.

For the next few hours they kept calling Michelle's cell phone number, praying that she would answer, and it would all be a bad dream.

Investigators believe that after talking to the two officers, Jonathan Nyce realized that he had made a big mistake, leaving a perfect set of footprints in the snow at the scene. So as soon as they left, he went down into his basement, closing the door behind him. He then sliced off the soles of his adapted moccasin boots, cutting them up into fourteen small pieces, using his workbench scroll saw.

As he was hiding the pieces in a box of Christmas decorations and other places around the basement, his daughter Samantha came down to tell him two more detectives had arrived.

18

"Lock Him into a Statement"

etective Daniel McKeown Jr. had just come home from dropping his daughter off at school, when his cell phone rang at 9:22 a.m. It was Lieutenant Francis Fechter, asking him to go to a fatal car accident on Jacobs Creek Road, only ten miles away from his house. On his way there he got another call, informing him that the fatal vehicle registration had been traced back to Jonathan Nyce.

"Knowing my prior history with the Nyces," said Detective McKeown, "they wanted me to make a positive identification of the body."

The detective hadn't thought about Jonathan and Michelle Nyce since August, when the Hopewell Municipal Court had ordered the no contact restraining order between Michelle and Alexander Castaneda.

Just after 9:30 a.m. he arrived at Jacobs Creek Road, which was already being sealed off from traffic as a possible crime scene. There he was met by Officer Louis Vastola, who carefully escorted him into the creek and up to the green Land Cruiser, with its engine still running.

"I saw a female, deceased, [and] it was Mrs. Nyce," he

later remembered. There was obvious head trauma and a tremendous amount of blood to the head of the victim."

After making a positive identification, McKeown walked back to the road, where he was greeted by his sister, Detective Karen Ortman, of the Mercer County Prosecutor's Office, who happened to be on duty that morning.

McKeown had known that his sister was working homicide, and there was a good chance she would get the call. Secretly he hoped that if it was a homicide, they would get to work a case together for the first time.

"It wasn't going to be brother and sister," said Detective McKeown. "It was going to be cop to cop."

"This is going to get interesting," said Detective Ortman, after hearing it was Michelle Nyce's body, and knowing a little of the background.

"Without a doubt," agreed McKeown.

Chief Chipowsky came over and appointed McKeown lead detective for the investigation, in light of his previous experience with the Nyce family. He ordered him and Detective Ortman straight to Keithwood Court to lock Dr. Jonathan Nyce into a statement.

The two detectives had grown up together in the small New Jersey town of Hazlet, in nearby Ewing Township. Their father, Daniel B. McKeown Sr., was an administrative law judge, and their mother a legal secretary.

Born in 1965, Dan is fifteen months older than Karen.

"Growing up," says Dan, "I would say I was probably a little overly protective of my little sister."

"But I was also very protective of you," said Karen.

Two years ahead of his sister at high school, Dan says he had several friends wanting to date the pretty dark-haired schoolgirl.

"And no, that wasn't going to happen," he chuckled. "It's just funny how at that time I'm watching over her like a hawk, and twenty years later, look what we're doing."

When Karen was a young girl, she wanted to be a politician or a lobbyist in Washington, D.C. But after graduating from Trenton State in 1988, she decided to make a career in law enforcement and entered the police academy.

Then in 1989 she joined the Mercer County Prosecutor's Office as a detective.

"My dad was friendly with the prosecutor at the time," she said. "Which was hard to live down the first few years of my employment. But I've since proven myself."

In 1990, she was named Detective of the Year by former Mercer County Prosecutor Dan Giaquinto. She is married to a Newark DEA special agent and has three young children attending the same elementary school as Alex and Trevor Nyce.

Her older brother Dan joined the Hopewell Township Police Department in 1990. But unlike the prosecutor's office, where everyone starts out as a detective, Dan had to put his time in on the squad before working his way up to the detective bureau four years ago.

Ten years ago, he married Karen's best friend Tracy, also a detective with the Mercer County Prosecutor's Office, and they too have three children.

Now brother and sister would team up for their first murder investigation together.

At 10:45 a.m., during the two-minute drive to the Nyce house, they discussed tactics as Dan briefed his sister about Dr. Nyce's preposterous $500,000 extortion claim six months earlier. They both realized the importance of locking Nyce into a statement.

"We knew he saw her last," said Detective Ortman. "When we went down there, we discussed—Whatever we have to do to lock him into a statement, we've got to do."

They parked their unmarked Hopewell police car in the street at the bottom of the driveway, where Sergeant Sherman and Officer Cserensak were waiting. The two detectives walked over to them to check if Jonathan was at home. Cserensak confirmed that he was in the house with two of his children, as well as a friend named Nancy Baeza, who had just arrived to see Nyce.

As they were talking, Baeza came out, got in her car and was driving away when they stopped her. They asked if she would stay and look after the children, as they intended to take Nyce to Hopewell Township police station to make a statement. She agreed, remaining in her car as the two plain-clothes detectives walked up to the front door and rang the bell.

"A little girl answered the door," said Detective McKeown. "She said that her father was in the basement, and we asked her to get him."

Samantha smiled, saying she would, and closing the door behind her. Then the two detectives waited outside in the freezing snow for about ten minutes, before Jonathan Nyce appeared at the door, barefoot, unkempt and looking in a terrible state.

"The thing that stood out in my mind was how cold it was, and Samantha saying he's down in the basement," said McKeown. "He comes upstairs and he's in barefoot and I thought, 'Jesus, he's got to be freezing.'"

Nyce immediately recognized McKeown. They shook hands and the officer introduced him to his sister.

"He struck me as like an eccentric scientist," Detective Ortman remembered. "'He just didn't care that it was really cold out."

They then explained why they were there, asking him to come back with them to Hopewell Township Police Department and give a statement. Nyce readily agreed, giving permission for Baeza to look after his children.

Although Sergeant Cseremsak had already told him Michelle was dead, Nyce now acted as if he didn't know, complaining that the police wouldn't tell him what hospital she was in.

"He was going through the motions," said Ortman. "He was still perpetuating the uncertainty about her. That kind of garbage."

When Detective McKeown offered to drive Nyce to the station, he accepted, requesting a minute to brush his teeth and put his shoes and socks on.

Although it is just one-and-a-half miles from Keithwood Court to the Hopewell police station, McKeown deliberately took a far longer route through Ewing Township. The direct one would have taken them along Jacobs Creek Road, where Michelle's body still lay in the vehicle. He did not want Nyce to see the crash scene and get distracted.

"As soon as we got in the car, he starts talking about her extra-marital affairs," remembers Ortman. "How we should be looking at the boyfriend and the boyfriend's wife. And I'm thinking to myself, 'What the heck is he talking about?'

"But of course I listened and then asked him questions to keep him talking, because obviously talking about the boyfriend made him comfortable. So I encouraged it, because I wanted to make him comfortable."

Nyce told them to investigate Enyo as a possible suspect, saying he had probably been with Michelle last night. He even speculated that Enyo's wife, Patricia, might also want to harm Michelle.

Then he began to ramble, telling them about the Sampaguita perfume company he and Michelle were starting and what an excellent Chanel saleswoman she was. He segued to Michelle's pregnant friend Amy, saying he didn't like her because she was "morally bankrupt."

"He was very judgmental about people, and that struck me," said Detective Ortman. "And very quick to bring others into this case."

In order to relax him and get him to open up further, Ortman began to flatter him about his scientific accomplishments.

"That's where I struck gold," she said. "I started telling him about how I really didn't know about science and how smart he seemed."

Warming to his favorite subject, Jonathan Nyce talked and talked, boasting about his achievements for the rest of the journey.

"Oh, he wouldn't shut up," observed Ortman. "On and on and on and on. And I thought, this is a safe conversation to have. I told him I thought he was magnificent, just to keep him talking."

◆ ◆ ◆

At 11:15 a.m., they arrived at Hopewell police station, going straight into Detective McKeown's office. The detectives sat around one desk while Jonathan Nyce was at the other, facing them. McKeown sent out for coffee, and while they were waiting for it to arrive, he explained the formal statement process to Nyce. Their questions and answers would both be typed into a computer and then printed out for his review. If he was satisfied, he would initial the bottom of each page and sign the last one.

They began taking the ten-page statement at 12 noon, and it took two-and-a-half hours to finish. Detective Ortman asked the questions, which were witnessed by her brother. After confirming that Nyce wasn't under the influence of drugs or alcohol, she asked what he knew about the "automobile accident" involving his wife.

He said he had last seen Michelle the previous day, when she'd told him she had to work late at Macy's. She had then planned to go out to the mall with Amy.

"Whenever my wife is out late, the kids sleep with me," he said. "My wife is a fairly unstable person and is out late frequently."

He said he had been "groggy" just after 6:00 that morning, when his mother had called to tell him the alarm company had contacted her. Then he'd gone back to sleep, knowing there was a ninety-minute snow delay that morning for schools.

When he'd finally gotten up, he had driven his 12-year-old son Alex to Timberlane School.

"I came home and started to get the other kids dressed when the police showed up," he wrote in his statement. "They told me they found Michelle's car."

Finally, he said, police had come out and told him that Michelle had been found dead in the SUV. After they'd left, he'd continued getting Trevor and Samantha ready for school.

"I didn't know what else to do," he explained. "I figured I'd send them to school, then ask my mom to come over."

On the way to the police station, Nyce had asked Detective McKeown if his wife had been wearing her glasses. Now asked to explain further, he said he would be "mad at her" if she hadn't been, as "she can't really see at all."

Then Detective Orton asked how he had first met Michelle, and Nyce's mood suddenly brightened.

"It was a real love story," he began, a thin smile coming to his face for the first time. "I was attending a conference in Hawaii and she was there just lying on the beach with a cousin. I went to go surfing, after leaving a meeting, and literally stepped on her foot."

Nyce then told the detectives how he had started EpiGenesis in North Carolina. He also mentioned Sampaguita.

Then Detective Ortman asked what time he had last seen Michelle yesterday.

"I last saw Michelle at about 4:00 p.m. exactly," he answered. "I found out that Samantha's gym class had not been cancelled due to snow, and the class was at 4:15 p.m."

He described leaving the house with his three children, while Michelle was getting ready for her shift at Macy's.

"It takes her two hours to get ready," he explained. "She has to be at work by 6:00 p.m."

After the one-hour gymnastics class he had taken his kids for pizza at T J's in Pennington, before they returned home, settling down in his bed to watch *Bruce Almighty*.

He was then asked if he had spoken to Michelle by phone during the evening. He said he and the children had left a message on her cell phone, after they were all tucked up in bed.

"I put the phone on speaker so everyone could talk," he explained. "She never responded to the message."

After the movie ended they had all gone to sleep in the master bedroom. But when he got up after midnight to use the bathroom, he realized that his wife had not come home.

"I got concerned," he said. "She's usually home by one a.m."

He said he had called her cell phone, but it had gone straight to voice mail, so he went back to sleep.

"My doctor prescribes me Ativan, known as lorazepam," he informed them. "Which I take since Michelle was having her affair and I was absolutely beside myself. When Michelle goes out, and if she's going to be late, which she tells me as she is going out the door, I will take one. Then I don't care.

"Michelle hooked up with the gardener," he said. "I know this because I was sitting in my car when I got a call on my cell phone from a man who played a tape of my wife having sex with another man."

He then repeated how Enyo had tried to blackmail him, demanding $500,000 for some video- and audiotapes of them having sex.

Detective McKeown, who had concluded after his thorough investigation that it had never happened, sat there mentally rolling his eyes, as Jonathan Nyce began embellishing his story.

"Also, I just remembered," he said, "that when we were eating at a restaurant one evening in July or August, Michelle told me that she remembered something that Enyo stated. He said to her, 'Don't worry. I'll take care of him and I'm not gonna tell you how I'm gonna do it, or you'll be scared.'"

Moving on, Ortman asked if he and Michelle had ever had "physical" arguments.

"Never," replied Nyce. "She would throw things at me once in a while, but I was pretty good at ducking. I never struck her in my life. She liked to pick at me. She always needed something to be angry about."

Then he was asked if they'd had a "normal" sex life.

"Yeah," he said. "We had a lot of sex. It was normal."

Finally the detectives asked if there was anything he wanted to add to his statement. Nyce said that a couple of weeks earlier, Michelle had wanted a new car, complaining she was being followed when she left work.

"She intimated that if it wasn't Enyo, it was one of his

friends," he said. "Maybe I should have taken her more seri-ously, I don't know."

The interview concluded at 2:20 p.m., and after reading the transcript, Jonathan Nyce initialed each page, signing that it was a "true, free and voluntary statement." It was wit-nessed by Mercer County Assistant Prosecutor and Chief of the Homicide Unit Tom Meidt.

During the interview both detectives had noticed numer-ous scratches and small cuts on Nyce's hands, and that his fingernails were torn and dirty. So McKeown asked if they could photograph his hands and take buccal swabs, and he agreed.

Then he called his parents in Collegeville, telling them what had happened, and asking them to come to his house as soon as possible. Jonathan Jr. and Emma Nyce had just re-turned from lunch with their dance instructor, after taking a class at a senior center. His mother told him she first had a 4:00 p.m. hair appointment, and then they would drive over.

At 4:00 p.m. Detective McKeown drove Jonathan Nyce to Timberlane School to collect Alex and bring him home. During the two-mile journey to Pennington, the detective deliberately did not encourage any further conversation, and they rode in silence.

"And then just out of the blue he says, 'You know, I really thought things were going to work out,'" remembered the detective.

"'OK, Jon, why do you think that?' And he explained they only argued when she talked about moving out."

He asked when Michelle had last threatened to move out, catching Nyce off-guard.

"Last night," he said.

But before McKeown could pursue it any further, they had reached the school and Alex Nyce was walking towards them.

During the ride home the conversation mainly focused on Alex's day. But at one point Nyce told his son that when they got home, there was something that they needed to discuss as a family, assuring him everything would be OK.

"Alex had no reaction," noted McKeown, "and nothing else was mentioned."

After dropping them off at Keithwood Court, the detective returned to Hopewell Township Police Department, informing his sister about their conversation and how Nyce said they had argued the night before.

"I had already begun working on the search warrants for the house and the Land Cruiser," said Detective Ortman. "I said, 'Make sure you put that in writing. That was completely inconsistent with him last seeing Michelle at four p.m."

19

Minimal Damage

By mid-morning, Jacobs Creek Road was a hive of activity, as the investigation into Michelle Nyce's death moved into high gear. By this time detectives were certain it was not accidental, and were treating it as a murder.

Two police cars sealed off a long stretch of the road, and a Crime Scene Investigation (CSI) team from the New Jersey State Police were on their way. A police helicopter hovered over the creek, taking aerial photos of the whole area. And Hopewell Township police officers had already taped off the scene with red accident tape, placing bright yellow flags alongside the footprints coming from the Land Cruiser.

At 10:30 p.m., Detective Geoffrey Noble of the New Jersey State Police Major Crimes Unit arrived at Jacobs Creek Road. "We had to set up a crime scene and assist the Hopewell Township Police Department," explained Detective Noble. "It was a very large crime scene." The bald, no-nonsense ten-year veteran would supervise, also acting as a liaison between the investigators and the crime-scene officers, ensuring that all information was shared.

When he arrived Detective Noble was fully briefed on what was known so far, before making his own inspection.

"Certain aspects didn't make sense," he said. "It was not consistent with a simple motor accident."

"My first observation was that there was very little damage to the vehicle," compared with the terrible injuries sustained by the dead woman inside, he later testified. "And I've investigated many accidents. There was not significant impact to the vehicle."

Detective Noble took careful note of the size 12 footprints leaving the passenger side of the car. As he walked around the Land Cruiser, which still had the engine running, he noted it was covered in blood, inside and out. Then he looked into the open driver's-side door and saw Michelle Nyce's frozen body.

"The victim was slumped to the side across the center console," he said. "There were significant amounts of blood from wounds to the forehead area."

He also observed the driver's seat was positioned as far back as it could go, making it impossible for Michelle's feet to have reached the pedals. And although she was just wearing stockings, there was a pair of shoes nearby on the floor.

Michelle was wearing a black suit jacket with her Macy's name tag still pinned on it, and a white Chanel ribbon affixed to it. There was a thick gold chain around her neck, and she was only wearing one gold earring. A blue ice scraper lay between her legs, and there was a large black suitcase lying on the back seat.

At 12:15 p.m. Detective Sergeant James Molinaro and Detective Patrick Thornton, from the Hopewell office of the New Jersey State Police, arrived to take over the investigation. Molinaro, a seasoned twenty-three-year veteran was in charge of the CSI unit. He immediately took charge of the investigation, with Thornton as his lead crime scene investigator.

First they met with Hopewell Police Chief Mike Chipowsky and several of his officers, before personally walking the crash site.

"I conducted an overall assessment," explained Detective Sergeant Molinaro. "Then I broke down the assignments."

As lead crime-scene investigator, Detective Thornton would be in charge of photographing the scene and fully documenting it, writing up notes for a later investigation report.

"I walked Jacobs Creek Road back and forth several times," Thornton later testified. "The Land Cruiser was located in the creek, partially submerged in the water."

He noted the Land Cruiser's tire track exiting off the road, through a dirt mound and down into the ravine.

"Where it had traveled there were leaves visible," he said. "I could see the path down to where it finally rested."

While the New Jersey police were collecting evidence at Jacobs Creek Road, the Hopewell Township Police Department began their own investigation.

At 11:45 a.m. Captain George Meyer assigned Sergeant Thomas Puskas and Detective Pental to interview Michelle's friend Amy Sumayang. At 1:30 p.m., Sergeant Puskas found her at the Post Office Remote Encoding Center in Princeton, where she worked as a data operator, and gave her the news of Michelle's death.

"Her reaction was very shocked," wrote Puskas in his report, "and slightly emotional."

Amy told the officers how she was supposed to have called Michelle the previous day, as they had planned to go out after she finished work. But she had been too busy to call, finally leaving a message on Michelle's cell phone at around 9:50 p.m. A few minutes later Michelle returned her call, also leaving a message, but Amy had finally gotten through to her in person.

She said Michelle had said she was going to Wegmans, but when Amy offered to meet her there, her friend did not want her to. Amy said she thought Michelle was probably going to meet a male friend named Enyo.

When Puskas pressed for more details about Enyo, she said she did not know where they'd met or where they'd gone on dates.

But she was more forthcoming about Michelle's relationship with Jonathan. She said Michelle had complained they had been fighting for five years, now arguing almost daily. But Michelle had never indicated she had been physically hit by Jonathan.

"During the course of the fights Michelle Nyce always asked for a divorce," wrote Puskas in his subsequent report. "[Amy] had no knowledge of any divorce filing by either person."

She also said Michelle had once found a condom in her husband's luggage after a business trip, and believed he may have been having an affair.

Puskas asked Amy about whether Michelle had vision problems, as Nyce had previously suggested. Amy said Michelle never wore glasses and had perfect sight.

Throughout the interview Amy, who was heavily pregnant, kept asking if Jonathan knew she was talking to them.

"It was quite obvious [she] was very concerned," noted Puskas. "When asked if she was afraid of Jonathan Nyce, she would only say he did not like her."

Back at Jacobs Creek, Detective Sergeant Molinaro was busy organizing his CSI team. At 12:30 p.m. he called in his highly experienced investigator, Detective John Ryan, who arrived two hours later.

"My assignment was to photograph and document some footwear impressions at the scene," he later explained. "There was a set located in the snow, heading southeast away from the vehicle, then up through the wood and ending on the roadway."

Starting from the road, Detective Ryan carefully photographed every footprint, using high-contrast black-and-white film, alongside a right-angle rule, so they could be printed to scale. Most of the footprints lacked detail, but as he got nearer the vehicle they improved drastically in quality.

He also made plaster cast impressions of six of the best footprints, so they could be fully documented.

After he had finished, Detective Ryan turned his attention

to Michelle Nyce's body, which had now been in the vehicle
for about twelve hours in the sub-zero temperatures and was
frozen solid.

"In her clenched left hand we found hair and fibers," he
said. "There were also hair and fibers on the side of the driver's seat, facing the door."

He collected swabs of blood and tissue from all over the
car, immediately placing them in a special container so they
didn't freeze, and cataloguing them into evidence.

Then he looked at Michelle's horrendous head injuries.

"In my experience, due to her injuries there should have
been some type of damage to the windshield and the dash-
board," he later testified. "These were very deep injuries.
Gouges in the forehead area."

At 3:20 p.m. Detective Sergeant Jeffrey Kronenfeld arrived to complete the New Jersey State Police CSI team,
which would now work around the clock for three days, with
little or no sleep.

It was a slow day at the newsroom of the Trenton *Times* and
Hopewell reporter Lisa Coryell had taken a long lunch. The
tough-talking attractive brunette returned to her desk to find
a handwritten piece of paper from the City Desk, saying:
"Woman's body found in creek frozen."

"It had come over the scanner, and as I cover Hopewell, it
was going to be my story," said Coryell.

She was briefed that, although it had initially looked like
an accident, foul play was suspected, and told to closely
monitor any developments in the case. That night Coryell
had plans to leave town for a birthday party in the Poconos
with her 13-year-old niece and her friends. But if it proved
to be murder, she knew she would have to stay and work the
story.

First she called up her police contacts to try to ID the accident victim.

"They weren't giving any information on who she was or
her identity," said the dogged reporter. "And I said, 'Look,

I've got six thirteen-year-old girls waiting to go to the Pononos. Just give me a heads-up on her name, so I can start knocking on doors."

Finally she persuaded her contact to give her Michelle Nyce's name and address, and by 3:00 she was out canvassing Keithwood Court, talking to residents.

"The neighbor across the street was telling me what a wonderful father he was," remembered Coryell. "How he had taken her child and his child out searching for Indian arrowheads in the woods."

But another neighbor named Melissa Weeks, who lived a street away from the Nyces, said everyone wanted to know what had really happened.

"Was it an accident?" Weeks asked. "Was it sickness? Or was it murder? Everybody's nervous because this happened in our back yard."

By afternoon, Larissa Soos and Jean Larini were desperate for more news of Michelle, still not knowing what had happened to their friend. They kept calling Jonathan Nyce's home and cell phone, but there was no answer. At 3:00 p.m. they decided to take matters into their own hands, going to Hopewell Township Police Department for answers.

"We thought we'd better make sure she's not in the hospital," said Larini. "We just don't want to accept that she's gone."

They sat in the waiting room for about forty minutes, before Captain George Meyer saw them in his office.

"We really wanted to hear what was going on," said Larissa. "They really didn't tell us anything. They were asking us questions and I'm like, 'Where is she? What happened?' They said were looking into things."

They asked Captain Meyer if they could to go to the Nyce home to take care of the three children, and were given permission.

They arrived at about 4:00 p.m. and found Todd Ridge Road closed off, with several Hopewell police officers stationed at the bottom of the driveway. After explaining that they were friends of the family, they were allowed through.

"Jonathan answered the door," said Larissa. "We were all crying and hugging each other. His hair was disheveled and his eyes were sore from crying. He was really grieving, and the kids were so sad."

When they had all composed themselves, Jean Larini asked when he had last talked to Michelle. Nyce said it had been about 4:00 p.m. the previous day, before she had left for work.

Then she asked him why he hadn't called the police when Michelle hadn't come home.

Nyce just said he had not, refusing to elaborate any further. Larini became suspicious, wondering why he was being so evasive.

"At that point I'm thinking, 'He's the one that did it,'" she remembered. "We just asked him again why he didn't call the police and report she's missing or not home."

He told them he had gotten up at 5:00 a.m. and begun getting the kids ready.

"He was hoping," said Jean, "she will pull into the driveway and have some excuses."

Then Nyce abruptly changed the subject, informing them that he planned to continue developing Sampaguita perfume as a tribute to Michelle.

"I thought, 'Oh my God,'" said Soos. "It was just so surprising that he would be talking about tributes so soon. He wanted to carry on with it, although she was dead—as a tribute? I was too upset to think about it. I just thought about the kids. He also made the comment that he thought his life was perfect. I was just really concerned about the kids."

Then he called the children into the living room, announcing that, as their mother was gone now, Larissa and Jean would be taking her place.

They asked if the kids had eaten lunch, and Nyce said he had cooked them macaroni and cheese after returning from the police station. And when they asked what they could do to help, he said the police were coming back, and his parents were on their way over to make funeral arrangements.

So they offered to take the children back to Larissa's for dinner, and to comfort them.

"And he said, 'That would be great, they need their motherly care,'" said Jean. "That's what he said."

Then Larissa took Alex and Trevor upstairs to pack some clothes, and Jean left Nyce in the kitchen, going down to the garage to collect Samantha's winter coat and boots from a closet by the door.

She was about to go into the garage when Jonathan Nyce suddenly came up behind her, looking as if he had seen a ghost. Then he stood in front of the garage door, barring her way, with a strange look in his beady eyes.

"He was just staring at me," said Larini, who bears an uncanny physical resemblance to Michelle. "He was so tall and I had no idea what it was. I just said, 'Oh, I'm sorry, Jon.' And I started crying again."

Later, when she discovered Jonathan had killed Michelle in the garage less than twenty-four hours before, she realized what a lucky escape she had had.

"I had goose bumps," she said. "Michelle and I look alike. We're the same size and we have long hair."

Larini believes that if she had entered the garage and seen any evidence of the murder, her life might have been in danger. Or perhaps when Jonathan saw her by the garage entrance, he thought he'd seen Michelle's ghost.

Then the two women took the three Nyce kids back to Larissa's house, leaving Jonathan alone to wait for his parents to arrive. On the way they drove along Jacobs Creek Road, passing by Michelle's body, still lying in the Land Cruiser.

It was already dark at 6:15 p.m. when Mercer County Medical Examiner Dr. Raafat Ahmad arrived at the death scene. Hopewell Township Fire Department had set spotlights around the Land Cruiser so the investigation could continue through the night.

Dr. Ahmad's investigator, Chris Merlino, had arrived

ninety minutes earlier, to start making preparations to remove Michelle's body from the creek and bring it to the
M.E.'s office for autopsy.

Born in Pakistan, the diminutive forensic pathologist had
been the County M.E. for twenty-five years, performing
more than three thousand autopsies in her career.

"I was told there was a body of a young woman found in Jacobs Creek," she remembered. "I had to go to pronounce her
dead, and see if her injuries were consistent with an accident."

It did not take long for Dr. Ahmad to determine that
Michelle Nyce had not died in an accident, and that it was
homicide.

"It was just inconsistent with a car accident," Dr. Ahmad
would later testify. "Her body was frozen rigid. It was sixteen degrees."

The doctor noted injuries to Michelle's forehead, as well
as blood smears on the steering wheel inside, and blood on
both doors.

"There was [also] blood outside the car," she said. "It
looked like it was staged."

At 6:30 p.m. Michelle was officially pronounced dead
and M.E. Investigator Merlino began preparing the body for
removal. Then Detectives Thornton and Molinaro picked up
Michelle's body from the driver's seat, carefully placing it
on a clean white sheet inside the body bag. Michelle's hands
and feet were then brown-bagged with red tape to preserve
any evidence that may have been left under her nails.

The detectives then zipped up the body bag and carried
the plywood board supporting Michelle's body out of the
creek and up the hill. It was then placed in the M.E.'s vehicle, and driven to Dr. Ahmad's office at Mercer County Airport for a viewing later that night in more suitable medical
conditions.

After the body had been driven away, officers secured the
Toyota Land Cruiser and loaded it on a flatbed truck. Then it
was brought to a nearby New Jersey State Police facility in
Hamilton for further inspection.

At 6:37 p.m. all the investigators convened at the

Hopewell Township Police Station to discuss progress so far, and how to proceed. By this time they were certain that Michelle had not died in Jacobs Creek, and that it was a secondary crime scene. Detective Karen Ortman was busy completing a probable cause affidavit for a search warrant for 1 Keithwood Court, now considered the primary crime scene.

At the meeting it was decided to go straight there and order Jonathan Nyce to leave until a judge could sign the search warrants.

"We believed there was something in the house," explained Detective Sergeant Kronenfeld, "and we wanted to make sure evidence was not destroyed."

At 7:23 p.m. Detectives McKeown and Ortman pulled into the Mercer County Medical Examiner's Office, located in shabby, nondescript Building 44 at Mercer County Airport in West Trenton, for a preliminary viewing of the body. Already there were Mercer County Assistant Prosecutor Thomas Meidt and most of the New Jersey State Police investigative team, led by James Molinaro.

Michelle's body lay on a medical trolley in a black vinyl body bag, which was then unzipped by Investigator Chris Merlino. Her body was still clothed and had been wrapped in a white sheet to preserve evidence.

Dr. Ahmad did a brief examination, pointing out to the investigators two deep open wounds on Michelle's bloodsoaked forehead, and another over her left ear. She also noted small cuts and lacerations all over her neck and under her chin.

"It was not a motor accident," Dr. Ahmad said. "There were injuries on the head and the forehead. She had defensive wounds on the inside and outside of her hands."

As the body bag was zipped up and placed in a freezer, Dr. Ahmad announced she would perform the postmortem at 9:00 the next morning.

• • •

That night Lisa Coryell was still working the story, to the frustration of her niece and her friends, who were all packed and ready to go to the Poconos. She'd interviewed Hopewell Township Police Chief Michael Chipowsky at 6:00 p.m. and he'd told her Michelle Nyce's death was murder.

She had also telephoned Jonathan Nyce at his house, and to her surprise he had picked up the phone and given her an interview. When she asked if he'd like to say something about Michelle, he'd replied, "We miss her very much. I miss her beyond any understanding."

The experienced reporter thought his quote was just plain "weird."

"I mean, how do you miss somebody who's only been dead a few hours?" she later asked. "Most people in a situation like that still refer to the person as if they're alive. And he's already talking about her in the past tense."

20

"Michelle Has a Wild Side"

At 8:31 p.m. New Jersey State Police Detective Sergeant Jeffrey Kronenfeld and Sergeant Thomas Puskas of the Hopewell Township Police Department walked up the front drive of 1 Keithwood Court to evict Jonathan Nyce from his home. They saw his brand-new red Hummer 2 parked in the driveway, as well as several other cars parked alongside it.

Several hours earlier, Nyce's parents, his brother Michael and sister-in-law Margaret had arrived to look after him.

"I didn't realize what was going on," his mother later remembered. "It just numbed me."

When the officers rang the doorbell, Emma Nyce answered and they told her they wanted to speak to her son. Then a barefoot Jonathan Nyce came to the door, wearing a blue-and-white–striped shirt and white pants. He looked tired, and his eyes were bloodshot.

"We asked him to vacate the premises," said Sergeant Puskas. "He had some questions."

Nyce seemed in a daze, unable to comprehend what was going on, asking if he had to leave. When they repeated that he did, in anticipation of the search warrants, he started "mumbling" about Enyo "terrorizing his family."

Then he wanted to call a lawyer, and stepped into the kitchen, picking up a Yellow Pages directory and looking through the attorney section. He finally found the number for Lee Engleman, the attorney who'd represented him three months earlier at the Municipal Court hearing, and dialed the number. When there was no answer he left a message.

"I have a serious problem," he told the attorney. "My wife, Michelle, was killed in a car accident over the weekend, and although I was safe in my bed, the police are all over my house right now. They have a warrant. I may need your help as to how to proceed."

Kronenfeld told him to collect clothes and essential belongings for him and his children, until they could return to the house. He was then escorted upstairs by officers, making sure that he was never alone.

He headed straight to the bathroom, but it was locked so he couldn't get in. Then he went into the master bedroom, retrieving a metal key secreted over the door sill. He took it, returning to the bathroom and opening the door.

"As we entered . . . I immediately stepped on broken clear glass," said Detective Sergeant Kronenfeld. "Jonathan Nyce advised that the kids were in the bathroom earlier and broke a glass. He advised that he locked the door so the kids would not step on the broken glass."

As the detectives looked on, Nyce cleaned his teeth and went to his bedroom closet, collecting a brown leather jacket, a pair of moccasins and some toiletries. He also picked up a bottle of his antidepressants and waved it in front of the officers, explaining it was Ativan, prescribed by his psychiatrist.

Jonathan Nyce was escorted downstairs into the living room, where he told his family they all had to vacate the house, as the police were going to carry out a search.

"I went upstairs to get clothes for the kids," said his mother, "and one of the policemen followed me. I said, 'You don't have to follow me.' He said, 'Oh, I have to.'"

At 9:06 p.m. Jonathan Nyce handed the keys to 1 Keith-wood Court over to Detective Sergeant Kronenfeld and drove off in his Hummer, followed by his brother and parents. For most of the next week, two Hopewell police officers stood guard outside the house, making sure nobody came in or out without permission.

At about 9:30 p.m. Jonathan Nyce and his family arrived at Larissa Soos' house to collect the children. Larissa had just cooked dinner and was in her basement with a couple of friends, conducting a scrapbook workshop.

"[Jonathan's] father said they can't stay in his house because they're looking around," said Larissa. "He said the word 'crime scene.' They were looking for stuff."

Nyce said that he was taking the children back to stay with his parents in Collegeville. Then his brother Michael took the kids upstairs to pack and Larissa's husband John came into the basement, saying Jonathan wanted to talk to her.

"There was Jonathan, me and my husband in our family room," remembered Larissa. "The first thing he said was, 'I hate to tell you this, but your friend has a wild side.'

"I was like, 'What do you mean?' "

He then revealed that Michelle was having an affair with a gardener, saying he regretted not telling them earlier, so they could have "talked some sense into her." Larissa was stunned, saying she had no idea. Then Nyce speculated that maybe Michelle had not confided in her because she respected Larissa too much, and knew she would not approve.

"He told me that Michelle was bi-polar and that she likes sex all the time . . . she was seeing a psychiatrist. She was coming home late."

Nyce also informed her that Michelle had been with her lover last night, and had seen him every night that week. And that whenever Michelle said she was going to the grocery store, she was creating an alibi to see her boyfriend.

"I was confused," said Larissa. "I don't know why I'm hearing this. My friend just died in a car accident. I felt like he was trying to convince me that Michelle was a bad person . . . he kept talking about this other life that she supposedly had. . . . my friend is gone. And her husband is saying all this stuff, and she's not alive to defend herself."

In retrospect, Larissa thinks the narcissistic Jonathan Nyce, always so concerned how he came over to other people, was already attempting to portray himself in the best light possible.

"I think, looking back," she said, "he's just trying to justify everything that will be unfolding in the next few months. Because at that time I wondered why he was saying this. I was just shocked."

At the end of the bizarre conversation, Jonathan Nyce asked Larissa and John Soos if they would consider taking care of his children, if anything happened to him. They told him this wasn't the right time to make such a major decision, suggesting they take it day by day.

Then Nyce got up from the couch, rounded up his children and they all left to drive to his parents' home in Collegeville to spend the night.

At 9:00 p.m., after handing in her story, Lisa Coryell drove the six young girls in her SUV to the crime scene on Jacobs Creek Road, on their way to the Poconos. It was a freezing, dark night, and she was allowed through the police barricades, stopping by the edge of the narrow road so they could see the floodlit crime scene below.

"They were just pulling the Land Cruiser out of the creek," she said. "The kids were scared to death. They knew she worked at the Chanel counter at Macy's, so all weekend they were talking about the ghost of Chanel and scaring each other."

21

"Not Cut and Dried"

On Saturday morning the Trenton *Times* ran the banner headline "Woman Found Dead in Creek: Police Are Treating Case as Homicide."

"A township woman was found dead in her sport utility vehicle," began Lisa Coryell's story, "and police are treating the death as a homicide."

It quoted Chief Chipowsky as not "comfortable" calling her death an accident, adding that investigators had found suspicious footprints in the snow, leading away from the crash.

Chipowsky said an autopsy to determine the cause of Michelle's death would be held soon, and his Hopewell PD, the New Jersey State Police, and the Mercer County Prosecutor's Office were jointly investigating.

"The nature of the incident," he said, "was not cut and dried as most incidents are."

The Nyces' Realtor Roberta Parker was also quoted in the story, saying their house had been on the market for three months at an asking price of $1.6 million.

"They were a beautiful couple," she said. "A team. I feel so bad for him and the children."

At 8:30 a.m., after reading the Trenton *Times*, Larissa Soos immediately called Jonathan Nyce at his parents' home. She and Jean had been up all night grieving for their dead friend. "We barely slept," said Larissa. "When I asked him if he was able to sleep, he said, 'Oh yeah, I took some medicine.'"

She asked when he planned to return to Keithwood Court with the children, and he complained that police were still "ransacking" the house.

Then she told him about the Trenton *Times* story.

"I said, 'Jonathan, they're calling it a homicide,'" she remembered. "I read the whole story out to him. He started crying and didn't say a lot."

After she had finished reading it, she asked again why he hadn't called the police when Michelle hadn't come home Thursday night. He explained he had taken his prescription medication, falling fast asleep until about 2:00 a.m., when he discovered Michelle still wasn't home. He wasn't worried, as she had done that before, and was expecting her to walk in at 7:00 a.m. with "some lame excuse."

He had then gone back to sleep, waking up again at around 5:00 a.m. and had stayed awake to prepare his children for school.

"Then he asked if Michelle's family had called," she said. "And whether we should ship [her] body back to the Philippines."

The Philippines is twelve hours ahead of the East coast, and so far Jonathan Nyce had made no attempt to notify Michelle's family of her untimely death. They only discovered it when a Filipino friend of Michelle's named Rudy Paglio saw the article in the Trenton *Times*, and immediately called his brother-in-law, who lived in Orion. He then drove to the Rivieras' home in Depensa Capunitan to tell them the sad news.

"We were told it was an accident," said Teodoro Riviera. "I then telephoned Jonathan and asked what had happened to Michelle."

His son-in-law informed him Michelle had died in a car accident, but Riviera was suspicious.

"So I started asking him questions," he said. "When did Michelle leave the mall? Where was she working? Did you know she was on her way home?"

Jonathan had no answers for any of his questions. Finally Riviera asked why he hadn't tried to find Michelle, or called the police. But Nyce replied he did not know where she was.

"When I stayed with them I had observed that Jonathan was always on his mobile phone," said Riviera, "always wanting to talk to Michelle. And now when she has an accident, he did not know. I knew something didn't sound right.

"So I already suspected Jonathan and thought he might have done something to the car to cause an accident. But it was only in my mind."

At 8:35 a.m. Chief Chipowsky assigned four of his best officers to canvass the streets around Keithwood Court. They were instructed to knock on doors, advising residents of Michelle Nyce's death and asking if they could recall seeing anything unusual between 8:00 Thursday night and 8:00 Friday morning. Neighbors were also asked for their impressions of the Nyce family, and any pertinent information about them.

An hour later, Mercer County Medical Examiner Dr. Raafat Ahmad began conducting Michelle Nyce's autopsy at her office at Mercer County Airport. She was assisted by Chris Merlino. Also present as witnesses were New Jersey State Police Officers Jeffrey Kronenfeld, William Scull, James Molinaro, Patrick Thornton and Detective Kevin Zorn of the Hopewell Township Police Department.

Dr. Ahmad began with a visual examination of Michelle's clothed body, before performing a closer examination of her clothing, using special infra red lighting. Then Detective Sergeant Molinaro carefully collected several hairs and fibers found on the clothing, marking them up and then placing them in sealed evidence envelopes.

An hour into the postmortem it was decided that

Michelle's body should be X-rayed before her clothing was removed. So her body was put back inside the body bag, and driven ten miles to St. Francis Medical Center on Hamilton Avenue, in Trenton.

After the X-rays, which did not prove significant, were taken, Michelle's body was returned to the medical examiner's office and the autopsy resumed at 11:45 a.m.

In her report, Dr. Ahmad wrote that Michelle Nyce was 5 feet 2 inches, weighing 100 pounds. Her body was lean and well preserved, although there was rigor mortis present. Her personal hygiene was good and her pubic area recently shaved.

Dr. Ahmad began by removing the brown bags from Michelle's hands and feet, and then taking off her clothing and jewelry. As each item was removed, it was photographed by Detective Thornton, before being placed in a sealed evidence envelope.

"Her clothing was taken as evidence," explained Dr. Ahmad. "She had black pants with blood smears and a red bra with bloodstains on the back."

Michelle was also wearing thigh-high stockings, with blood on the feet and sole areas.

"[That] was very significant," said the medical examiner. "She was walking or running in the blood."

Then the doctor cleaned up Michelle's bloodied face and body, to make a closer examination of her terrible injuries.

"Her face was covered in blood," Dr. Ahmad later testified. "There was blood to the hair, face and hands. There was blood everywhere. After we removed her clothing, we cleaned her up."

The medical examiner found three lacerations to the forehead, so deep that her skull was visible. There was also a massive injury to the top of her head, which had caused a thirteen-and-a-half-centimeter skull fracture, going from the top of the eye socket to the base of the skull. This horrific injury, Dr. Ahmad would later testify, could have been caused by a baseball bat.

Michelle had been brutally beaten and her whole body was black and blue.

"There were multiple bruises on her left arm, and contusions," said Dr. Ahmad. "On her left hip there was a cluster of purplish bruises. Contusions to her right knee and multiple bruising to her left and right elbows and her nails were blue. Her right eye was swollen and there were injuries present to the lips."

She also found injuries on the inside and outside of Michelle's hands and wrists.

"She was protecting her vital areas from the assailant," the doctor explained. "These were defensive wounds. It was a reflex action. When she was attacked, her hands went up to protect her face. She was trying to defend herself."

Michelle had also suffered brain damage, probably caused by "somebody beating or punching" her, as well as heavy internal bruising to her spleen, pancreas, adrenal gland and lymph nodes.

"I removed the top of the skull," said Dr. Ahmad. "There was hemorrhaging underneath in the brain. Her brain was covered in blood, caused by massive blunt force trauma. There were one hundred cc's of blood that leaked into the brain as a result of the injuries to the top of her head."

But perhaps even more disturbingly, Dr. Ahmad found clear evidence that Michelle had not died quickly.

"The presence of bloody froth in her lungs," explained the medical examiner, "indicates that she was alive and breathing in her own blood for ten minutes after she sustained her injuries. She was having difficulty breathing. Her brain was injured, her skull was injured, but her heart was still beating."

Towards the end of the autopsy Dr. Ahmad identified an additional deep head wound that had been hidden by Michelle's long blood-matted hair, in which her other gold earring had been found.

At 3:59 p.m. Dr. Ahmad completed the postmortem, recording in her autopsy report that Michelle Nyce had died of massive blunt force injuries to the head with fractured skull, contusions of the brain and intra-cranial bleedings.

Methacton High School in Collegeville, P.A., where Jonathan Nyce was best known for his baseball skills and being the tallest boy in the school.
Credit: John Glatt

Love-struck Jonathan Nyce courted Michelle Riviera in the Philippines by mail for more than a year before he flew over to marry her.
Credit: John Glatt

In June 1990 a triumphant-looking Jonathan Nyce, 41, married 23-year-old Michelle in a civil ceremony at Orion City Hall. Later she told friends how nervous she was about the marriage. It would be many years before she discovered his real age. *Credit: The Riviera Family*

Jonathan and Michelle with their children, Alex, Trevor and Samantha, always played the part of the perfect family. Not even their best friends knew the terrible truth about Michelle's affair and the breakdown of their marriage.
Credit: The Riviera Family

Larissa Soos holds a plant given to her by Michelle, just a few days before her death.
Credit: John Glatt

A rare tender moment between Jonathan and Michelle. After her killing Jonathan would be excised from the picture, which would compose the front page of pamphlet handed out at her memorial service
Credit: Larissa Soos

The Macy's store in Lawrenceville, N.J., where Michelle worked behind the Chanel counter and finally found independence from her possessive husband.
Credit: John Glatt

In March 1999, Jonathan Nyce made the cover of Princeton-based *U.S.1* newspaper, in an in-depth profile where he was tipped as a potential player in the $9-billion asthma market.
Credit: Craig Terry, U.S.1 newspaper

Michelle's father, Teodoro Riviera, a few days after he flew to America in April 2004, seeking justice for his daughter's killer
Credit: John Glatt

Michelle adored her children and often took them swimming to the Jersey Shore.
Credit: Larissa Soos

Jonathan and Michelle often went out to elaborate dinners with friends. Here they are enjoying a night out with John and Larissa Soos.
Credit: Larissa Soos

Jonathan Nyce's tortured handwritten poem, written a couple of days after he discovered Michelle was having an affair with their gardener. *Credit: John Glatt*

Mount's Motel on U.S. 1 in Lawrenceville, where Michelle spent the final hours of her life with Miguel deJesus.
Credit: John Glatt

Police immediately suspected foul play, after seeing Jonathan Nyce's size 12 footprints leaving the Toyota Land Cruiser. *Credit: New Jersey State Police*

Jonathan Nyce's mug shot after his arrest for Michelle's murder. *Credit: Mercer County Prosecutor's Office*

The Nyce's luxury $1.6-million home just hours after Jonathan Nyce killed his wife, Michelle, in the garage. *Credit: New Jersey State Police*

The brother-and-sister detective team of Karen Ortman and Dan McKeown worked together to solve the Nyce case in record time. *Credit: John Glatt*

Mercer County Superior Court, where Jonathan Nyce was convicted by a jury of passion provocation manslaughter. *Credit: John Glatt*

Emma and Jonathan Nyce Jr. at their home in Collegeville in August 2005. Throughout the trial they who stood by their eldest son, convinced of his innocence. *Credit: John Glatt*

Jonathan Nyce looks more like a lawyer than a murder defendant as he leaves Judge Wilbur Mathesius's courtroom just prior to jury selection. *Credit: Martin Griff/ The Times of Trenton*

Nyce defense attorney Robin Lord dramatically makes a point during her opening arguments on the first day of the trial. Behind her Judge Mathesius listens intently. The two would often clash during the lengthy, often emotional trial. *Credit: Paul Savage/ The Times of Trenton*

On the stand Michelle Nyce's lover,
Miguel deJesus, was shown
gruesome picture of her dead body
by prosecutor Tom Meidt.
Credit: Frank Jacobs III/
The Times of Trenton

Defendant Jonathan Nyce angrily stared down his
rival Enyo, who testified about having sex with
Michelle the night she died.
Credit: Martin Griff/ The Times of Trenton

The defense's forensic pathologist,
Dr. John Adams, argued that
Michelle's injuries had been the
result of a fall and were
not suspicious.
Credit: Michael Mancuso/
The Times of Trenton

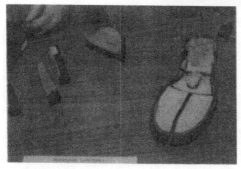

The soles of the boots
Jonathan Nyce wore the night
of Michelle's death. When
police started asking
questions he cut them into
more than a dozen pieces,
hiding them around his
basement.
Credit: John Glatt

Judge Mathesius continually warned Robin Lord during the trial. Here he makes a heated gesture telling the tenacious defender that certain questions would not be allowed in his courtroom.
Credit: Paul Savage/ The Times of Trenton

Mercer County Sheriff Kevin Larkin places handcuffs on a crest-fallen Jonathan Nyce straight after he was found guilty of passion provocation manslaughter.
Credit: Frank Jacobs III/ The Times of Trenton

Michelle's distraught sister, Melodia, and father, Teodoro, are comforted by a victim services counselor after Jonathan Nyce is sentenced to a minimal eight years in jail for causing the death of his wife. They had wanted life
Credit: Paul Savage/ The Times of Trenton

Michelle's nieces and nephews at her final resting place in the village of the Filipino village of Orion, near where she was born.
Credit: The Riviera Family

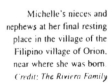

"The manner of death is homicide," she wrote. "Brutally beaten."

At 10 a.m. that morning, Detective Dan McKeown and Sergeant Michael Cseremsak began searching for the elusive Enyo. The previous night Detective Geoffrey Noble and Sergeant Hoskiss had attempted to find him, going door-to-door at the tough Windsor Castle Apartment complex, where he was supposed to live.

"We spoke to numerous people," said Detective Noble, "but there was no forthcoming information. At 1:00 a.m. we gave up."

This time McKeown and Cseremsak tried to locate him through his common-law wife, Patricia Abad. First they went to the Princeton Medical Center, where she was employed, but were told she had the weekend off. The human resources department gave the detectives her address at the Princeton Arms East apartment in Cranbury.

They arrived at midday, immediately spotting a 1991 Nissan Maxima, which was registered to a Miguel deJesus, Enyo's real name. They knocked on the apartment door. A Mexican man answered, and then Patricia Abad came into the foyer.

"She invited us in," said Detective McKeown. "[We] explained why we were there and I asked if she had recently seen her husband. She [said yes], then turned and pointed to Enyo, who was sitting on the couch."

McKeown then asked him to come back to Hopewell Township Police Department to give a statement. Abad insisted on going too, and followed them in her car.

They drove in silence for the half-hour journey to the station. But when they arrived at 12:30, Enyo asked to call his lawyer, Gary Jodha, who said he was busy until 3:30. So Enyo was allowed to leave, after promising to return with his lawyer later that afternoon for questioning.

At 5:50 p.m. Enyo and his lawyer walked into the police department two hours late, and were taken into an interview room. A few minutes later McKeown and Noble arrived to conduct the interview.

Enyo described how he had first met Michelle when he came to plant trees, and how they had started an affair. He said that after the Hopewell Township Municipal Court ordered him to have no further contact with Michelle for two years, he had not seen her for almost two months. But then in October she had called him, and they had soon started having sex again.

He readily admitted being with Michelle Thursday night, explaining that she had called him for a date. He said they had met in the Quakerbridge Plaza parking lot, going to Mount's Motel, where they'd spent two hours together in a rented room.

After the encounter, he had driven her back to the Quakerbridge Plaza at 12:30 a.m., where he kissed her goodnight before she drove home.

Enyo told the detectives he then began to cover his tracks, so Patricia would not know he'd been cheating on her.

"I called a friend, Edgar," he said. "I said, 'If my wife is looking for me, let her know I'm having a drink with you.'"

Then he drove to the Jim's Diner on Highway 130 in East Windsor.

"I stayed twenty minutes and drank two Heineken beers," he said. "So she could smell the alcohol in my body."

At about 1:15 a.m. he drove home, where Patricia and his daughter were asleep. But as he was getting undressed for bed, Patricia woke up, ordering him to sleep on the couch because he was drunk.

"She doesn't like it when I drink," he explained. "Because I snore."

He said the first he'd heard of Michelle's death was that morning at around 10:00, when a friend arrived at his door with a copy of the paper. The friend told him the police were searching for him and he was scared, calling his attorney for advice.

He was then asked if Michelle had ever mentioned her husband being violent towards her.

"She told me that he used to chain her against the bed and beat her up," Enyo told the detectives. "I noticed a scratch on her right leg that was about two to three inches long."

When he had asked about it, Michelle said Jonathan had done it, saying she was scared of him because of his violent behavior.

"She was afraid of him sometimes because he got so mad," said Enyo. "He was so much bigger than her."

At the end of the interview Enyo and Gary Jodha signed his typewritten statement and he was allowed to go home.

After the autopsy was completed, Detective Sergeant Molinaro, Detective Thornton and Sergeant Scull went to the New Jersey State Police, Troop C Headquarters, in Hamilton, where Michelle's 1997 green Toyota Land Cruiser had been towed the previous night.

Earlier the search warrants for 1 Keithwood Court and all three Nyce vehicles had been signed by Mercer County Superior Court Judge Wilbur H. Mathesius (who uses the name William), and investigators were now ready to move in.

At 5:30 p.m. they removed a grey vinyl tarpaulin that had been placed over the vehicle, and began their examination. They noted the only damage was a scraped bumper bent inwards, and the driver's-side indicator was hanging by a wire. There were minor scratches and dents, par for the course for a vehicle with 114,707 miles on the odometer.

"I saw no major damage upon this vehicle," Sergeant Scull later wrote in his report, "which caused me to believe [it] hit something and came to an abrupt stop, an element usually observed during investigation of a fatal motor vehicle accident."

They then looked inside the vehicle, taking care not to disturb the large amounts of dried blood all over it, later to be examined by Detective Thornton for blood spatter. Again it was noted how the driver's seat was way back, positioned for a far taller person then the diminutive victim.

After photographing everything both inside and outside

the Land Cruiser, the detectives collected twenty items of
potential evidence. These included: the large bloody suitcase in the back seat; a Forever 21 denim jean jacket from
the rear floor; a travel tag with the name Jonathan Nyce under the driver's seat; two purple and black ice scrapers; two
pairs of high-heeled shoes on the driver's floor; Michelle's
Coach purse with her ID and several credit cards; her $1,100
watch in the front console; a transparent bag, containing a
cell phone; and two other cell phones from the passenger's-side front door.

Then they turned their attention to the large black suit
case, measuring thirty inches high, twenty-one inches wide
and fifteen inches deep, and weighing about 75 pounds. It
had blood on all six surfaces, and they suspected that blood-
soaked clothing had either been placed under it or on top.

The case was then opened and Detective Sergeant Molinaro carefully removed and inspected each item, while
Sergeant Scull wrote down a brief description.

Inside were numerous items of Michelle's clothing, as if
she had packed it in a hurry. There was an assortment of Victoria's Secret underwear, including several pairs of thigh-
high stockings, a black silk robe, seven brassieres, four
thongs and a garter belt. There was also a pink knit Hello
Kitty bag, a floral bag containing various Chanel products,
and several jeans, pants, sweaters and shirts. There were no
toiletries in the case, although some were found in a bag by
the passenger's-side door.

At 7:40 p.m. it was decided to stop the search and resume
the following day, when blood spatter analysis could be done
in daylight.

While one team of detectives was busy searching the Land
Cruiser, a second converged on 1 Keithwood Court at 5:25
p.m., where they now believed Michelle had been killed. A
thirteen-strong joint task force combining state police investigators and Hopewell Police Department officers led by Detective Sergeant Kronenfeld, met in the drive. They would

spend the next three days combing every inch of the huge house for evidence.

Soon after they arrived, an animal control officer removed several of the Nyce children's pets from the freezing basement, including the family's pet dog Copper, a dove and a ferret.

Detective John Ryan began by taking numerous photographs of the exterior of the house, before going inside at 6:05 with the other investigators.

"I did a preliminary walkthrough with Sergeant Thomas Keyes to get a feel for the residence," he explained. "I was taking mental notes of where items of evidence were."

When they entered the basement they immediately noticed blood on the door jamb and the floor. There were numerous other reddish-brown marks on the snow blower, wet vac and garbage recycling bucket.

"After the initial walkthrough of the scene we formulated a game plan," said Detective Ryan. "Our task was to process the garage, as we felt most of the physical evidence was there."

Sergeant Kronenfeld was responsible for processing the rest of the twenty-one-room colonial house.

"We were looking for an instrument or a weapon," said Kronenfeld, "that might have been used to make the damage to Mrs. Nyce."

Kronenfeld methodically led his team of investigators around every room of the house. Although it was a lavish place with no expense spared in the furnishings, he noticed that it was unkempt and dirty, needing a good cleaning.

They started on the main floor, going straight into the music room to the left of the tiled vestibule. Inside they saw an electric organ, a piano, several electric guitars on stands and a set of drums. At the other end of the music room lay Michelle's custom-built gymnasium, full of the most up-to-date work-out machines and a wall of free weights.

They retraced their steps back into Jonathan Nyce's office, to the left of the vestibule. Inside was a desk with a computer, a book case and a metal file cabinet. Then Kronenfeld opened the desk drawer, discovering Nyce's tortured handwritten "stainless steel heart" letter to Michelle, dated July 12, 2003. He was so excited he called Detective Ryan upstairs from the garage to show him.

Then at the top of the bookcase they found a .380 handgun with three magazines containing ten rounds of ammunition.

Downstairs in the unfinished basement, running the entire length of the house and accessed by a rear stairwell, they discovered a worktable with an electric scroll saw. There were numerous boxes scattered on the floor, as well as various items of furniture and file cabinets.

"I noted the appearance of fresh paint applied to the floor," noted Kronenfeld in his report. "The paint appeared to have been applied to specific areas of the walls, leaving large portions unpainted."

In the three-car garage, where Nyce's 2001 Audi TT sports car was still parked, Ryan was also finding valuable evidence. After setting up fluorescent lights, he began photographing and then examining the large garage.

"There was blood on the door frame, going from the house into the garage," Ryan would later testify. "It appeared the floor had been wiped up."

He also took special note of a shelving unit in the garage, holding a baseball bat, which looked like it had blood on it.

"We had no idea what caused the injuries to the victim's head," he said. "And [the bat] had a dark-colored stain on it, so we collected it."

He also found a plastic bag in a blue garbage container on the wall of the garage, with numerous blood-soaked white paper towels, as well as another roll of bloody paper towels nearby. Lying on the garage floor, in a white plastic bag, were yet more bloody paper towels. And in a recycling bucket nearby they found a frozen white sweat sock with suspected blood and hair on it.

There was blood spatter on the ground near the Audi TT, and investigators noted an empty bottle of peroxide lying on the garage floor, as if a clean-up had been attempted.

Upstairs in the living room, investigators found a

soaking-wet pair of men's black pajama bottoms, stuffed behind the couch.

"It was unusual to find a wet pair of pants behind the sofa," said Detective Ryan. "A washing machine was found on the second-floor laundry room, with some reddish-brown tinted water and a sample was taken."

When detectives searched a man's closet in the second-floor master bedroom, they discovered a pair of Sebago Dockside boots whose sole pattern was similar to the ones found in the garage.

And early Sunday morning, six hours into the search, they discovered Jonathan Nyce's crudely doctored birth and marriage certificates, in a woman's closet in the master bedroom.

"Both had been altered to read '1958,' instead of '1950,' " said Ryan.

At 3:30 a.m. they halted the search. "The investigators were exhausted," said Kronenfeld. "And it was decided it was better to come back the next day."

When they left, a Hopewell Police Department officer guarded the house, with orders not to let anyone inside.

At 9:00 p.m. Saturday night, Detective Karen Ortman telephoned Jonathan Nyce at his parents' home, requesting he return to Hopewell Police Department immediately for a second interview. But there was a heavy snowstorm in Pennsylvania and Nyce explained that conditions were too treacherous for driving. So it was agreed he would come at 9:00 the following morning.

But Hopewell detectives were taking no chances that their prime suspect might make a run for it, or even attempt suicide. So they asked the Collegeville Police Department to place him under round-the-clock physical surveillance, until he could make the trip back to New Jersey.

22

The Interrogation

At 8:00 Sunday morning, Detective William Scull arrived at Hopewell Township Police Department. His assignment was to interrogate Jonathan Nyce and get a murder confession.

The highly experienced interrogator, in his late thirties, had spent two days in meticulous preparation. On Friday he had visited the Jacobs Creek Road crash scene, before attending Michelle's autopsy and then helping to process the Land Cruiser. Late Saturday night he went to 1 Keithwood Court, where he was walked through the scene by Detective Ryan, who pointed out all areas of interest.

He had also met with Detective Geoffrey Noble, who had briefed him about his interview with Enyo, the last known person to see Michelle alive. And he had read Jonathan Nyce's statement to Detective Ortman, regarding the death of his wife.

"As a result of my direct observations and knowledge of ongoing investigative efforts," he wrote in his report, "I was under the belief that Doctor Nyce was a suspect in this apparent homicide, and that it was probable that Michelle Nyce was murdered within her home."

Before Nyce arrived, Scull met with Dan McKeown, who would sit in on the interview to make the suspect feel more relaxed.

"The purpose for me being there was, they were afraid Jonathan would go cold," said McKeown. "And because he knew me, he was comfortable and I could add anything if needed."

The interrogation was conducted in the Municipal Building's Township Committee Room, across the lobby from the police department. In the center of the well-lit rectangular room was a round wooden table, which they would all sit around. Both detectives were armed with weapons concealed in their business suits.

At precisely 9:00 a.m. Jonathan Nyce walked into the lobby of the police department, with his father and brother Michael. He was dressed casually in a well-pressed shirt, slacks and a brown leather jacket.

Detective McKeown greeted them and then led Nyce down the lobby into the conference room, where Scull was already waiting.

"I had made sure the table was clean," said the methodical detective. "I introduced myself and we shook hands, and I thanked him for coming in to further discuss this investigation."

Detective Scull seated Nyce to his right with his back facing the door, while Detective McKeown was to his left. Then, after reading him his Miranda rights, Scull asked if he was under the influence of any drugs or alcohol. Nyce, who had made no secret of taking lorazepam, now appeared irritated by the question.

"No," he snapped, "I haven't taken any."

Scull began the interview by simply asking him, "Why are you here?"

Nyce replied that he wanted to know what had happened to Michelle, and who did it to her. He said he wanted to move on and bury her.

"I informed him of the status of the investigation," Scull would later testify, "and that it was all pointing to him."

For the next twenty minutes the detective calmly outlined the case against him so far.

"I addressed the accident scene," said Scull. "And told him we did not believe it was an accident. The blood evidence in the vehicle is not consistent with her being injured in the car. And that there was blood on the outside of the car."

Detective Scull told him he knew his garage door had been open when police had first arrived. An officer had seen him close it with a remote control from the Hummer, so as not to draw attention to it. He also informed him about all the blood evidence now being recovered from the garage, as well as evidence of a clean-up.

"I told him it had not been cleaned up well," said Scull. "And [blood] was still visible to the naked eye. I informed him we had recovered wet pants behind the couch, and broken glass, and that the search was continuing and detectives would be searching every inch of his house."

Sitting just three feet away from the detective, Nyce stared stoically at him, as the damning evidence against him mounted.

Detective Scull was well aware his adversary was a highly intelligent man, and should not be underestimated. So he carefully pointed out it was impossible to be certain it was Michelle's blood, until the samples were analyzed in a laboratory. He also informed him no fingerprints had yet been taken, but assured him they soon would be. And one of the detectives' top priorities was finding the boots that had made the footprints leaving the crash vehicle.

"I had to get his trust," explained Detective Scull. "I informed him that we had not yet obtained cell phone records, but assured him we will know every call and every voice mail left."

Finally he told Nyce that police would interview his children, family, friends and neighbors, as well as Michelle's, and any other person considered relevant to the investigation.

"It appears you guys think I'm involved in the death of my wife," Nyce said calmly.

Scull replied that all the evidence was proving he was.

Then Nyce asked the detective if he should get an attorney. Detective Scull said he could not advise him, as it would be improper, and that it must be his decision.

"I said obviously we do believe he is the primary suspect," said Scull. "He said he did not wish to get an attorney."

Then Jonathan Nyce said the police were looking at the wrong person, suggesting they concentrate on Enyo and his wife. And he told them about Michelle's affair with the gardener and the alleged extortion attempt, which Detective McKeown had investigated.

He now claimed Michelle had been so scared of Patricia Abad that she'd disabled the light bulbs in the garage opener, so she couldn't be seen when she came home at night.

Nyce said he was being framed by Enyo and his wife for Michelle's death. But Detective Scull said it was "totally ridiculous" that someone would frame him for murder, and then remove her body from the house.

"I essentially laughed at him," said the detective. "I told him it had to be the worst frame-up ever. It didn't make any sense."

Once again Nyce asked if he should get an attorney's opinion about his theory, and Scull repeated that it was not his place to advise on this, but agreed it was an important decision.

At this point Jonathan Nyce asked the detective if he could go home, so he could think about what he was going to say to be more helpful.

"I told him no," said Detective Scull. "Then I told him there was probable cause to arrest him and charge him with the murder of his wife. I spoke of all the evidence pointing to him. I told him the evidence wouldn't tell us the victim's actions, he'd have to tell us the truth."

The detective explained that, although the investigation had reached the level of probable cause, there were certain blanks only Nyce would be able to fill in.

"I gave examples," explained Scull, "such as the stress

Michelle's infidelity may have placed on their relationship, any statement that she had made or action she may have taken that could have contributed to her death.

"Alternatively, I stated her death may have been the result of a premeditated plan to punish her for her infidelity."

Then, trying to draw him out, Scull said he did not feel this was the case here, suggesting Nyce use common sense to determine if withholding information about Michelle's death would "aggravate or mitigate" his present situation.

Suddenly, realizing the overwhelming evidence against him, Jonathan Nyce tried to make a deal.

"He said he would be willing to provide a statement, implicating him in the death of his wife," said the detective, "if he would only have to serve a short time in jail, so he could be with his children again. I told him that I wasn't even going to present that to the prosecutors, and that my job was to find the truth."

Nyce's whole bearing had changed since he had walked into the room so confidently an hour earlier. At first he had been "generally stoic" and "making eye contact," but he now appeared insecure and nervous.

"At this point I noticed a definite change in his demeanor," said Scull. "He was deflated, his confidence wavering. He was sitting lower in his seat and there was no eye contact."

"I did not kill my wife!" Nyce kept stating. And when the detective asked him to define the word "kill," he replied, "To shoot, stab or choke someone."

The detective then employed another psychological tack to break down Nyce and get a confession.

"I needed him to understand there was no way he was going to convince me he was not involved in the death of his wife," he explained. "There was no mincing of words. The frame-up was ridiculous. He's an intelligent man."

Scull drew a parallel between the futility of attempts to convince him he was not involved in Michelle's death and the subsequent cover-up, and trying to persuade him the color of the interview room wall was black when it was

white. Nyce had to agree he could not be convinced the wall
he was looking at was a different color than it was.

"I addressed his superior intellect," explained Detective
Scull, "and obvious ability to think logically and analyti-
cally. I asked him if he would believe me if I said I was not
involved, in spite of all the evidence to the contrary, if our
roles were reversed.

"After a few moments of silence, he said, 'Probably not,'
halfheartedly adding that he was telling the truth."

At this crucial point in the interrogation there was a
knock at the door, and Captain George Meyer beckoned. Detective Scull called a break in the interview, asking if Nyce
wanted anything to eat or drink. When Nyce said he did not,
Scull walked out at 10:24 a.m., leaving him alone with Dan
McKeown.

Outside, Captain Meyer told Detective Scull that Lee Engleman, the attorney Nyce had called Friday afternoon, had
just talked to Michael Nyce, who was now in the lobby. Engleman wanted to represent Nyce, and had sent a message
advising him not to talk to the police until they had spoken.

Captain Meyer then handed Scull a torn piece of white
paper with Engleman's phone number on it.

Realizing the potential legal pitfalls this could create at
any future trial, Scull sought the advice of Mercer County Assistant Prosecutor Tom Meidt, who was also at the police station. Later the detective explained that although he knew he
had a legal obligation to inform Nyce about Engleman's telephone call, he did not have to relay his instruction not to talk
to the police. Meidt agreed with his analysis of the situation,
and after ten minutes away Scull returned to the interview.

At 10:31 a.m. Detective Scull placed the piece of paper
with the attorney's phone number on the table in front of
Nyce, telling him Engleman had requested he call.

"I informed him," said Scull, " 'You have to make a decision, and if you want, you'll be provided with a phone.' He
didn't want to call and pushed the paper away. He said he
just wanted to be helpful."

Then the detective asked him how Michelle's death

would affect their three children in the long term, and didn't they have a right to know the truth?

"It was my impression that he was a doting father," explained the detective. "I told him, 'If you're so concerned about your children, don't you want the truth?' "

Nyce replied that if Scull was so sure he had murdered Michelle, he should arrest him now and learn the truth at the trial.

The detective presented him with a hypothetical scenario. He asked Nyce to imagine someone arrested for an unspecified crime, resulting in a trial. The evidence introduced by the prosecution was very strong and supported a guilty jury decision.

On the stand the defendant testified to a version of events that downplayed his involvement in the crime. But unfortunately the defendant had not given this account to the police when initially questioned.

Then Scull asked Nyce if he would believe the defendant's statements, if he was on the jury.

Nyce agreed he would probably not believe the defendant, and then Detective Scull brought the scenario back to the death of his wife, suggesting that if he told police the truth about what happened that night, it would carry more weight than if he waited until trial.

"I asked Jonathan Nyce what was stopping him from providing his version of what happened that night," said Detective Scull. "He did not answer. I believed there was something stopping him from giving his version. I thought, 'What's the issue? What do I have to do to bridge the chasm?' "

There was a long silence as Nyce sat there contemplating his situation. Then, almost in a whisper, he asked if Michelle had been with Enyo that night.

"I did not answer immediately," said Scull. "Instead I asked him if being provided with this bit of information was what he needed to speak the truth. He stated that it *may* be."

Then the detective confirmed that Michelle had been unfaithful that night, and Nyce asked if it had been with Enyo.

The detective did not respond, instead turning to Dan McKeown, who had not said a word so far in the two-hour interview.

"And Jonathan looked over to me," remembered Detective McKeown. "And I said, 'Jonathan, I haven't lied to you since I've known you. She was.' Then he lost it."

First he began to cry and he started hyperventilating and sniffing, as if on the verge of a complete breakdown.

After a couple of minutes he asked how he could be sure they were telling the truth. Detective Scull said there was nothing he could say to convince him one way or the other.

"[I suggested] that he draw upon his own feelings and intelligence," explained Scull. "I advised him to reflect on our time together and assess if we lied to him in any way."

Then Jonathan Nyce became extremely emotional. His eyes welled up with tears and he started quietly sobbing, without saying a word.

"It was a quiet time," remembered Scull. "He was emotional in the room. Then I injected two other factors. In addition to Michelle Nyce being with Enyo that night, we knew he had called his wife, and her response had been to turn off her cell phone. I also knew that Michelle had doused herself in perfume just prior to her returning home, and I believed he had smelled that perfume.

"I believe he wanted to talk about it. He wanted to be helpful—he needed to know what Michelle was doing that night."

"I didn't mean to kill her," Nyce suddenly said, and began mumbling incomprehensibly about what had happened in the garage that night.

"He was hysterical," remembered Detective Scull. "His nose was running. He was sobbing. After allowing him to compose himself, I informed him that we needed to know what had led up to the murder of his wife."

While detectives were interrogating his son, Jonathan Jr. also met with investigators on the other side of the municipal building. He was interviewed by Detective John Pizzuro of the New Jersey State Police and Sergeant Thomas Puskas of Hopewell Township PD, about any relevant information he had about his son and daughter-in-law. He seemed uneasy and evasive throughout the fifty-minute interview.

"It was obvious Mr. Nyce Jr. was being cautious," Sergeant Puskas later wrote in his report. "He was clearly uncomfortable and protective of his son, while speaking to us."

Nyce's father was specifically asked about the burglar alarm going off at 6:00 a.m. Friday morning. He said his wife, Emma, had taken the call from the alarm company, and called Jonathan immediately. She had told him their son was "groggy," and didn't know which zone in the house had tripped the alarm.

When Sergeant Puskas asked if the alarm company had told them which zone it was, Jonathan Jr. said he was not sure. But a little later he remembered them saying it had been set off in the basement.

For the rest of the interview Jonathan Jr. was vague and unspecific. He denied ever discussing Michelle's death with his son or his reaction to her affair and the alleged extortion matter.

Finally, Sergeant Puskas asked if Jonathan was very upset about what had happened to his wife.

"No more than usual," his father replied.

At 11:40 a.m. Jonathan Nyce finished giving detectives his version of Michelle's death, and how he'd tried to stage it as an accident. He started off giving few details, so Detective Scull tried to focus him, asking question after question, until he elicited a clearer account.

Now he claimed he had acted in self-defense after Michelle had attacked him with a stiletto-like object. Her death had been unintentional, and he'd decided to make it look like an accident, to protect his children from discovering that their mother had tried to kill him. After putting her body in the Land Cruiser, he'd driven it to Jacobs Creek and over the edge into the water, before walking home.

He had then attempted to clean up Michelle's blood in the garage, using paper towels and rags dipped in hydrogen peroxide. Later he admitted hiding a stuffed plastic trash bag of paper towels that he'd used to clean up Michelle's blood behind a chimney flue in the basement. And he said he had worn a pair of moccasins when he'd driven his wife's body to Jacobs Creek.

But Detective Scull was certain he had still not gotten to the truth, and Nyce was deliberately being evasive.

"All of my attempts to have Jonathan Nyce walk me through his clean-up actions and decisions, step-by-step, proved futile," Detective Scull later wrote in his official report. "He repeatedly attempted to redirect any such questions by providing the reason *why* he chose to make Michelle's death look like an accident, dodging all attempts to detail his clean-up efforts."

Now the detectives needed him to repeat it all on audiotape as a confession, which could be used at any future murder trial. And they also wanted to compare the two versions for any discrepancies, as they still did not believe he was telling the truth.

Detective Scull called a short break and sent in for water, before briefing him about the procedure they would use to take the statement. First he would be reread his Miranda rights, and then they would discuss how he had met Michelle, and details of their relationship, to gain perspective. Finally they would talk about how she had died and what he'd done afterwards.

Nyce asked for a piece of paper to make notes, to help him gather his thoughts. He was given a legal-size piece of white lined paper and a pen. Then the detectives left him alone in the interview room, while they briefed the other investigators on the fast-moving developments, so they could resume searching the basement, armed with this new information.

By himself in the interview room, Jonathan Nyce began scribbling short notes on the paper. Some of them were indecipherable, but some were not and were highly disturbing.

"I wish you were dead!" wrote Jonathan Nyce while the

detectives were out of the room. Whether that comment was directed at Michelle or the detectives—or even at himself— remains unclear, for he was never questioned about it.

His other pre-statement jottings went as follows:

> Long disappointment
> > home
> > school
> Beautiful Marriage for 10 years
> 3 beautiful ch Alex 11, Trevor 10, Sam 5
> NC [to] NJ
> July 5th weekend
> I can show you what . . .
> I can be
> Marriage Vow
> Larissa = wonderful friend
> Amy = Terrible friend
> Bought 6 houses & Duck Farm/Emergency Food Shipment
> Vacation to: Angola, Grand Cayman, San Jose, San Diego, Orlando
> Threats by Enyo against me . . . HE . . . me to Michelle

When he left Jonathan Nyce in the interview room to gather his thoughts, Detective Scull met with Detective Sergeant Kronenfeld and other members of his investigative team. He informed them Jonathan Nyce had now confessed to killing his wife, revealing that he had hidden key evidence in his basement. He'd also admitted that the shoes he'd worn during the crime were still at 1 Keithwood Court.

At 12:06 p.m. Kronenfeld and eight other investigators arrived at Jonathan Nyce's house to continue their search. They immediately went down to the basement, moving a set of file cabinets in front of the chimney flue.

"There was a black metal trap door," Kronenfeld later testified. "Inside was a plastic bag with paper towels wet with blood."

Detective John Ryan would later describe how the investigator discovered the hidden cache of evidence.

"We found numerous paper towels with debris and staining in the bag," he said. "It was a brown shelving unit placed in front of a metal trap door. The plastic bag was stuffed inside."

After finding this the team turned their sights to Nyce's Hummer, which yielded no significant evidence.

At 3:35 p.m. the detectives suspended the search once again, until they could bring in special detection equipment now required. The residence was then secured, with two police officers placed outside around the clock.

23

"I Didn't Want to Hurt Her"

At 12:03 p.m. Detective William Scull turned on his audiotape recorder, placing the microphone in front of Jonathan Nyce, who, in a tearful wavering voice, began recounting his version of Michelle's death to the two detectives sitting either side of him at the round table. It would take him one hour and forty-three minutes to deliver his often emotional statement, during which he continually alternated between sadness, anger and remorse.

After getting him to sign the Miranda form, Scull attempted to put him more at ease by asking how he'd met Michelle in the first place. Even now Nyce maintained the pretense that they'd met in Hawaii, as well as embellishing the tale even further.

"I was attending a meeting of the American and Japanese Cancer Societies," he told them. "I am a scientist. I develop new drugs. It was a long meeting and I decided that I would take a break from the meeting and I rented a surfboard and headed to the beach, and was silly enough to step on Michelle's foot. We started a conversation. We started communicating and I married her in 1991."

Then gently, Detective Scull asked about their marriage and any problems that might be relevant to what had happened.

"Well, Michelle was a wonderful woman," Nyce began. "She was a wonderful wife for over ten years."

He told how they had "married overseas," before settling down in Greenville, North Carolina, where he was an assistant professor. He described the early days of their marriage as "idyllic," saying he had felt a "blessed man." Then they had had three children, and he'd been a great success at East Carolina University, discovering a "whole plethora of new drugs."

He appeared to gain confidence as he told the detectives about EpiGenesis and his business prowess, boasting of raising $65 million and shepherding two drugs to clinical trials. He described himself and Michelle during that period as "just the happiest couple you could imagine," with everyone jealous of their happiness.

Warming to his subject, he described his company's move to New Jersey as part of a high-stakes business expansion.

"Things were going very well," he declared. "I got very close to a billion-dollar deal with Glaxo Wellcome."

Then he told how his marriage had started falling apart, blaming Michelle's growing greed. He said that when she applied for American citizenship and saw "all these numbers rolling in," she thought she would be able to do whatever she wanted.

"I said this wasn't true," he said. "But we moved into an expensive neighborhood . . . then Michelle began to unravel psychologically."

In her "quest for eternal youth," she made a new set of teenage friends to socialize with. He described how she had recently taken him to an 18-year-old debutante's coming-out party.

"And Michelle is thirty-four," he explained, "and I'm fifty-three. It's not a place that feels comfortable for us."

Then he turned to his philanthropy, and how he'd helped Michelle's impoverished family back in the Philippines. He claimed he had built six homes, a school, a children's playground and financed a duck farm business. He told the detectives how one of Michelle's sisters had starved to death, and how he'd personally seen the family's "extreme poverty" when he'd visited almost a year earlier.

"They were starving," he said, claiming he had sent a $6,000 emergency food case package on his return.

He then told how a boardroom shuffle had led to his firing from EpiGenesis, and his new careers, writing children's books and developing a perfume company with Michelle and several of their friends.

Then he turned to June 2002 when, he said, his and Michelle's relationship had begun to unravel.

"Michelle would pick fights about many things," he explained. "And I told her on many occasions, 'You know how it looks, honey, like you're picking a fight about nothing. Why do this?' Her father was living with us at the time. I had paid for him to come over. Michelle was not working. She chose to just have free time with her friends."

Then he recounted her affair with Enyo and how he'd gone to the FBI after the two phone calls, demanding $500,000 for video sex tapes of Michelle. And he even tried to give the impression that Detective Dan McKeown, now sitting next to him, had sided with him against Michelle.

"Dan indicated to me at that time that he did not trust anything that Michelle said," he conspiratorially told Detective Scull.

Then Scull asked if he felt he was a good husband and father.

"I think I have been a wonderful husband to Michelle," he declared. "I feel I've been an outstanding husband, father to my kids—and they will tell you that."

Exactly forty minutes into his statement, Detective Scull changed C-90 audiotapes, and they moved on to Friday morning's tragic events. Jonathan Nyce began by reiterating his earlier statement to police. He had spent the day with

Michelle and his three children, later going sledding with the children before taking them to Samantha's gym class.

Michelle had been preparing for her Macy's shift when he'd left at 4:00 p.m., and when he returned home three hours later, she was gone. After watching *Bruce Almighty* in bed with his kids in the master bedroom, they'd called Michelle's cell phone, but it had gone straight to voice mail.

He'd then taken a lorazepam and gone to sleep. Prompted by Detective Scull, he explained it was an anti-anxiety drug prescribed by his psychiatrist. He added that he always took some if he thought Michelle was out cheating, so he wouldn't care and could sleep.

"I mean, that's how good of an anti-anxiety compound it is," he told them. "It lets me do almost everything else, until I am asleep."

At about midnight, he continued, he had woken up and realized Michelle had not returned home. He couldn't remember if he had made a second call to her, but then, dressed in a tee-shirt and black pajama bottoms, he'd gotten up for a drink of water, before returning to bed.

At about 2:00 a.m., baby Samantha asked him to make her a milk bottle. And while he was preparing it in the kitchen, he'd heard the "crunching" sound of Michelle's Land Cruiser tires coming up the driveway in the snow.

He walked through the connecting door from the kitchen into the garage to speak to her, as he suspected she might have been cheating. The garage door was shut, he remembered, and Michelle was still inside the vehicle.

"She opened the door," said Jonathan Nyce, "and she was dressed differently than in Chanel clothes, I mean, boots and things. The first thing I said was, 'Silly, where's your glasses?'

"And she told me, 'Fuck you!' So I said, 'Where were you?' And she told me, 'Fuck you!' again. I said, 'Come on, honey, you know it's late. Just tell me where you were.'

"And I was on my lorazepam, so I'm not getting upset. She said something like, 'You know, I'll do whatever I want!'"

Jonathan Nyce then speculated that Michelle was high on ecstasy or some other drug, advising the detectives to test for narcotics.

"Her eyes were really big," he told them. "She acted very different. Although I have seen her act in a similar way in the workout room, when she has stoked herself on caffeine.

"Then for some reason she called me a fucking freak. I don't know why. I was just asking her questions about where she was."

Then he came towards her to help her out of the Land Cruiser, as the floor was slippery, Michelle took something out of her Chanel bag and "lunged" at his face and his neck.

Pressed by Scull for more information about the weapon, Nyce said it was in her right hand, describing it as "sharp" and "shiny." He thought it may have been a stiletto or a letter opener.

"If I hadn't moved," he said, "She would have gotten me all the way through. It would have gone through the middle of my throat. And she's very, very strong and fast. She's a physical trainer."

Then, according to Nyce, she prepared to attack him again.

"I saw her bracing her legs and her feet for a lunge," he said, although the only light came from the interior of the Land Cruiser. "And again, her face is very different than I have ever seen it before. It's worse than I've ever seen her on a caffeine fix. She's got tight pants on and I can even see the muscles in her legs. All this just seems to be in slow motion."

Then as she lunged at him again with the stiletto, he grabbed her shoulder and waist, hauling her out of the Land Cruiser onto the concrete floor.

"I threw her down too hard," he sobbed. "She just flew out and hit with a sickening thunk of her head on the concrete floor. I mean, I gave her a good push, but I expected some defensive maneuvering."

Nyce said he saw Michelle's blood as she fell face down on the concrete, but she was still alive and mobilizing for yet another attack.

"She was still flailing with the knife," he explained. "So I said, 'Honey, just hold still.' First I put one knee on top of her, and then I said, 'Wait, I'll get bandages.'

"I mean, I didn't know she was going to be hurt. I didn't."

Nyce said he ran to a nearby closet for bandages, and tried to dress her wounds, but she kept flailing at him. He then pushed her head down hard into the concrete, as he tried unsuccessfully to wrestle the knife away from her.

"I didn't want to hurt her," he said, "but I'm trying to be effective at disarming her and being able to render assistance. I just wanted to try and control her."

This time she lay motionless, and he put his knee to her back and pushed down, driving her head into the floor.

"I was kneeling too hard on her, so I got off," he said. "I started talking to her and trying to get the wounds stopped."

He then went off to get tissue paper to stem the bleeding, but was too late.

"I knelt down and I felt her pulse," he said. "And she wasn't breathing. She was dead. I've done this before. I was at a couple of accidents where I've rendered first aid."

He said he spent around fifteen minutes trying to revive her.

"I kept checking her pulse," he sobbed emotionally. "I checked it everywhere to make sure my hand wasn't warm. To make sure I wasn't missing it. We have a stethoscope somewhere, I was looking for it."

He said that, out of respect for his dead wife, he placed a brown jacket on top of her, as she was starting to get cold.

Then Detective Scull asked him point blank whether he had intended to kill Michelle.

"No," he said, "I never had a bad thought really in my heart, but she's dead. I never have an aggressive thought in my heart."

The detective then asked his plan of action, as Michelle's battered body lay at his feet.

"I'll tell you," said Nyce, sounding more composed. "What went through my mind is my children. How will I explain to them that Mommy tried to kill me? Is there something worse I could say than that Mommy tried to kill me? So I said, 'It's better that I just run her into a tree.' "

He tearfully explained how his head was clouded by the lorazepam, and he wasn't thinking straight. He said he took off her blue parka ski jacket as he lifted her into the driver's seat of the Land Cruiser, placing her behind the steering wheel. After transferring her suitcase from the passenger front seat into the back, and still dressed in his pajamas, he got into the passenger seat.

Then, using his left hand to manipulate the gas pedal with a medium-sized ice scraper he found in the car, and his right to steer with, he reversed out of the garage, veering off the driveway and all over his front yard.

"I didn't steer so well," he admitted, adding that he was wearing a glove on his left hand, but nothing on his right. "But it was fairly easy to control. I accelerated with the [ice scraper]."

So with Michelle's body propped up beside him, he drove about a mile to Jacobs Creek Road. He also said he was holding Michelle's stiletto weapon in his right hand and threw it out the window at some point.

Asked his thoughts during the drive, Nyce said he contemplated suicide, but decided against it for the sake of his children.

"I only [had] two thoughts," he explained. "Not to let my family know that my wife wanted to kill me. And the second one was, Where do I have to crash the vehicle?

"My first choice was the . . . Jacobs Creek area and just die. Make it a hard crash and die there too. I almost did that. But then I decided my boys and girl needed me. I decided to go further on and I just found a place where there were no side rails . . . And just went off. [I] thought while I was doing it I'd be killed, but . . . I needed, you know, I, I had to take the kids. I was not thinking."

Then Jonathan Nyce started crying uncontrollably, taking several minutes to compose himself.

"The last thing I wanted is for my kids to know Michelle was becoming increasingly unstable," he told the detectives.

"I want my kids to have good feelings about their mother no matter what."

He said that although he had not gone directly home, he couldn't account for where he'd been for the half-hour it took him to reach Keithwood Court. But once back he took two more lorazepam, and began cleaning up Michelle's blood all over the garage with hydrogen peroxide.

"I straightened up," he explained. "I cleaned up a little with a paper towel and put it in a white bag, put it in a blue plastic [recycling bin]. You know, I was in a state. I figured I would go back the next day and clean up the rest of it."

Then he went upstairs, took a shower and carefully sneaked back into bed with his children. When the alarm went off at 6:00 a.m. Friday morning, it was "the real thing," he told the detectives, suggesting someone may have been following Michelle.

Then Detective Scull pressed him for more details of his clean-up, saying investigators had already found dirty rags and blood-soaked paper towels in a white trash bag in the garage.

"I'm surprised at being so stupid," he said. "But that could be consistent, because I was in a pretty bad state."

Scull said Nyce had earlier mentioned two garbage bags full of bloody paper towels, and wanted to know what he'd done with the other one.

"I put it in the ash chute in the fireplace in the basement," he said. "I did a pretty crappy clean-up job, as you know. I put it in white plastic garbage bags and stuck it in the weekly trash. I mean, that's as stupid as you can get."

Then he was asked what footwear he was wearing that night.

"I don't believe I had boots," replied Nyce. "I'm pretty sure I only had shoes on."

Detective Scull then pointed out they had found a "pretty good" boot tread pattern in the snow by the vehicle, and asked if the pair that had made the tracts would still be in the house.

"I suppose they would," he said, "because I didn't take anything off and discard it. I don't remember wearing boots. But, I mean, I was in a terrible state."

He said none of his children woke up while he was cleaning up, or had any knowledge of anything that had happened.

At 1:31 p.m. Detective Scull turned off the tape recorder and inserted the third and last tape, for the final sixteen minutes of Jonathan Nyce's dramatic confession. Now Detective Scull asked Nyce to tell him anything else that might be relevant to Michelle's tragic death.

"All I can say is that I love my wife completely," he sobbed. "I took the marriage vows very seriously, 'in sickness and in health.' I felt she was in sickness and I was going to stand by her.

"In practical terms she had this lover. I felt that if she would only stop and come back to the family, I would put this behind me. According to her [Enyo] was only the second lover in her life; me being the first. And I've had more lovers than that back when I grew up.

"I mean, I had been totally faithful to her all the time we were married," he said. "Before the Fourth of July excursion, I said, 'Look, Michelle, whatever you've done, you don't even have to tell me. Just stop it and I forgive you. I said the same thing to her [Thursday] night. She just laughed at me. And that's just about when she lunged at me with whatever it was she had.

"But the bottom line is, I have not a bad thought in my heart about her. I was more trying to catch her. I know I pushed her to the ground, but I was more just trying to control her so that I could be a loving influence.

"But I pushed too hard and she hit the floor in a way I never expected. I never expected her not to put up her hands, or catch with her feet or something. I never expected that she would hit the floor with her head like that. [I'm] sorry for this accident. I didn't mean it to happen. I love her still."

Now sobbing uncontrollably, Jonathan Nyce said he wished he could spend the rest of his life with Michelle, and he had fully expected her to pull through her sickness and return to normal.

"She fell into a bad crowd," he said. "She had to be able to come home . . . just look at the faces of her children eventually and say, 'What I'm doing [is] wrong.'

"And we were all four of us waiting for that to happen. And then this happened. I just can't believe it."

At 1:48 p.m. Jonathan Nyce finished his statement. But before turning the recorder off, Detective Scull once again asked if he wanted to call attorney Lee Engleman, whose number was still on the table in front of him. Nyce just pushed it away, saying he didn't want to.

Then, after signing all three tapes, Nyce asked for some time alone with his father and brother Michael, before he was formally arrested for Michelle's murder. Scull said he could, but only under police supervision.

Detective Dan McKeown then conducted a body search in the interview room, and led him out into the lobby where Nyce's family was waiting. It was a highly emotional moment, as he told them he was being arrested for Michelle's murder.

"I saw him lean forward," said Detective Scull, "speak to them for about thirty seconds. Then they all burst into tears and hugged."

Jonathan Nyce was then taken across to the Hopewell Township Police Department processing room, where Detective McKeown fingerprinted him and took mug shots.

"He was almost in a trance," remembered Detective McKeown. "Now he asked if he could talk to his attorney."

The detective remained in the room as Nyce called Lee Engleman, leaving a message on his answer machine, explaining his dire situation.

Then Detective McKeown and Officer Chris Kascik drove Jonathan Nyce to the Mercer County Correction Cen-

ter in Lambertville, New Jersey, to spend his first night behind bars.

One hour later Chief Michael Chipowsky announced that
Jonathan Nyce had been arrested for the first-degree murder
of his wife. He congratulated his detectives for their "dili-
gent work," calling the arrest "a quick conclusion."

"The detectives and everybody involved have given their
all," he told reporters.

He said the three Nyce children were staying at their Uncle Michael Nyce's home in Pennsylvania.

"It's unfortunate, because now we have other victims,"
he said. "These three children will have no parents. They're
orphans."

The press was then given a copy of the State of New Jersey's probable cause complaint warrant, signed by the Mercer County Superior Court judge on call, William
Mathesius, who formally set Nyce's bail at $2 million cash.

It stated that there was probable cause to believe Jonathan
Nyce did "purposely and knowingly cause the death of his
wife, Michelle Nyce, by forcefully removing the victim from
the driver's side compartment of her automobile and throwing
said victim face-forward to the ground until such time that the
suspect heard a thud that 'made me sick,' thereby causing the
death of Michelle Nyce. A crime of the first (1st) degree."

Mercer County Prosecutor Joseph L. Bocchini Jr., whose
office would prosecute Jonathan Nyce, called the crime
"appalling."

"I vow that my office will prosecute this case as thoroughly as it was investigated," he declared. "Investigators
worked non-stop since this began."

Late Sunday afternoon, Larissa Soos finally got through to
Michael Nyce, who was back at his parents' house in Collegeville. She had been trying to reach Jonathan Nyce all day

to find out what was happening, and if she could do anything to help with the children when they came home.

He told her Jonathan was still at the police station, waiting to be "transported." Astonished, Larissa asked him what he meant and Michael told her he had been arrested for Michelle's murder.

"He said that it was an accident," remembered Soos. "She was coming home late every night and was having an affair. And he snapped.

"They were arguing. They were on each other and she fell down and hit her head and he panicked. He drove her body to the creek and Jonathan is waiting to be charged. He made it seem tamer than I later read."

Larissa was stunned when she heard police had arrested Jonathan for Michelle's murder, and it would be days before she could rationalize it.

"When the brother told me about it, my life just went wild," said Soos. "And I was really crying, I'm like, 'Well, how can he do it? Maybe he snapped and didn't know what he was doing?'

"But then later, making it look like an accident, he had to know what he was doing . . . I guess I felt sorry for both of them. Right now I'm in the middle trying to figure out why this would happen."

Then Michael announced his family had decided to have Michelle cremated in America, and would take care of all expenses. But Larissa knew it was customary for Filipinos to be buried in their hometown by their family, an important mark of respect.

So after putting down the phone, she immediately called Michelle's father in the Philippines, to tell him Jonathan had been arrested, and warning him Michelle would be cremated in New Jersey unless he stepped in.

"She told me that it was not an accident," said Teodoro Riviera, "and Michelle had been murdered. It was already in my mind that nobody else had done it but Jonathan, and after that I find out that he did kill my daughter."

When Riviera heard about the funeral plan for Michelle, he was livid.

"They wanted to cremate Michelle," he said. "I want her back here."

Larissa told him to call Michael Nyce immediately if he wanted Michelle's body returned to the Philippines, so he did.

"I told him, 'Michael, I'm Teodoro Riviera,'" he remembered. "'I ask you a favor for me—don't cremate my daughter!'"

In an emotional conversation, Riviera asked for his daughter's body to be returned home, offering to fly to the States to collect it. When Michael asked him why he wanted to come to New Jersey, Riviera became angry.

"So I answer," he said, "'Why are you asking me that question? I am the father. She is my daughter and my responsibility.'"

Nyce said he couldn't understand what he was saying, as the line was bad. And Riviera asked if it was because he did not want to. Then Nyce said he'd call back later to discuss it further, putting down the phone.

Soon afterwards, the Nyce family talked to several reporters, who called their house for comment after Jonathan's arrest.

"He is a very gentle person, family-oriented, loves his kids," said Michael Nyce. "Our focus right now is the kids."

But his mother, Emma, was more forthcoming, saying her eldest son was "a great provider" for Michelle and her family back in the Philippines.

"[But] she always wanted more, more, more," she sobbed.

24

"I Don't Get It . . . They Seemed So Happy"

Monday was Martin Luther King Day, and Hopewell Township residents woke up to discover one of their most respected citizens had been charged with murdering his wife. The Trenton *Times* led with the story on its front page under the banner headline, "Husband Charged in Death," while the more sensational *Trentonian* tabloid had "Hubby Charged in Hopewell Slay."

The *Trentonian* quoted an unnamed Nyce neighbor, speculating the twenty-plus-year age difference had something to do with it.

"When you're in your thirties," observed the neighbor, "you still have a lot of spunk left in your life. I mean, she was beautiful. She had smooth olive-colored skin. Everybody would go to Macy's just to look at her."

The story painted Jonathan Nyce as overly possessive and controlling with Michelle.

Roz Clancy told of casting Michelle in a commercial, and Jonathan refusing to allow her to do it. Then in mid-interview Clancy broke down in tears, telling the reporter how close Jonathan and Michelle had appeared to be.

"I don't get it," she said, "they seemed so happy.

"When I heard about it, I went into shock. She was warm and playful and loving. Her husband was quiet and gracious. He sort of sat in the background and enjoyed watching the family."

Another identified Nyce neighbor told the Trenton *Times* it was hard to believe Jonathan Nyce was capable of such a horrendous crime.

"I'm so surprised," she said. "He was such a caring father and husband, and also because he seemed smarter than this."

Added her husband, "He was so low key. He seemed like an intellectual."

That morning, Sergeant Puskas was sent out to check all the storm drains and Dumpsters along any possible route that Jonathan Nyce might have taken early Friday morning. He was looking for the sharp, shiny object Nyce had alleged Michelle had lunged at him with, or any other relevant items of clothing or footwear that he may have discarded.

"We had to visualize," Sergeant Puskas later explained. There was still snow and ice on the ground and "I had a difficult time looking, as the drains were frozen and you couldn't lift the grate."

Monday afternoon Detective Dan McKeown, Detective Karen Ortman, Captain George Meyer and Detective Kevin Zorn together walked the entire length of Jacobs Creek Road, searching for the alleged weapon and the ski parka coat Michelle had been wearing when she had left Macy's the night of the murder.

"[It was a] brain-storming effort," said Captain Meyer. "We walked the neighborhood, but I wouldn't call it a search."

The team also measured the distance from 1 Keithwood Court to the crash site, as well as the distance of the route Nyce said he had used when he had driven Alex to school Friday morning.

• • •

Early Tuesday morning Jonathan Nyce pleaded not guilty via a TV hookup from Mercer County Correction Center, at his arraignment in front of Judge Bonnie Goldman. A large television had been set up in the crowded courtroom, showing Jonathan Nyce morosely slumped over a bench, wearing a regulation orange jumpsuit, a burly prison guard hovering behind him.

After being advised of his rights, the one-time millionaire meekly told the judge, "I would like to apply for a court-appointed attorney," as he couldn't afford a lawyer.

Suddenly Jonathan Nyce could no longer contain himself, and began rambling, apparently to try to justify his confession.

"Well, the reason I spoke with police officers," he began explaining, "without any benefit of any attorney at all, the other day was that I . . . I told them very directly that my wife . . ."

At that point Judge Goldman cut him off, advising him to keep his mouth shut until he could talk to a lawyer, so he wouldn't dig an even deeper grave for himself.

At 10:08 a.m. investigators returned to 1 Keithwood Court to resume the search. This time they were looking for boot soles to match the footprints leaving the crash scene, and the stiletto.

Outside the house two police cruisers idled in the driveway, where Jonathan Nyce's shiny red Hummer was still parked. Nearby was the children's play set and a tire swing hanging from a tree.

Led by Detective Sergeant Kronenfeld, the seven-strong team of investigators resumed searching the basement. This time they concentrated on walls, ventilation shafts and air-conditioning ducts, where evidence could have been hidden.

Soon after they began, Sergeant Puskas noticed a large

old NordicTrack box at the north end of the basement, containing a collapsed plastic Christmas tree and fairy lighting.

"On top of these items was another object," he recalled. "[It was] part of a shoe sole."

He immediately summoned the other investigators over to examine the fragment of black sole.

"The fact that we found a portion of a sole was pretty significant," said Kronenfeld. "Then we looked in the basement for various portions of a shoe. There were numerous pieces of the shoe found all over the basement."

Over the next hour investigators found a total of fourteen pieces of sole, including one with the size "12" printed on it.

"I did not see any uppers to the soles anywhere," noted Kronenfeld in his report. "However, on the workbench was a small scroll saw, and fragments of black rubber substance were noted about the bench and saw, along with another piece of shoe sole."

When he arrived on the scene, Detective John Ryan found a pair of sole-less moccasins hidden behind the workbench.

"It appeared the footwear had been glued to those shoes," said Detective Ryan. "Then the bottom of the Brahma boots had been sawed off and glued on the moccasins. Then they'd been removed and cut into fourteen pieces."

Detective Ryan easily put all fourteen pieces together like a jigsaw puzzle, forming two complete soles. Forensic tests would eventually determine that they were Jonathan Nyce's custom-made hybrid moccasin/Brahma combination boots, matching the footprints leaving the Land Cruiser at the crash site.

The detectives finally completed their search at 4:00 that afternoon, and the following day the keys to the home were returned to the Nyce family.

While investigators were still searching the basement, Detectives McKeown and Ortman met Jonathan Nyce Jr., his son Michael and nephew Ryan outside the house. The previously agreed plan was for them to go into the house and collect the children's clothing and favorite toys. Then the detectives would follow them to Collegeville, where they could interview the three children about anything they might know about their mother's death.

Jonathan Nyce's father and brother remained in the driveway, while the two detectives escorted Ryan into the house to collect the items.

Then they all drove to Hopewell Township Police Department to collect a Mercer County victim support counselor named Susan Meyer, who would accompany them. The detectives then followed the Nyces' car south along the New Jersey Turnpike. But during the one-hour drive to Pennsylvania, everything changed.

"Michael's attitude to us began to change drastically," explained Detective McKeown. "Right now, we were becoming the enemy."

After receiving their ticket at the Pennsylvania Turnpike tollbooth, Jonathan Nyce Jr. pulled over to the shoulder of the entrance ramp and stopped. McKeown and Ortman pulled up behind him, observing Michael having an intense conversation on his cell phone.

"And I said to Karen," remembered Detective McKeown, "we're not taking the kids."

About five minutes later, Michael Nyce got out of the car and walked back to the detectives. He told them he had just talked to his attorney, and been advised not to let them interview the children. He returned to his car and took off down the turnpike, leaving the detectives to return empty handed, as they had no jurisdiction to interview the minors without permission.

"This was frustrating," said McKeown. "There's no doubt in my mind that at least one of the children must have heard or seen something. And they would have been able to offer more insight into what really happened that night."

Six weeks later, Detective Karen Ortman finally got to interview Alex, Trevor and Samantha, in the presence of their father's defense lawyer, Hal Haveson, and a pediatric psychiatrist.

"They had been instructed on what to say," said Detective Ortman. "We were not even allowed to conduct the interview. We had to have a psychiatrist do it."

On Tuesday morning grief counselors visited the Bear Tavern and Timberlane Schools, to help Alex, Trevor and Samantha's classmates cope with what had happened. As Monday had been a national holiday, it was the children's first day back at school since Jonathan Nyce's arrest. Many of the children had known Michelle, as she had frequently attended school functions, and her children's friends often visited their home.

That night at a Hopewell Valley Regional Board of Education meeting, Superintendent Nick Lorenzetti paid tribute to Michelle Nyce.

"It is with a deep sense of regret and sorrow," he told the meeting, "that we acknowledge the sudden and tragic death of one of our parents."

The following day the mayor of Hopewell Township, Vanessa Sandom, announced plans to establish a trust fund for the Nyce children's education. Describing Michelle's death as a "horrible, senseless tragedy," Mayor Sandom asked the town to pray for the children.

"Whenever a family in our community experiences a tragedy of this magnitude," she said, "the entire community shares their grief. I know I speak for everyone in our community when I say that the Nyce children are in our hearts and our prayers."

25

"I Have No History of Physical Violence"

By Wednesday, the Jonathan Nyce story had gone national, with *The New York Times* and *New York Post* both making it a major story. "Entrepreneur Confesses to Killing Wife, the Police Say," ran the *Times* headline at the front of the Metro section.

"The developer of a new asthma treatment who was ousted a year ago from the research company he founded has admitted killing his wife in the garage of their million-dollar house and then trying to make it look as if she had died in an auto accident, the police said on Tuesday," breathlessly began the article.

After a brief résumé of Nyce's career, the article said that the Hopewell Township Police Department was still trying to decide his motive. Chief Chipowsky said that they were speculating it was motivated by either Nyce's financial problems, or his belief that Michelle was having an affair.

The article also carried a brief interview with EpiGenesis' new financial officer Joanne Leonard (no relation to Nyce friend and assistant Sherry Leonard), distancing the company from its founder.

"I can confirm that he left in March 2003," said Leonard, and that we have had no contact with him since then."

Predictably, the *New York Post* took a far more sensational approach, carrying the headline "Deadly Jealousy—N.J. Doctor Saw Wife as Cheat."

The *Post* had interviewed Larissa Soos, who speculated that Jonathan, convinced his wife was having an affair, had "snapped."

"If she was having an affair, she never confided it to me," Larissa told *Post* reporter Jeane MacIntosh. "But really, she's just very friendly and very naïve."

Describing Nyce as "overprotective" and "jealous," Soos said that whenever she was out with Michelle, Jonathan would call her cell phone, checking up on her. Then Michelle would hand it to her, so she could talk to Jonathan and prove she was there.

Larissa said that Michelle's friends first suspected Jonathan when they discovered he had not reported her missing. This was totally out of character, as he usually wanted to know where she was twenty-four hours a day.

Later, the Nyces' long-time friend Andy Sjamsu said everyone was in shock when they heard about Jonathan's arrest.

"How were we all so totally blind that we couldn't see it?" he asked. "The fact is nobody was around to see it as it really was. What's wrong with this picture? Every time people came over they would be the picture-perfect family, and then go back I guess."

On Wednesday morning, Mercer County Superior Court held a bail reduction hearing for Jonathan Nyce, and for the first time the prosecutor's office revealed their theory of how he had murdered his wife, and his motive.

Once again Nyce appeared via a closed-circuit TV hookup from Mercer County Correction Center. The public gallery of Judge Charles Delehey's courtroom was packed with reporters and television cameras. Also in attendance were

Jonathan Nyce Jr., Michael and Jonathan's other brother David, who had flown in from his home in North Carolina.

Assistant Prosecutor Tom Meidt told the court how Nyce had accused Michelle of starting the deadly struggle by flailing at him with a stiletto knife. Initially, said Meidt, Nyce had denied any involvement in Michelle's death, telling police about her affair and speculating that her lover was responsible.

But in a second interview he had admitted killing her, claiming it was an accident.

"He said they engaged in a struggle," the assistant prosecutor told the judge. "And he ended up smashing her head on the garage floor. He said she continued to flail at him with the knife, and he continued to smash her head on the floor."

Then, after killing her, he had put her in the driver's seat of the Land Cruiser, using an ice scraper to control the pedals, and driving the car with his other hand.

The assistant prosecutor revealed that police had found blood all over the garage, as well as a bloody trail up to the second-floor bedroom, where they believed he'd showered after murdering his wife. Bloody paper towels and a sock had also been found in a recycling bin, as well as empty bottles of hydrogen peroxide.

He also revealed that Michelle had been involved in an affair for more than a year, and had spent the hours before her death with her lover, Enyo. He also piqued reporters' curiosity by mentioning that Jonathan Nyce had first discovered the lover and his identity six months earlier, when the couple had argued about it.

After outlining the case against Nyce, Tom Meidt urged Judge Delehey not to reduce his $2 million cash bail, describing the defendant as a "flight risk."

This time Nyce was represented by attorney Lee Engleman, who denied Nyce would flee.

"The facts suggest self-defense," argued Engleman, adding that his client had no criminal record. "His children need him now more than ever. He will be the primary caregiver. In fact, he was before as well. There was really no one else who provided appropriate care for those children."

Then, in another dramatic outburst, defying both the judge and his own attorney, Jonathan Nyce insisted on addressing the judge.

"I have no history of physical violence ever against any person," he said, looking close to tears on the TV screen placed by the judge's bench. "I never ever had ill will toward my wife. This, what happened, was a pure accident."

Then Judge Delehy agreed to cut his bail in half to $1 million cash, denying Engleman's request that his client be allowed to post bond rather than cash, so he could go home. The court also refused Nyce's application for a public defender, finding that his financial need had not been proven.

The case would now go to a grand jury, who would decide whether Jonathan Nyce should stand trial for Michelle's savage murder.

After the hearing, Lee Engleman said his client still could not afford $1 million bail, as he had few liquid assets. Then he hurriedly left court, refusing to discuss the case with reporters any further.

But Mercer County Prosecutor Joseph Bocchini Jr. held a press conference, discounting Nyce's account of Michelle's death as a lie.

"Our investigation . . . revealed no knife," he said. "It is our belief that the knife is a figment of his imagination. Her head was slammed face-first into the garage floor, so the theory of her flailing with the knife doesn't fit."

The prosecutor added it was certainly possible he would seek the death penalty, and it would be in the hands of a death penalty committee, made up of himself and his senior staff.

Then a couple of reporters headed to Hopewell Township Police Department to interview chief Chipowsky. The chief said he was delighted by such a swift resolution to the case, applauding the cooperation between his department, the New Jersey State Police and the Mercer County Prosecutor's Office.

"A department of our size doesn't maintain the resources for an investigation of this magnitude," he explained.

Then without consulting the prosecutor's office, and regardless of the consequences, the chief handed reporters a copy of Detective McKeown's explosive July 2003 police report, outlining his investigation into Jonathan Nyce's allegations that Miguel deJesus had tried to extort $500,000 in return for videotapes of Michelle having sex.

This took the story to a scandalous new level, and the following day it would make newspaper headlines around the world.

"Sex-Tape Blackmail—N.J. Doc Eyed Wife's Lover In Plot Before Slaying Her: Cops," screamed the *New York Post*'s headline on Thursday.

The page lead, complete with a sexy photograph of Michelle, said Dr. Jonathan Nyce was "the victim of a $500,000 blackmail attempt" by Michelle's gardener lover. Calling Miguel deJesus a "deadbeat dad," it accused him of threatening to sell tapes of his sexual encounters with Michelle if Nyce didn't pay him.

The story also gave details of her affair with Enyo, including how they had met when he went to her house to plant trees. And it quoted Assistant Prosecutor Tom Meidt's testimony at the bail hearing that Michelle was returning from a "late-night motel rendezvous" with him when she was confronted by her husband and murdered.

The Trenton *Times*'s Lisa Coryell, who had interviewed Michelle's sister Melodia in the Philippines, broke the story that Jonathan Nyce had first met Michelle through a newspaper advertisement, and not as a result of a romantic accident on a Hawaiian beach. From now on Michelle Nyce would be branded a mail-order bride, exploding the myth she and Jonathan had carefully cultivated for the last fifteen years.

When Michelle's friends read the lurid stories, they could not believe this was the same woman they had known, finding it impossible to fathom her double life. They despaired that she could not have reached out to them for help before it was too late. But it's a Filipino personality trait never to discuss problems, and they even have a word for it, "*hiya*," meaning embarrassment.

"If only she could have mentioned it to me," said Jean Larini. "Maybe I could have talked to her and tried to sort it out."

Larissa Soos said she learned about the alleged extortion threat in the newspapers.

"There's so much I didn't know," she said. "I feel sad because I didn't realize how sad and miserable her life was. I understand she didn't want to burden her friends with that, but I wish she could have opened up to us."

Andy Sjamsu said he'd had to hide the newspapers from his children in the days after her death.

"I thought it was a joke," he said. "It was so bizarre. Where did she get the time to be screwing around with the gardener?"

Back in North Carolina, her friends were shocked to learn about Michelle's adulterous affair. In hindsight Kuny Brothers believes Michelle was ashamed, explaining why she'd suddenly dropped her old friends without explanation.

"Maybe it was because she was having the affair and she knows that I wouldn't have approved," said Brothers. "This may be why she didn't let me know where she was. I think she probably was unhappy because [Jonathan] was so into his work, but a lot of foreigners don't like to discuss their unhappiness."

And Sandy Chakarthi, Michelle's former workout partner and friend in Greenville, said she was shocked when she heard about her murder.

"I didn't try to pass judgment," said Sandy. "I think she was isolated up there, and lonely. Somebody took a liking to her and it felt good, and that's what happened. Many people have affairs, but nobody deserves to be killed over it."

Their friends were also hurt by the fact that Jonathan and Michelle had always lied about how they had really met.

"I kind of think that's another shame thing," said Kuny Brothers. "I guess she was a mail-order bride, but she told me that he was on a medical conference in Hawaii and they met on the beach. And that's another thing I was angry about. It was really shocking."

26

Going Home

Over the next week investigators doggedly continued interviewing witnesses and pursuing new leads. On Thursday, January 22, Detective Dan McKeown re-interviewed Enyo at the Mercer County Prosecutor's Office Homicide Unit on South Broad Street in Trenton. Also present were his attorney, Gary Jodha, Assistant Prosecutor Tom Meidt, Detective Karen Ortman and Detective Geoffrey Noble.

Finally he was asked to clarify his various nicknames and aliases. He explained that his real name was Miguel deJesus. Michelle used to call him "Enyo" or "honey," and he employed the aliases "Sergio Martinez" and "Alexander Castaneda," to avoid paying child support. He also admitted procuring and using a New Jersey driver's license in the name of Alexander Castaneda.

After completing his statement and signing it, Enyo was allowed to go home.

"At this time there is no evidence to substantiate extortion charges," said a spokeswoman for the prosecutor's office.

Everybody wanted to know more about the mystery gardener who appeared to have driven Jonathan Nyce to murder. Reporters spent days trying to track him down, with little luck. They went to several addresses that had connections to Alexander Castaneda and his three alter-egos, but the closest they got was to his attorney Gary Jodha.

"My guy wrecked a home and he's not proud of that," Jodha told Lisa Coryell of the Trenton *Times*. "If the police thought he'd done this, he'd be behind bars. Extortion is very heavy stuff."

Jodha said his client was "ashamed" of what he'd done and had now gone into hiding, as he was "scared" of Jonathan Nyce.

The following day Detectives McKeown and Ortman interviewed Larissa Soos at her home. She told them how she and Jean Larini were supposed to have met the morning of Michelle's death for their scrapbook club. When she called at 9:00 a.m. to check on Michelle, Jonathan had answered and said she'd been in a car accident. Larissa told the detectives that from then on, his behavior and actions seemed strange and out of place.

She was especially upset when Jonathan began to attack Michelle for being sex-mad and bi-polar.

"I was so confused," she told the detectives. "You can't imagine how I'm feeling. We considered ourselves sisters."

On Saturday, January 24, six days after Jonathan Nyce was arrested, Michelle's family announced they wanted custody of her children, so they could raise them in the Philippines. They had hired a Filipino attorney to investigate how to go about it.

"We want the children to come here," Michelle's sister Melodia told Lisa Coryell by phone from the Philippines. "We think it will be good for the children that I am to be the one to take care of them."

Since the evening their mother had died, Alex, who celebrated his twelfth birthday that week, Trevor, 10, and 5-year-old Samantha had been staying at their Uncle Michael's house in Eagleville, Pennsylvania. Although the children were still officially registered at Bear Tavern and Timberlane Schools, school officials did not expect them to return.

Hopewell Valley District Superintendent Nick Lorenzetti was in daily contact with Michael Nyce, closely monitoring the counseling they were receiving. The children's classmates were collecting a care package of cards, toys and pictures to send to them.

The Riviera family's Filipino lawyer, David Paguio Jr., said he had warned them it might be hard to fight for custody in the New Jersey courts. He was searching for a New Jersey attorney to act on their behalf.

"We have different laws here," he said. "I need someone who is an expert in laws there."

Since Jonathan Nyce had been charged with murder, his family had distanced themselves from Michelle's. Originally they had promised to pay for her funeral, but when Teodoro Riviera demanded her body be returned to the Philippines, they promptly withdrew the offer.

"I suspect he had a change of heart and stopped talking to us," said Larissa, "because of all the stories that are coming out in the papers about his brother."

Now she and Jean Larini were making plans to have her body flown back to the Philippines, as well as trying to raise the $13,000 needed for transportation. And they had already selected a casket at the Cromwell–Immordino Memorial Home in Hopewell, N.J., so her parents could begin preparations in Orion.

But Michelle's body still remained under police guard at the medical examiner's office, until her husband's defense lawyer could arrange for a second autopsy to help his case.

On Wednesday, January 28, more than one hundred people gathered at Princeton Community Church in Hopewell Township to celebrate Michelle Nyce's short life. It was a brutally cold night for the special memorial service, organized by Larissa Soos. None of Jonathan's family or the

Nyce children attended—they would hold their own a week later. Although the Nyce family were staunch Catholics, it was decided that having the service in a non-denominational church would have been more to Michelle's liking.

"It was a pretty sobering event," said John Tredea, who covered it for the weekly *Hopewell Valley News*. "I don't know how many of the people there actually knew her, but they were showing their support."

On the front of the program was a picture of Michelle, her head rising out of the sea. Originally Jonathan had been behind her staring at the camera through beady eyes, but now he had been exorcised by Photoshop.

Alongside the picture was a poem, especially composed for the occasion:

> *God's finger touched her and she slipped away from earth's dark shadows to a brighter day.*

The service began with a eulogy by Pastor Andy Mahoney, delivered from the pulpit in front of a giant photograph of a smiling Michelle.

"Michelle was us," he began. "She was a mom raising her children. She was a wife. She was a friend who laughed with those she loved. She smiled an infectious smile."

An emotional Larissa Soos then stepped up to the pulpit to eulogize her best friend.

"We all have one thing in common why we're all here tonight," began Larissa, choking back tears. "Michelle had touched our lives in some form or another. Some of us may have known her for three years or more. Others maybe just a few months or less.

"Michelle had friends from different walks of life— young or old, men or women, rich or poor. Michelle may have the looks of a model, but she is easygoing and down to earth. Her smile can light up any room. Her laughter can warm your heart . . .

"Tonight, I want to celebrate how she lived and not how

she died. Tonight, I want to tell you about my best friend, my sister, and a great mom to Alex, Trevor and Samantha.

"Michelle, wherever you are now, you will always be a STAR to me. This is your night! This is your community.

"I may have lost my best friend, my sister, but one thing no one can take away is my wonderful memories and friendship that Michelle and I have together.

"That's how I will always remember my dear Michelle Nyce!

"Rest in peace, my dear Michelle . . . Until we see each other again."

Sandy Chakarthi was Michelle's only friend from Greenville, North Carolina, who attended the service, and she addressed the mourners. Sandy had read about the murder in a newspaper and phoned Hopewell police for details of the funeral, and was put in touch with Larissa Soos.

"When she moved up here she was so frightened of being alone," Sandy told the congregation. "She didn't know anyone. But I can see tonight she made friends, lots of friends."

Then she spoke of visiting Michelle in Hopewell, after not seeing her for several years.

"She greeted me with open arms and a smile, as if no time had passed," she said. "But I could tell there was an underlying sadness. I couldn't tell why. I lost track of her after that. Until now."

At the end of the service Larissa screened a video she'd made, using photographs of Michelle with her children. Not surprisingly there wasn't a single shot of Jonathan Nyce, who was conspicuous in his absence.

On Tuesday, February 3, the medical examiner finally released Michelle's body to Larissa Soos, who had been given special power of attorney by Teodoro Riviera. She was now planning to have it transported back to the Philippines the following week.

The previous afternoon, renowned forensic pathologist

Michael Baden, the former chief medical examiner of New York City, who stars in the HBO series *Autopsy*, examined her body. He had been brought on by Jonathan Nyce's defense lawyers Lee Engleman and Hal Haveson.

Baden's examination was attended by Mercer County Medical Examiner Dr. Raafat Ahmad, and eight of the case investigators from the New Jersey State Police and Hopewell Township P.D.

They walked into the examination room to find Michelle's body covered by a white plastic sheet. Then M.E. Investigator Chris Merlino removed it and it was photographed by one of the detectives. After that Dr. Baden spent the next hour and twenty minutes examining the wounds, photographing them and describing them in detail to attorney Haveson.

According to a New Jersey State Police report documenting the examination, Dr. Baden described the injuries to Michelle's right hand as "offensive" wounds.

That same day Larissa Soos hired New Jersey attorney Joel Mayer on behalf of the Riviera family, as the first step in filing a wrongful death suit against Jonathan Nyce. She had been asked by Teodoro Riviera to find an attorney to represent the family, and Mayer was recommended by the Filipino-American Association.

He had agreed to work on a contingency basis, immediately launching a search to assess all Jonathan Nyce's financial and realty assets.

"Her family has retained me to file the wrongful death action," explained Mayer. "One of the first concerns I have is the status of Jonathan Nyce's debts versus his assets."

He then planned to go to court to freeze them, so Nyce wouldn't have the opportunity to hide them.

Mayer was also working with another law firm in the Riviera family's upcoming battle for the Nyce children's custody. He had tried to talk to Michael Nyce about the children seeing their mother for the last time for closure.

"But so far these efforts have been unsuccessful," he said. "That's unfortunate."

Michelle's body now lay in a casket at the Hopewell funeral home, and most afternoons Larissa, Jean and several of their friends would go to visit her.

"We'd bring cake and coffee to the funeral home," said Soos, "and hang out around Michelle's casket."

Later that week there was a small private memorial service for Michelle at the funeral home, which was attended by Jonathan Nyce's parents, brothers and three children. The children spent more than an hour alone with their mother's closed casket in a private chapel, as they said their final goodbyes.

Michelle's casket remained closed as her face was so badly injured, morticians could not reconstruct it.

"The injuries were so severe, especially in her face and forehead," said Larissa Soos. "The funeral director said it would be best that we remember Michelle the way she was, beautiful and lovely."

Larissa and some of Michelle's other close friends attended the memorial service, and there was some tension between them and the Nyce family.

"It was awkward," said Larissa. "Michael Nyce was supposed to be doing the funeral, but he never mentioned anything about shipping her body back."

During the service Emma Nyce cried uncontrollably. The children spent much of it playing in the basement of the funeral parlor.

"The boys knew she was dead," said Larissa. "But it didn't seem to have clicked with Samantha, who was running around the whole time. They were all very quiet staring at the casket."

Before they left, the children all kneeled down in front of their mother's casket and said a prayer. They left through a side door to avoid the press.

A few days later there was another private service for the Nyce family and friends, presided over by a Catholic priest.

On Friday, February 13, her body was finally shipped back to the Philippines, paid for by donations from friends and well-wishers, as well as $5,000 from the Victims of Crime Compensation Board.

Earlier that day there had been a fourth memorial service, attended by Consul General of the Philippines Cecilia B. Rebong, who drove down from New York.

After the service, Michelle's casket was placed inside a hearse and driven to Newark International Airport, where it was flown on Northwest Airlines Flight 667 at 6:12 p.m. to Manila's Ninoy Aquino International Airport.

On February 16, exactly one month to the day after her murder, Michelle arrived in Orion, where her family organized a traditional Filipino funeral for her, attended by the mayor, the chief of police and other local dignitaries.

27

Robin Lord

On Friday, February 6, Michael Nyce contacted a Trenton-based criminal attorney named Robin Lord, asking her if she would take over his brother's defense. Lord immediately agreed to represent Jonathan Nyce, after visiting him at Mercer County Correction Center.

It would be the most high-profile case the New Jersey state capital had seen since 1997, when convicted sex offender Jesse Timmendequas was found guilty of brutally murdering 7-year-old Megan Kanka of Hamilton, New Jersey. He is now on death row. That notorious murder trial ultimately led to the formation of "Megan's Law," requiring convicted sex offenders in many states to register with local authorities, and Lord helped prepare the defense case.

Now the tough, flamboyant defense lawyer, who had already carved a formidable reputation for herself in New Jersey, would finally step into the national spotlight. She would be the perfect lawyer to represent the always-controlling Jonathan Nyce, and keep him in check in the courtroom.

Robin Lord and her partner Patrick Whelan, who handles the civil side, run their law office on South Broad Street,

Trenton, directly opposite Mercer County Superior Court. The area has become known as "Bail-bond Row," but Lord is no stranger to the tough Trenton street gangs, many of whom have been her clients over the years.

"A Jersey girl right down to her bullet-proof nails," read a recent profile of her. "A leather-tough liberal . . . a defender of the dreadful," it continued.

Petite and always immaculately dressed in designer suits, the red-haired lawyer is controversial and larger than life. Hyperbole is central to the Robin Lord "us-against-them" philosophy, and the fortyish mother of two is a mass of colorful contradictions. Vehemently anti-police—she almost sadistically delights in trying to humiliate them on the stand—Lord's husband Steve is a deputy Monmouth County sheriff, a former prison officer and an aspiring actor, who has occasionally appeared on the soap opera, *One Life to Live*.

"He roots me on and hopes my clients go to jail," said Lord, who has a keen, often sarcastic sense of humor.

Born Robin Kay in Hazlet, New Jersey, as a little girl she dreamed of being an attorney and following in the steps of her heroes Clarence Darrow and William Kunstler, whose portraits hang over her desk. Her mother and biggest fan Janet Kay, remembers her as a "mouthy" child who always spoke her mind.

"Even in elementary school, Robin was strong willed and strong in her beliefs," remembered her mother, who is often in court to watch her in action. "She'd argue those beliefs just as she does now."

As a child her family nicknamed her "Sarah Bernhardt," because she was so dramatic. And if a teacher ever gave her a lower grade than she thought she deserved, she'd go and argue her case, often resulting in her getting a better grade.

At 14 she ran away from home and was finally found by local police, who brought her home. This apparently was the start of her dislike of police officers, who she then accused of harassment.

At Raritan High School she wrote an open letter to the

police entitled, "Rules to Follow by Police Officers So That Teenagers May Look Upon Them As Their Enemy." The largely satirical letter won her an "A" when she presented it as a school paper.

In 1979 she graduated top of her class, going to Syracuse University to major in legal studies, a major she claims to have largely tailored for herself. Four years later, Robin headed west to Oklahoma City University Law School, finishing first in her freshman class. Then after spending a summer working for the Brooklyn Legal Aid Society, she transferred her legal studies to the Hofstra Law School in Hempstead, New York, graduating a year early in 1985.

After working as a law clerk in the Office of the Monmouth County Prosecutor, she finally landed a job with the county public defender's office.

"It was a dream come true," she remembered. "I was representing those who couldn't afford to hire someone to defend them."

There, Lord found a great champion and mentor in the late veteran attorney Barbara Lependorf, who unsuccessfully defended Timmendequas for the murder of Megan Kanka.

"She's not always as diplomatic as she might be," Lependorf once said about Lord. "She comes on like gangbusters, which sometimes offends people. She puts a lot of judges on the defensive."

In the early 1990s she left the public defender's office to go into private practice, and has had a string of sensational victories, becoming known locally as the patron saint of lost causes. She is obsessively thorough in her prep work for a trial, often knowing the scientific text books better than the experts.

Her M.O. of finding weaknesses in the prosecution case and then exploiting them his made her the bane of Mercer County law enforcement, who have often accused her of unethical behavior.

"The majority of police officers lie," she told Lisa Coryell for a Trenton *Times* 2002 profile of her. "They lie on police reports, they lie when they testify. They do it because they have to lie to get convictions. That's their perception of justice. It's not mine."

Lord is also the consummate performer in the courtroom, providing juries with many a *Perry Mason* moment. In one notorious 1995 episode, she gave the finger to a Superior Court judge, after she disagreed with one of his rulings.

"My job is not to judge whether people are guilty or innocent of the crimes they are charged with," she once said, "but to make sure justice prevails. And justice prevails when people are given a fair trial."

She has also said that many clients don't tell her if they are guilty, as they mistakenly believe she won't fight as hard for them.

Now that she had joined the Nyce defense, the Mercer County prosecution team knew they had a formidable opponent who would stop at nothing to get her client off.

On Wednesday, February 11, Robin Lord asked Superior Court Judge Maria Sypek to release her client on a $1 million bond, saying he had no prior convictions and was not a flight risk. Judge Sypek, in her position as the presiding judge of the criminal division of the courts, would be handling all the preliminary hearings in the case. In the event a grand jury handed down a murder indictment, it would be turned over to Superior Court Judge Wilbur Mathesius.

"I want Dr. Nyce to have the opportunity to post a one-million-dollar bond and go home to his children," she told the judge in her first appearance on behalf of Jonathan Nyce. "I believe the cash-only stipulation is a misapplication of the law."

Judge Sypek denied her request, but agreed she would reconsider, if Lord could prove there was no danger Nyce would make a run for it.

Soon after taking over the Nyce defense, Lord embarked on a public relations campaign to reverse the negative perception of her client in the media. She told reporters that he speaks to his three young children by telephone from the Mercer County Correctional Center every single night.

"And every conversation ends with the kids asking, 'Daddy, when are you coming home?'" she said. "They send him pictures and notes."

Lord also announced that Dr. Michael Baden, who was part of the O. J. Simpson Dream Team, as well as working on the JonBenét Ramsey and Chandra Levy cases, had joined her defense team. She told reporters that he had already conducted his own examination of Michelle Nyce's body.

"He has not formulated an opinion yet," said Lord, who is friends with Dr. Baden's attorney wife Linda Kenny. "He's awaiting additional evidence to evaluate."

One week after Judge Sypek denied Jonathan Nyce bail, Robin Lord was back in court arguing his case. She appealed to the judge to release him on a bond, saying he could not come up with $1 million in cash.

"They have his passport, Judge," she declared. "Where's this man going? He's going nowhere."

Lord said if he were to be released, Nyce would stay with his family in Pennsylvania and be willing to wear an electronic surveillance device and meet any other stipulations the court set.

"We just want out," she said. "He has no assets that would give this court cause for concern that he is a flight risk. He is a responsible father."

But Assistant Prosecutor Tom Meidt disagreed, saying Nyce has business contacts all over the world and might flee the country if he were released.

"He said he pounded his wife's head into the concrete floor of the garage," Meidt told the judge. "Took a break to get bandages, then came back and further pounded her head onto the floor."

Lord reiterated that Nyce's statement had said Michelle's

death was an accident, and he was defending himself after she'd attacked him with a knife.

"At worst," she said, "it's a crime of passion, which is manslaughter."

Six days later, Judge Sypek handed Lord her first victory in the case, agreeing to allow Nyce to post bond and be released on bail until his trial. But in her decision Judge Sypek doubled Nyce's bail to $2 million, also ruling that if he ever made bail he should have supervised contact with his children.

"My concern is that he might want to take them," she said. "Be it abroad, to be with them evermore."

Lord said her client couldn't afford to make bail right away, and would be asking for a reduction.

She also announced that she was beefing up her defense team, adding Maria Noto as her co-counsel. Noto is president of the New Jersey chapter of the Washington, D.C.–based National Association of Criminal Defense Lawyers.

Lord's long-time private investigator John Coy, a twenty-nine-year veteran of the Trenton Police Department, was already working the case. Lord would set him loose to fully investigate Michelle Nyce's private life, looking for as much dirt as possible.

For Robin Lord knew that ultimately she would have to put Michelle Nyce's lifestyle on the stand if an upcoming grand jury decided there was a case to answer. That would be the only way Jonathan Nyce would win.

28

The Dirt Flies

On Monday, March 1, attorneys representing Michelle's family asked a Superior Court judge to freeze Jonathan Nyce's assets, so he couldn't use them for his defense. The same day, Michael Nyce and his wife, Margaret, filed papers seeking the temporary legal custody of the three children, who were now living with them.

Attorney Paul Norris, representing Teodoro and Trefisa Riviera, said they had no personal interest in their son-in-law's estate, and were acting solely in their grandchildren's interest.

"If Jonathan Nyce, in his defense, uses up all the assets or hides his assets," explained Norris, "we now have three children who have no assets and no parents."

Robin Lord's partner, Pat Whelan, countered the motion, arguing that his client had made no effort "to hide, steal or divert his assets."

In fact, maintained Whelan, Jonathan Nyce was in the process of setting up trust accounts for his children.

In a separate civil court motion, Michael and Margaret Nyce said they were far better equipped to look after the children than Michelle's family. They pointed out that the children had never been to the Philippines, and the only member of their maternal relatives they had ever met was their grandfather.

The following day Civil Court Judge Neil Shuster froze Jonathan Nyce's assets until a court-appointed administrator could identify them. The judge appointed an attorney to catalogue his assets and prepare a report, so he could decide whether to make it permanent. He also appointed a separate attorney to oversee the children's legal interests.

Nyce's defense team then asked the judge to allow some of his money to be used to continue to pay them for their services.

"We're hopeful the judge will allow Jonathan Nyce reasonable expenses to defend himself in the criminal and civil arena," Pat Whelan told reporters after the hearing.

The next day there was another blow to the Nyce defense, when Judge Sypek denied a motion by Lord requesting access to his incriminating statement to police. The judge ruled that it was not the defendant's constitutional right to place the statement into discovery.

"It's extremely unfair," Lord complained to reporters. "Why don't they turn the statement over? Because they know if they wait it's more to their advantage. The prosecution can poison public opinion as to the guilt of Dr. Nyce and continue to stand on their soap box making allegations."

Earlier the judge had asked Assistant Prosecutor Tom Meidt for a status report on the state's case against Nyce.

"We're moving as quickly as we can," he said. "I expect we will have our investigation complete in less than six months."

Two days later, Robin Lord took the unprecedented step of subpoenaing Tom Meidt in a civil court action, to force him to hand over the confession.

Calling Lord's move "unusual," Meidt joked that he had never had to hire an attorney to represent him before.

"I was surprised to receive the subpoena," said Meidt. "I just don't believe Robin Lord should have access to the statement."

Lord hit back, accusing the prosecution of taking "great liberties with the English language," in their interpretation of her client's statement.

"We're confident," she said, "that in the civil arena that we're in now, the statement will show the court that there is not a reasonable likelihood of success on the merits that this was an intentional killing."

But on March 15, Civil Court Judge Neil Shuster decided that Lord was not entitled to see her client's confession before a grand jury indictment. In his ruling the judge suggested she discover what was in it simply by asking her client.

"The interest of the state in preserving the evidence in this matter," wrote the judge in his ruling, "far outweighs the defendant's right to obtain a copy of his alleged confession."

On Monday, March 15, Teodoro Riviera, now 63, moved to the United States to improve the family's chances of gaining custody of his three grandchildren. He arrived at Newark International Airport with just $6 in his pocket, and was met by Larissa Soos, who had found him a small studio apartment on East Broad Street in Hopewell Borough to live in.

"I came here to get justice for my daughter," he said. "And the custody of her kids. I am very poor, but I will find a job. I will provide for them."

Riviera said his wife, Trefisa, planned to join him as soon as he could get her necessary immigration papers, and together they planned to set up a proper home for the children. He strongly denied Robin Lord's accusation that he was only interested in his son-in-law's-money.

"It's not that I want money," he said. "I want the kids because I love the grandkids."

Riviera claimed that he had difficulty reaching his grandchildren by telephone from the Philippines, as the Nyce family were reluctant to let them talk. Finally Michael Nyce had agreed to put them on the telephone, after first making him promise not to discuss their mother's death. Apparently they had still not been told their father had been charged with her murder, but only that he was helping the FBI solve it.

"He said to me," said Riviera, " 'Do not talk to them about who killed their mother.' When I talked to them, they were crying, and Samantha said, 'Grandpa, do you know that my mother is dead?' I told her I knew and I said, 'Don't worry, Sammy, I will come to America.' "

Riviera said he believed Alex, Trevor and Samantha were being brainwashed by the family, who were trying to turn them against Michelle.

"They're telling them their mother was a bad mother," he said.

Michelle's softly spoken father said he now planned to take an active part in both the civil and criminal cases against his son-in-law. He denied Michael Nyce's accusations that the children didn't know his side of the family, and would not be happy in the Philippines.

"Michelle wanted them to visit the Philippines," he said. "But Jonathan said no. He took their passports and hid them. My family is not here, but the children know them through pictures."

One week after he arrived, Teodoro Riviera went to the Hopewell Township Police Department's detective bureau, where he was interviewed by Dan McKeown and Karen Ortman. He told them how he had personally witnessed Jonathan Nyce's explosive temper, and how Michelle had desperately wanted a divorce.

He said everything was fine in 2002, when he first moved in for seven months. But when he returned in June 2003, two months after Nyce was fired from EpiGenesis, everything had changed.

"They were always fighting," he told the detectives, saying the recurring themes of their arguments were "jealousy" and Nyce being at home all the time and not looking for work. He also told them the real story of how Jonathan had pursued his daughter through correspondence and then flown to Manila, marrying her one week later.

He complained that his son-in-law had exaggerated everything he claimed to have done for the family, and it had been Michelle who had sent them money out of her own allowance.

"All I know is, Michelle sent the money," he said. "Michelle helped us build six houses."

He also claimed he knew nothing about his daughter's affair, although he said in 2002 she had introduced him to a man called Alexander Castaneda, and they'd all dined together in a Japanese restaurant.

He also told the detectives about his son-in-law's temper tantrums and how Michelle had once shown him a hole in the wall outside the master bedroom.

"[Jonathan] hit the wall," said Riviera. "When I left in January the hole was still not fixed."

On Wednesday, April 14, three months after Michelle's death, a Mercer County grand jury indicted Jonathan Nyce for first-degree murder, and a second count of tampering with evidence. If convicted, Nyce could spend the rest of his life in prison.

The indictment was announced by Mercer County Prosecutor Joe Bocchini, who said his office was now ready to take the case to trial. The state's case to the grand jury was presented by Assistant Prosecutor Tom Meidt, who called just one witness, Detective Dan McKeown.

After Detective McKeown's sworn testimony, Meidt proposed that the grand jury indict Nyce on first-degree murder and fourth-degree tampering with evidence offences. But he emphasized that the indictment was just a proposal, instructing them on the different levels of homicide they could select.

"[The function of the grand jury is] to determine," he told them, "whether, based on the nature of the injuries inflicted, the acts afterward, and all the evidence that was presented to you, whether it's murder or passion provocation manslaughter. The proposed indictment right now is murder."

Robin Lord welcomed the grand jury indictment, saying she could now start preparing Jonathan Nyce's defense.

"We're very excited that the prosecutor's office finally decided to move this case forward," she declared. "Now we will have the opportunity to have all the discovery and the police reports and conduct a more intelligent and thorough investigation. Once that is accomplished, we are confident the state will not be able to prove that Dr. Nyce is guilty."

Michelle's father said he was also pleased with his son-in-law's indictment.

"I feel good," he told a reporter. "This is what we need. We need for Jonathan to be found guilty of killing Michelle."

The following day Jonathan Nyce was arraigned in front of Mercer Superior Court Judge Maria Sypek, where he pleaded not guilty to first-degree murder and tampering with evidence. Shackled and handcuffed with a padlocked chain around his waist, the once stout man appeared to have lost a lot of weight in the three months since his arrest, and his baggy gray suit looked several sizes too big.

During the brief arraignment he stood silently, as Robin Lord officially entered his not guilty plea. But he seemed in good spirits, often conferring with her and even sharing a joke at one point.

At the hearing, Lord said she planned to ask the court to suppress Nyce's confession, on the grounds that police contravened his Fourth and Fifth Amendment rights. The Fourth protects citizens against illegal searches and seizures, and the Fifth protects people from incriminating themselves.

When asked outside the courtroom why she wanted her client's statement ruled inadmissible, Lord replied, "Because it's not true."

A week later Robin Lord went on the attack, attempting to discredit Michelle and her father, during her fourth attempt to have bail reduced. The hearing, once again in front of Judge Maria Sypek, began with Tom Meidt explaining that Nyce had yanked Michelle out of the Land Cruiser with such force, he had left bruised impressions of his fingers on her left arm.

He revealed for the first time that Michelle had tried to

defend herself, and had abrasions and bruises on both hands to prove it. He also divulged that she and Jonathan had argued about her plans to leave him the day before she died, and police had found a packed suitcase of her clothes in the back of her SUV.

"This was no accident," said Meidt.

Then Robin Lord got to her feet, asking for his bail to be reduced, calling the prosecution case weak. "It's one thing to say, 'This is our theory of what happened,'" she told Judge Sypek. "It's quite another to say, 'This is what Dr. Nyce confessed to us.'"

She denied Nyce had ever said in his statement that he had repeatedly smashed Michelle's head on the concrete garage floor.

"It was a horrible, horrible accident," she declared. "Dr. Nyce tells of how his wife pulled into the garage, how he went up to her car and Michelle had a crazed look in her eyes, as if she were on drugs. She started cursing at him . . . she reached into a bag, took out a sharp, pointed object and started to lunge at Dr. Nyce and, as a reaction, he grabbed ahold of her and she went to the ground, possibly hitting her head on the car on the way down."

Lord also questioned the admissibility of his statement, claiming her client was on prescribed antidepressants when he made it.

Then Judge Sypek reduced Jonathan Nyce's bail to $1.7 million, meaning he would now have to find just over $100,000 to go free until his trial. But it was a hollow victory for Lord, who told the judge that her client had no access to money.

"We have our assets frozen by a man who claims to have the best interest of the children in mind," she told the court. "But we've investigated quite to the contrary. Our investigation has shown that Mr. Riviera is hardly a fit parent. There is evidence that he was involved with a mail-order bride scheme, involving fifteen-year-old girls."

At this point Tom Meidt stood up to object and Judge Sypek cut her off in mid-sentence.

"I'm bringing it to the court's attention," said Lord defiantly.

Later, outside the courtroom, reporter Lisa Coryell asked Lord to elaborate on what evidence investigator John Coy had uncovered.

"We'll have our opportunity in court to try this case," she replied.

The following day Teodoro Riviera defended his good name, calling Robin Lord "a liar." Speaking from Larissa Soos' house, he said he had come to America to get justice for Michelle, and it had nothing to do with money.

"These allegations that I was involved with the mail-order brides," he said. "Where did they get the evidence? I arrived here on March fifteen. Now if I was involved with fifteen-year-old girls, do you think I'd come to America? No. I'd be in prison now."

He said his civil attorney, T. Sandford Durst, who was representing the family in the child custody battle, called him on his way to work after reading Lord's accusations in a newspaper.

"I felt hurt," he said. "I could not understand why this is happening after everything I've been through."

A few hours later Durst publicly challenged Lord to substantiate her outrageous claims, saying he was considering a slander suit. He said he'd written her a letter demanding evidence to prove her "baseless and offensive" allegations.

"If you make a statement like that," he said, "you'd better have a damn good reason for saying it."

When Lisa Coryell asked Lord about the letter, she said she would not be responding to it.

"I have nothing to say to them," she snapped. "I'll try my case in court, where I try all my cases."

On hearing her response, Durst said he would advise his client of his legal options.

"We believe [this] is a defamatory comment and a baseless attempt to destroy his character and reputation," said Durst.

On Monday, April 26, Sandy Durst organized a press

conference for Michelle's father, so he could set the record straight. Speaking quietly in halting, broken English, an often emotional Teodoro Riviera publicly denied any involvement in trading mail-order brides or being a gold-digger.

He told reporters that he had immigrated to the United States to fight for the custody of his three grandchildren. He also denied Robin Lord's claims that he and his family had been destitute when Jonathan first met Michelle. He said his son-in-law was not the savior of his family, and Michelle had sent money, allowing them to have a better life.

Then Durst produced the affectionate letter Jonathan Nyce had given Riviera the previous Christmas, prior to his return to the Philippines. Referring to him as "Dad," Nyce had told him what a "pleasure" it had been having him live with the family, inviting him to come back whenever he liked.

The following day Pat Whelan countered, claiming Riviera was too angry and bitter to care for his grandchildren. Although Mercer County Family Court Judge Jan Grall had sealed all the papers relating to the custody case, the Trenton *Times* apparently were leaked a letter from Whelan to the court.

In the letter, Whelan claimed that before her death, Michelle, as well as Jonathan, had sought to limit their children's contact with her family in the Philippines. He wrote that his client would never consent to Teodoro Riviera having any legal authority or unsupervised access to his children.

"Mr. Riviera," wrote Whelan, "due to his misplaced belief that our client intentionally killed Michelle Nyce, has not hidden his direct hostility towards our client. The court should be concerned that Mr. Riviera, due to his anger and bitterness, will not be sensitive to the needs of the children."

Whelan maintained that the children's Uncle Michael and Aunt Margaret, who had been appointed temporary guardians, were "uniquely qualified" to raise them permanently.

"Our client," he wrote, "believes that his brother and sister-in-law understand what it takes to raise the children to become happy, healthy and successful adults."

* * *

The battle of what little remained of Jonathan Nyce's assets continued into May, after Superior Court Judge Neil Shuster refused to free any of it up so he could pay for his defense. Pat Whelan, now handling the civil part of the case, told the judge that it was in the Nyce children's interest that their father should be well defended.

But the three children's court-appointed guardian, Ed Slaughter, told Judge Shuster he disagreed, saying the money should remain intact for their future. He recommended the judge permanently freeze Nyce's assets, so he couldn't use them to defend himself. In a court-ordered report, Slaughter wrote it was likely that Jonathan Nyce would be found civilly, if not criminally, responsible for Michelle's death.

"Depletion of the family estate in order to pay for an expensive criminal defense is, thus, not in the best interest of the Nyce children," read his report. "It is imperative for their welfare that the family estate be preserved to the greatest extent possible."

A week later Michael Nyce hired an attorney named Adwoa Sanderson to represent the children in the custody case. "I certainly think it harms the children," Sanderson told reporters, "if their father doesn't get the best defense and can't return to them. I don't think it's in their best interest to tell them, 'Well, Daddy couldn't get an attorney because we had to set aside $700,000 for you.'"

As he languished in the Mercer County Correction Center, Jonathan Nyce spent his days helping Robin Lord prepare his defense and writing fairy tales for his children.

"He wrote them stories, beautiful stories," said his mother, Emma Nyce. "Especially Samantha. He'd write her a beautiful little story and mail it to her. And [the children] would also write him stories and letters and send him pictures. Alex would always send a picture of him and his dad holding hands."

29

Skirmishes

On Tuesday, July 6, 2004, Mercer County Superior Court Judge Maria Sypek handed Jonathan's Nyce a get-out-of-jail free card, by reducing his bail to $750,000. Two weeks earlier for the fifth time, Robin Lord had argued her client was broke, appearing pessimistic the freeze on his assets would be lifted until after the outcome of his criminal trial.

"Right now, Mr. Nyce has zero assets," she told Judge Sypek.

But Assistant Prosecutor Tom Meidt disagreed.

"I've never seen a [murder] defendant with the assets this defendant has."

It was a major victory for Robin Lord, and now Nyce's family had to come up with at least $75,000, which is nonrefundable, for the bail bondsman to secure his freedom. Judge Sypek ruled that in the event he was released, Nyce would have to stay in New Jersey and be fitted with a permanent global positioning device, so he could be monitored around the clock.

Still in custody a week later, a gaunt-looking Jonathan

Nyce attended another hearing, where Lord argued for him to be allowed to stay with his parents in Collegeville. She told the judge that as 1 Keithwood Court had now been cleared out and was up for sale, he would otherwise have to reside in a hotel, which would not have a switchboard capable of handling a global tracking device.

Judge Sypek ruled with Lord, now paving the way for Nyce to return home to his parents.

At 4:00 p.m. Friday, August 6, Jonathan Nyce walked out of Mercer County Correction Center after almost seven months' incarceration. Looking pale and haggard in a loose-fitting suit, he was then escorted in his stocking feet to Robin Lord's law offices, where, less than an hour later, he gave an impromptu press conference to previously tipped-off reporters.

"I'm relieved to be out," he said, sitting in the cramped front office, sipping a Diet Coke and eating a nutrition bar. "The first thing I'm going to do is to go home and hug my children."

When asked why he was not wearing shoes, he explained that the jail had misplaced them.

Robin Lord said she was delighted the judge had set him free, so he could see his children again.

"This is the beginning of the end of his nightmare," declared Lord optimistically. "He's innocent, and innocent people don't belong in jail."

As a condition of bail, Nyce was only allowed supervised visits with his children, and could not stay with them overnight.

Lord said she would be appealing this restriction at a later date. Now that he was free, she said, he would be able to assist preparing his defense more effectively than he been able to behind bars.

After the press conference, where Lord refused to allow her client to answer any questions about Michelle's death, she walked him next door to the AA Bail Bonds office, where a black plastic global positioning ankle device was fitted, out of the view of press cameras.

From now on Jonathan Nyce would be electronically monitored every ten seconds, and would have to remain within two hundred feet of his parents' home.

But unfortunately, due to a miscommunication between Mercer County Correction Center and the prosecutor's office, no one connected to the case had been warned he had been released. When Teodoro Riviera read about it in Saturday's newspaper he was very upset, terrified that his son-in-law might attempt to harm him.

"He was scared," said Larissa Soos, who also learned about it from the media. "He thinks, 'What if Jonathan escapes' and tries to harm him? I don't know why they didn't warn us, so we could be prepared."

Soos said her major concern was that Nyce would attempt to contact her and try to explain himself and what had happened to Michelle.

"I think his lawyer will advise him that it would be foolish for him to do so," she said.

Larissa also wondered how long it would be until Alex, Trevor and Samantha Nyce discovered the truth—that their father was facing the prospect of life imprisonment for the murder of their mother.

"Michael has never told them what happened," said Larissa. "They know their dad is somewhere where he can't come home right now. He talks to them on the phone or writes letters, but other than that, I don't think they have really told the kids anything."

On Thursday, October 14, Robin Lord fired the first salvo in her battle to clear Jonathan Nyce of murder. She filed the first in a series of motions, asking Mercer County Superior Court Judge Bill Mathesius, who would preside at the upcoming murder trial, to rule her client's confession inadmissible. She also asked Judge Mathesius, who had signed the original search warrant, to rule all evidence police had discovered at the Nyce house inadmissible.

"They held Dr. Nyce in custody and got a warrant of

probable cause and questioned him for hours prior to obtaining a statement," read Lord's motion. "This was a violation of his Fourth Amendment rights."

She also accused the police of refusing him access to an attorney, thereby violating his Fifth Amendment rights.

"The Assistant Prosecutor advised the police not to inform Dr. Nyce that his lawyer at the time called in and asked that he be told to stop talking immediately," wrote Lord. "I was outraged when I read that in the police reports."

She also claimed police had illegally searched 1 Keithwood Court before getting a search warrant. And after Judge Mathesius had finally issued one, they continued illegally searching for days.

"They held the house hostage," argued Lord, "searching the premises not just for one day, not just for two days, not just three days but for four complete, consecutive days. They kicked the family out for six days."

In a third motion filed the following week, Robin requested that Judge Mathesius dismiss the case, accusing Assistant Prosecutor Tom Meidt of deliberately misleading the grand jury to get an indictment. She claimed that although Meidt had explained to the grand jury they could indict on lesser charges of passion/provocation manslaughter, aggravated manslaughter and reckless manslaughter, they had only been given the option to vote for murder.

Additionally, claimed Lord, the assistant prosecutor had deliberately turned off the official transcription machine five times during his discussion with grand jury members. In her motion, Lord said that when she read the 160-page transcript of the grand jury hearing, it was clear jurors were "troubled and confused." In fact, wrote Lord, one grand juror said, "I do not believe that he tried to murder her."

Responding to the defense's accusations, Meidt pointed out that, after hearing all the evidence, the grand jury had found probable cause to indict Jonathan Nyce for murder.

"I presented a fair case and the jury returned an indictment," Meidt told the *Trentonian*. "I'm not trying to go tit-for-tat with her . . . I don't see her making any headway with this."

◆ ◆ ◆

Now back living with his parents in the house he grew up in, Jonathan Nyce retreated into a world of make-believe. He spent his days reading voraciously and writing stories for the children, or assisting with his defense. He even expressed the wish to one day write a book about him and Michelle and everything that had happened to them.

At 7:00 every night, he and his parents settled down in front of the television to watch *Jeopardy*.

"He knows all the answers," said Emma Nyce. "I don't care what you ask him, he has all the answers."

Under his bail conditions, he was unable to spend any time alone with his children, who were now living just five miles down the road with their Uncle Michael and his wife, Margaret.

His brother had a demanding, full-time job as a highway foreman for the Pennsylvania Department of Transportation. Margaret was Director of Child Life Services at St. Christopher's Hospital in Philadelphia. They both worked long hours, so Jonathan Nyce was unable to see his children as much as he would have liked.

"It was hard on all of us," said his mother. "Because he couldn't see the kids every day like he wanted to. And it was hard on the kids too. Michael had a rule, and that's how it stood. It was fine because the kids did good at school and he saw them whenever he could."

Emma Nyce said her three grandchildren had now settled down in their new Pennsylvania schools, and were doing well. Since their mother's death, they had all been seeing a psychologist every two weeks, and had come to terms with it.

"I'm sad to say they never, ever talk about their mother," said Emma. "And we keep telling them she's up in heaven and not to worry about her. She's all right."

She said Samantha, now 6, had recently drawn a picture of her whole family, leaving out her mother.

"She just wrote the word, 'Mommy' in there," said Emma. "That's Samantha."

* * *

On Tuesday, November 30, Jonathan Nyce and his father drove from Collegeville Pennsylvania to Mercer Superior Court in Trenton for a hearing to determine if the murder charges against him should be thrown out. The hearing, in Judge Bill Mathesius' second-floor courtroom, would consider whether Assistant Prosecutor Tom Meidt had manipulated the grand jury to get an indictment.

Known locally as "Wild Bill" from his days as a controversial rough-and-tumble New Jersey politician, Judge Mathesius, 65, lived in Hopewell Township, not far from his defendant. He began his career working for the FBI in 1961, and after a short spell as a clerk to a U.S. District Court judge, he became Assistant United States Attorney for the District of New Jersey, heading up the Trenton office.

In 1970 he was appointed Mercer County's first assistant prosecutor and chief trial attorney, before being made Mercer County prosecutor in 1973.

Two years later he left to take up a private law practice as a New York–based special counsel for American Express, as well as adjudicating contested cases for the New Jersey Department of Civil Service.

In 1980 he moved into the political arena, being elected Mercer County executive, in charge of more than 2,500 employees and overseeing an annual budget of $150 million. During his eleven years running Mercer County, Mathesius was outspoken and was known as a loose cannon, gaining him his "Wild Bill" moniker.

In 1991 he joined the faculty at Princeton University's Woodrow Wilson School of Politics and did some private counseling, before being appointed a judge at Hopewell Township Municipal Court.

Nine years later, in 2002, he was appointed a judge at the Mercer County Superior Court bench, where he soon butted heads with the State Supreme Court over a 2002 opinion he wrote regarding an appeal for a death row inmate. The case involved a convicted killer named Ambrose Harris, whose

1992 random murder of 22-year-old artist Kristin Huggins had shocked Trenton.

In November 2004, the New Jersey Supreme Court took Judge Mathesius to task in no uncertain terms, labeling his comments about the New Jersey death penalty "outrageous, sarcastic and pejorative." Additionally, the Supreme Court also criticized his references to its former members as "gratuitous personal attacks."

Now the also-controversial defense attorney Robin Lord would cross legal swords with Judge Mathesius during the trial of Jonathan Nyce. It would not be the first time the two had faced off against each other in court, as Judge Mathesius had presided over several murder cases involving Lord since he came to the bench.

Judge Mathesius explained that he had been hand-picked by his superiors to preside over Robin Lord's cases.

"They wanted one person for Robin," he explained in his chambers at Mercer County Superior Court. "They wanted her not to be able to play one judge off another."

Judge Mathesius said he personally liked Robin Lord, and respected her professionally.

"I enjoy her," he said. "I think she's very bright, but I don't know that she enjoys me as much. She goes as far as you'll let her."

And there would be many skirmishes between the two at this hearing, to decide if Jonathan Nyce's grand jury had been railroaded into a murder indictment.

Tall and balding in a pressed pinstripe suit, Nyce looked like he'd aged twenty years since his arrest. Sitting on the edge of the front bench, to the left of the small courtroom next to Lord, he showed no emotion the entire hearing. After Judge Mathesius had taken his seat, Robin Lord stood up to argue for a dismissal.

According to the defense attorney, the jurors had intimated that they'd wanted to consider lesser charges than murder, but were not given the opportunity by Assistant Prosecutor Meidt.

"He left a clear impression that it was an all-or-nothing proposition," declared Lord. "He should have told them they could indict on a lesser charge."

Lord claimed that Meidt was afraid that Nyce would be indicted for passion/provocation, which carries minimal jail time of 5 to 10 years, instead of murder, which is 30 years to life.

Assistant Prosecutor Doris Galuchie, who would co-prosecute the Nyce case with Tom Meidt, denied that grand jurors were ever misled or manipulated.

"They knew what they had to consider," she told Judge Mathesius. "If they didn't want to indict on murder, they could have no-billed that and gone on to consider other options."

Lord also accused Meidt of prosecutorial misconduct, claiming that the audiotape machine recording the jurors' deliberations had been continually switched on and off, leaving some interactions unrecorded.

"We don't know what happened while the tape was shut off," she observed.

Shrugging her shoulders, Galuchie accused Lord of merely making "a mountain out of a molehill," saying it was an "exceedingly fair" presentation to the grand jury.

Three days later Judge Bill Mathesius rejected Lord's arguments for dismissal out of hand, labeling her accusation "a hyperbole of significant proportion." In a ten-page ruling, he found that Assistant Prosecutor Meidt was not guilty of any misconduct, and there had been nothing untoward regarding his handling of the grand jury.

"Despite defendant's claim, the law demonstrates that not only is this not prosecutorial misconduct but rather it is a standard and permissible practice in New Jersey."

The judge also found that Meidt had exercised no "improper influence" over the audio recording of the proceedings, and Jonathan Nyce had not been denied a fair grand jury hearing.

Tom Meidt welcomed the ruling, saying that Robin Lord's motion was "completely exaggerated," and he had been vindicated by Judge Mathesius.

• • •

A week later, on Tuesday, December 7, Robin Lord was back in Judge Mathesius' courtroom for a three-day hearing, arguing that the police had illegally searched Jonathan Nyce's house. She claimed that all the blood-soaked incriminating evidence found should be ruled inadmissible, as they had been obtained without proper search warrants.

"You had the body [of a woman] who had an affair and had marital problems," she told Judge Mathesius. "Obviously the husband is always the first suspect . . . But there were no concrete, well-founded reasons to suspect him."

Nyce sat stoically next to his lawyer as she argued that police had ordered him and his family out of 1 Keithwood Court before they even had a search warrant. Then, after getting one, they had spent days searching the house.

New Jersey State Police Sergeant Jeffrey Kronenfeld was called as a witness, and Lord aggressively questioned him about the investigation and the necessity of evicting Nyce from his home prior to the warrant being signed.

"We believed something happened in the house," the detective told the court. "We wanted to make sure the evidence in that house was maintained and not destroyed."

Tom Meidt told the judge that the police had done nothing wrong in having Nyce vacate his home, or in their execution of the warrant. He pointed out that "evidence was clearly being destroyed," mentioning the cut-up footwear and the trash bags full of bloody paper towels.

On the second day of the hearing, tempers flared between Robin Lord and Judge Mathesius as the defense attorney called Mercer County Prosecutor's Office Detective Karen Ortman to the stand. Seeking to discredit her detective work on the case, Lord claimed that she had had no real evidence that a crime had been committed in the house.

Detective Ortman explained that from the beginning, investigators did not believe Michelle's death was accidental. And the footprints from the crash site, going up to Jacobs

Creek Road toward the Nyce home, had made detectives believe something had happened in the house.

As Lord relentlessly fired question after question at the detective, Judge Mathesius repeatedly refused to allow them, shouting at her several times in exasperation. Finally Lord gave up in frustration, storming back to her defense table.

"This is an exercise in futility," she complained to the judge. "I have no further questions. I can't go anyplace with this witness, because you're misinterpreting [the laws]."

At the end of the day the judge ordered both counsels to "get your witnesses ready," saying he was determined to conclude the hearing tomorrow, even if they had to stay until 10:00 p.m.

On Thursday morning, Robin Lord argued that police had violated her client's rights by ordering him out of his house, and that the fact they had found his wife Michelle's body less than a mile away and discovered the Nyces had serious marital problems was not enough probable cause for a search.

"He had a right to stay in that house," she declared, "and not be evicted before they executed a warrant."

She accused investigators of packing up and removing boxes of letters, computer files and other paperwork having nothing to do with the case.

At one point Judge Mathesius grew so incensed with Lord's persistent claim that the investigators' fears that Nyce might destroy evidence were insufficient grounds to remove him from his house, that he got up from the bench, throwing his arms into the air in theatrical exasperation.

"It's all under the rubric of evidence," he said angrily. "You can call it what you want. You can call it rice and beans. Whatever you want to call it, it's all evidence."

"[Dr. Nyce] had a right to eat that rice and beans," Lord replied, without missing a beat.

"Did he have a right to choke his wife with those rice and beans?" asked the judge.

"He didn't kill his wife," Lord said, as her client looked on without a trace of emotion.

At the end of the hearing, the judge said he would rule on Robin Lord's motion within a week, announcing that Jonathan Nyce's trial for the murder of his wife would begin on March 7, 2005.

Jonathan Nyce spent Christmas with his family in Pennsylvania, with the dark cloud of his upcoming trial hanging over his head. He swapped presents with his children under the tree, pretending everything was normal. But it was Alex, Trevor and Samantha's first Christmas without their mother.

"They never ask for their mom," maintained Emma Nyce. "They only did after it first happened."

The children's grandmother said they were aware of the charges against their father, and have adjusted to their new life. They were also all doing well at their new schools in Pennsylvania, she said. Alex had inherited his father's gift for science, while Trevor enjoyed football and loved art.

"Samantha excels in everything she does," said Emma.

She said they no longer see their old friends in Hopewell.

"They did in the beginning," said their grandmother, "but then it got too busy for us all."

30

"He Was Not Shocked"

Ultimately, it took Judge Bill Mathesius more than a month to rule against Robin Lord's motion that the Nyce home had been illegally searched, and therefore all evidence should be inadmissible at trial. On January 10, 2005, in a seventeen-page written opinion, the judge ruled against the defense, finding that information gleaned from the Jacobs Creek crash site had given investigators "good reason" to suspect the house was the primary crime scene.

"The course of action taken by the State and local police was reasonable and lawful," the judge wrote. "The motion to suppress evidence is denied."

On Tuesday, March 8, Robin Lord's third motion, to have Judge Mathesius throw out Jonathan Nyce's statement prior to his arrest, resulted in a sensational week-long Miranda hearing. Lord, who would always refer to it as a "statement," as opposed to prosecutors' contention it was a "confession," called a procession of police witnesses to the stand in a stunning prequel to the actual trial.

Lord argued Jonathan Nyce had been deprived of his fundamental right to have an attorney present when he was interrogated by Detective William Scull the Sunday after Michelle's death.

Her first witness was Hopewell Township Police Department Sergeant Mike Cseremsak, who described how he had been sent to Keithwood Court after Michelle had been found dead in her Land Cruiser. The bald, bespectacled officer told the hearing how Jonathan Nyce had been out when they had first arrived, taking his son Alex to school. When he returned they met him at the top of the driveway, following his Hummer 2 to the front of the house.

Cseremsak said Nyce looked "disheveled," with his hair in "a mess" and the fly of his jeans open. After being instructed by his superior, Lieutenant Fechter, he had given Nyce a standard Miranda warning before telling him his wife had died in an accident.

"He was not shocked," said Cseremsak. "He did not get upset. It was almost a neutral reaction."

Asked when he had last seen Michelle, Nyce said it was the previous afternoon when she'd told him she planned to go out with a girlfriend after her evening shift at Macy's. And it was not "unusual" for Michelle to stay out all night.

As Cseremsak was leaving, Nyce finally broke down, turning red and starting to cry.

Lord's next witness was the case's lead investigator, Detective Dan McKeown. Under Lord's questions, McKeown described how he had first been summoned to Jacobs Creek to identify whether the dead woman in the Land Cruiser was Michelle Nyce. After doing so, he and Detective Ortman had then gone to the house and been kept waiting ten minutes before Jonathan Nyce finally appeared.

Later that morning he and Ortman had taken a voluntary nine-page statement from Nyce. When Lord asked why he had not told him his Miranda rights, McKeown said there was no need.

"He was not under arrest," he explained. "He wasn't being charged."

On the second day of the Miranda hearing, Robin Lord called Jonathan Nyce's interrogator, Sergeant William Scull, to the stand.

Under Lord's questioning, Scull said he had asked Nyce at least four times during the two-hour interview if he required an attorney. Each time he said he did not want one, although mentioning several times that maybe he should seek legal advice.

"I truly believe Doctor Nyce wanted to tell us what happened to his wife," said Sergeant Scull.

He then described how Nyce had finally broken down and confessed to killing Michelle accidentally, after being told she had doused herself in Chanel perfume just before leaving Enyo to return home.

"He began to full–out cry," Scull told the judge. "And he stated that he didn't mean to kill her."

Then Robin Lord asked the detective why he hadn't passed on attorney Lee Engleman's phone number to her client, and relayed his message to stop talking to the police. Scull said he placed the number on a piece of paper in front of Nyce, who then pushed it away. He said he was not legally obliged to do anything further.

"I believed with Mr. Nyce's supreme intelligence," said Scull, with more than a hint of sarcasm, "I wouldn't have to convince Mr. Nyce of anything."

Free on bail, Jonathan Nyce arrived each morning at the Superior Court with his father, carrying a battered leather briefcase. He looked more like a lawyer than a defendant facing a first-degree murder charge. While on bail he was free to come and go as he pleased, and each lunchtime he and his father would walk across South Broad Street to lunch in a pizzeria.

The next day, Judge Mathesius ordered Jonathan Nyce's complete confession to be played in open court. For the first time, Nyce's own version of events were made public.

While the three cassette tapes were being played, Nyce often became emotional, turning red and holding his head in his hands.

"I wish she was alive," the judge heard him sobbing. "I wish everything would have stayed the same. I loved her very much. I still do."

Much of the confession—which took an hour and forty-five minutes to play—was inaudible to reporters sitting in the back of the court. But there were many sensational new details of the case that would make the front pages of both Trenton newspapers the next day.

"Nyce Confession Airs Marriage Struggles," trumpeted Lisa Coryell's Trenton *Times* story.

"Accused murderer Jonathan Nyce," it began, "spent the months prior to his wife's death trying to keep up with her penchant for partying and fun—spending late nights at dance clubs and taking Viagra."

Six days later, the pre-trial Miranda hearing reconvened, with Robin Lord calling Nyce's former attorney Lee Engleman to the stand. Engleman said Jonathan Nyce had left a message on his phone asking for legal assistance on the day of his wife's death.

"I have a serious problem," Nyce was heard saying in the message, which was played in court.

For the next two days they had played phone tag, until Sunday morning when Engleman discovered Nyce was at Hopewell Township Police Department.

Engleman said he had spoken to Michael Nyce, who informed him that Jonathan was being questioned by detectives. He then left a message for the police to stop the interrogation and have Nyce call him immediately. Engleman told Lord that police had ignored both instructions.

Assistant Prosecutor Doris Galuchie then asked the lawyer why he'd called Hopewell Township Police Department on the telephone, instead of going there in person.

"They don't have to act as your messenger," Galuchie told him. "Why didn't you take the next step and go?"

Engleman replied that he'd expected the police to honor his directive to stop the interrogation.

After the lunch break, Michael Nyce took the stand. Under oath he testified that Engleman had called his cell phone, asking him to get a message to his brother, telling him to keep quiet until he arrived.

On the fifth and final day of the hearing, Robin Lord wound up her case to declare Nyce's statement inadmissible at his upcoming murder trial, now scheduled to begin June 7. She accused the police of refusing to allow her client to have an attorney present at his interrogation, and claimed her client had "spill[ed] his guts," after Sergeant Scull had intimated it would improve his chances at any subsequent trial.

"The case law says you don't have to say any magic words," she told Judge Mathesius. "Any reasonable interpretation [of a request] will do."

Lord argued that when Nyce had told Sergeant Scull that maybe he should talk to an attorney, all questioning should have stopped. She claimed that instead he was told why an attorney might not be in his best interests, a direct violation of the Miranda rule.

For the prosecution, Doris Galuchie maintained that Nyce had never asked for an attorney, and when police had asked him if he wanted one, he'd said no.

"I cannot think of a fact pattern more illustrious of the police," she said, "doing exactly what they were supposed to do than the testimony we have heard."

Judge Mathesius ended the marathon Miranda hearing, asking both sides to submit their written arguments to him by April 11, promising to rule on them within a week.

A month later the judge issued a thirty-one-page ruling, deciding that jurors at Jonathan Nyce's upcoming murder trial would be allowed to hear his confession. In a major victory for the prosecution, the judge totally exonerated the police, finding that Nyce had been treated well and none of his legal rights had been denied.

"The police acted appropriately and within the limits of the law," wrote the judge. "At no time did an officer involved in this case overstep his bounds and negatively affect Nyce's constitutional rights; quite to the contrary there was an abundance of courtesy, professional respect and a substantial regard for the defendant as husband, witness and, finally, suspect. In every appropriate instance, Nyce was informed of his rights and thereafter waived them."

When Robin Lord learned of the ruling, she told Lisa Coryell of the Trenton *Times* that Judge Mathesius had made a mistake that would guarantee her client an appeal, in the unlikely event he was found guilty.

"The court erred," she declared. "Both [Dr. Nyce's] Fifth and Sixth Amendment rights were violated repeatedly by law enforcement members, as well as members of the prosecutor's office. The end result is a coerced statement that is inaccurate, unreliable and just not true."

Now that Judge Mathesius had ruled against all three of Robin Lord's motions, Jonathan Nyce's trial was ready to begin on the seventh of June—almost eighteen months after the tragic death of Michelle Nyce.

31

Jury Selection

On Tuesday, June 7, 2005, at 9:30 a.m., 150 prospective jurors assembled in the Ceremonial Courtroom, on the fourth floor of Mercer County Superior Court, to begin selecting a jury for the Jonathan Nyce murder trial.

Mercer County Superior Court's normal jury pool allotment for a murder trial is 85, but Judge Bill Mathesius had asked for more, taking into account his prior experiences with Defense Attorney Robin Lord.

"They don't like you to waste money on bringing in a lot of jurors," explained the judge. "But I knew Robin . . . so I said I want one hundred and fifty jurors and I got one hundred and fifty jurors."

Court officials were already speculating it would be the most complicated jury selection in Mercer County history, predicting it might take a week or more to find the required twelve jurors and four alternates.

Two floors below in Judge Bill Mathesius' courtroom, the defendant arrived early with his father Jonathan Jr., and lawyer Robin Lord, to agree on the questions for prospective jurors.

Although facing 30 years to life, Nyce looked calm and unfazed as he sat taking notes at the brief hearing. He was dressed in an immaculately pressed business suit, his well-groomed sandy gray hair neatly combed over his bald spot.

The trial was expected to last at least a month, and the case had already amassed a staggering five thousand pages of discovery. The prosecution had already given the judge notice of its intention to call ninety-four witnesses, and so far the defense planned twelve.

Both sides agreed there would be difficulties picking a jury, due to pre-arranged vacations and other commitments. And with all the media coverage the case had received both locally and nationally, it would be tough finding Mercer County residents who had never heard the name Jonathan Nyce.

"Obviously if you're alive in this county," said Mathesius, "you've heard of the case."

Both sides agreed the prospective jurors should be questioned about their views on adultery and divorce, as well as if they'd ever been to the Philippines and had any prior knowledge of the case.

Then everybody filed out of the courtroom to go two floors up where the 150 prospective jurors were waiting.

"It's wild," said Jonathan Nyce Jr. in the elevator on his way to the fourth floor. "It's a hard one."

It was a scorching hot day, and the packed Ceremonial Courtroom was sweltering. The largest courtroom in the four-story building, it is only used for big trials generating extensive media coverage. Court TV had expressed early interest in televising the Nyce trial gavel to gavel, but as the jury in the Michael Jackson child molestation trial was still out, they had passed.

To the left of the court at the defense bench sat Jonathan Nyce, flanked by his attorneys Robin Lord, Pat Whelan, their investigator John Coy and paralegal Tamara Melendez. To their right was the prosecution table, with Assistant Prosecutors Tom Meidt and Doris Galuchie next to Karen Ortman, who had recently been promoted to Sergeant, and Detective Matt Norton, who had taken over her old job in the prosecutor's office.

Behind the defense table sat Jonathan Nyce Jr. and Emma Nyce, who would be joined by various relatives and friends throughout the trial.

And at the front of the courtroom, with a large Stars and Stripes flag to his left and the yellow New Jersey State one to his right, was Judge Bill Mathesius, presiding over what would be his final criminal case. The sixty-five-year-old judge bore more than a passing resemblance to Warren Beatty, with his carefully blown-back gray hair and black robes.

He first thanked the prospective jurors for coming to this "sixty-year-old annex in a hundred-year-old ancient building." And then he advised them, if selected, to bring warm clothes, as the Ceremonial Courtroom had its "own climate," bearing little relation to the temperature outside.

Then the judge asked who had heard of the Jonathan Nyce case, and almost half the jury pool raised their hands. Selection then began and as the court clerk called each of their numbers, the prospective jurors got up from their seats in the public gallery to go into the jury box to the right of the courtroom by the door. There they would be questioned by the two prosecutors, who had twelve challenges, and Robin Lord, with twenty.

By the end of the first day of selection, the prosecution had eliminated seven candidates and the defense six, including an FBI employee and a retired serviceman who had once served in the Philippines.

The next morning when the remaining potential jurors were seated, Judge Mathesius admitted forgetting to instruct them not to read newspaper accounts of the case. And when he asked how many had read media coverage of the previous day's selection process, the majority admitted they had.

Robin Lord then moved to have the entire pool dismissed, complaining that one prospective juror had actually read a newspaper account of the case aloud in the jury room the day before. To repair any damage, the judge had to spend additional time questioning each member of the pool to see if they had been prejudiced by exposure to trial coverage.

"I'm kind of kicking myself in the rear for not mentioning this," he told the court.

By 5:30 that afternoon, both sides had agreed on a jury. Ironically the final juror selected was the very last one left in the original 150-strong jury pool, who, like Jonathan Nyce, happened to be a biophysicist with a Ph.D.

Out of the selected jurors, fifteen were white and only one black. They included a retired civil engineer, a construction superintendent, a juvenile corrections officer, a commercial pilot and a nurse's aid.

Before dismissing them, Judge Mathesius ordered the sixteen jurors to be back in their seats at 10:30 the next morning for opening statements.

32

"What Is the Price of Infidelity?"

Jonathan Nyce's much anticipated trial began with an explosion of legal pyrotechnics, in both the prosecution and the defense opening statements.

Outside, there was a heat wave, with temperatures in the high 80s, as they had been for almost a week. The curtains of the Ceremonial Courtroom were drawn, shutting out the blazing sun.

It was standing room only when the defendant walked in with his father, brother David and attorney Robin Lord, just after 10:15 a.m.

Looking gaunt and apprehensive, Nyce carried a shabby old leather bag, while Lord, totally focused on the daunting task at hand, wheeled in several boxes of legal papers she'd brought from her law offices.

The genial sheriff's court officer James Freeman, who was in charge of the courtroom, checked everybody coming in at the door with a metal detector. The front row of the public gallery was packed with television and newspaper reporters. In front of the jury box, by the entrance to the court, were TV cameras and crews from Channel 6, the

Philadelphia ABC affiliate, and a local New Jersey cable news channel.

At exactly 10:30 there was a hushed silence, and everybody stood up as Judge Bill Mathesius walked into the courtroom, taking his seat on the proscenium, overlooking his court. After attending to a few minor matters of court business, he sent for the jury, who filed in, taking their numbered seats in the jury box.

Then the judge asked Assistant Prosecutor Doris Galuchie to proceed with her opening statement. Dressed in a smart suit and glasses, her short hair brushed back, the bookish-looking Galuchie stood up from the prosecution bench, and walked towards the sixteen jurors, already giving her their full attention.

"What is the price of infidelity?" she asked, looking straight at the jury. "What is the cost of betrayal? What penalty is imposed when a wife is caught cheating on her husband?

"When you're Mrs. Jonathan Nyce, you pay for your extra-marital indiscretions with your life. When you're Mrs. Jonathan Nyce, your husband brutally beats you to death by smashing your skull into a concrete floor. When you're Mrs. Jonathan Nyce, you die at the age of thirty-four in your own home, while your children are upstairs sleeping. When you're Mrs. Jonathan Nyce, your husband doesn't just kill you, he thereafter maligns your character and lies to the police, your family and your friends, all in an effort to literally get away with your murder."

Galuchie told the jury Jonathan Nyce had first met Michelle when she was 21 and half his age, and how they had married in the Philippines. She described how Nyce's business meant he was often away from home traveling, leaving Michelle "lonely and unhappy."

Then, in the summer of 2002, Michelle had "befriended" a gardener, whose nickname was Enyo. They had embarked on a sexual affair and her husband had found out. On the last night of her life, Galuchie told the jury, Michelle had met Enyo after finishing work at Macy's, and they'd had sex in the Mount's Motel on Route 1.

Afterwards Michelle had taken a shower and returned home.

"Waiting for her," said the assistant prosecutor, "was a jealous and angry defendant. They argued, the defendant demanding to know what she had been doing. Michelle finally told the defendant that she was leaving him. She went so far as to pack a suitcase during their argument."

Galuchie described how Michelle had taken the suitcase into the garage and had tried to place it into her Toyota Land Cruiser, and was then attacked by her husband.

"She was never able to leave the defendant," she told the jury. "She may have tried to get in the car, but the defendant yanked her out. [He] grabbed Michelle and threw her down into the concrete, smashing her skull."

She told the jury they would hear about terrible injuries Jonathan Nyce had inflicted on his wife. There were three "gaping lacerations" to her forehead and another deep one at the top of her head, as well as several fractures to her skull, one of which was more than five inches long. She had also suffered brain injuries, a broken bone in her face, and internal injuries, as well as numerous bruises and abrasions all over her body.

"While the defendant was inflicting these fatal blows," she said, "Michelle's kids were upstairs sleeping."

She then moved on to the ghoulish way Nyce tried to cover up his crime, by loading his wife's dead body in the Land Cruiser. He'd then driven her around the snowy rural roads of Hopewell Township, searching for a suitable place to stage "an accident."

"Picture this, if you will," she asked the jury, many of whom were taking notes. "Michelle's dead body is actually placed in the driver's seat of the car by the defendant. He sits in the passenger seat, leaning over her, steering the car and operating the gas and brake pedals with a long ice scraper. This is how he chose to operate."

She said Nyce had finally found a break in the fence along Jacobs Creek Road, and driven the vehicle down a steep embankment into the creek below. Then he calmly got out of the Land Cruiser and walked home through the snow, leaving Michelle's body to be discovered the next morning, frozen solid.

But once he reached home he had much work to do, said the assistant prosecutor.

"He had a lot of blood to clean up," she explained. "There [was] blood all over that garage."

She told the jury Nyce had used hydrogen peroxide, paper towels and rags to clean up his wife's blood, most of which were later found by the police. After he had finished, he went upstairs to bed with his children, sleeping soundly until the next morning.

She said that when Michelle's body had been discovered and police first went to interview him at his house, Nyce was more interested in telling them about Enyo and pointing the finger at him. She said he had repeatedly lied to police, even about how he had first met Michelle. And he had tried to portray his wife as "psychologically unstable," sex-mad and "bi-polar," although she was a "normal, sweet young woman."

But then, said the assistant prosecutor, Nyce had begun to slip up on his own lies. First he had told Detective Dan McKeown he had last seen Michelle the previous afternoon, and later saying they had "fought" about her moving out that night.

"[That was the] first of many mistakes you'll hear from Jonathan Nyce," she said.

Finishing up, Galuchie urged the jury to focus on the "two real issues" of this case: Did Jonathan Nyce murder his wife? And did he tamper with the evidence to try to cover it up?

The fact that Michelle had had an affair was irrelevant, she said, except as a motive for her murder.

"Infidelity never justifies murder," declared Galuchie. "Personal opinions regarding Michelle's affair have no place in this case."

She said the trial was all about the defendant's "conduct" and whether he murdered his wife.

"Michelle cannot tell you what happened the night she

died," she said. "Listen as the evidence speaks for her. Listen as the evidence establishes that the six-foot-four two hundred and forty-pound defendant threw his five-foot-two one hundred pound wife head first into a concrete floor. Listen as the evidence tells you that Michelle struggled to save her own life. Listen as the evidence tells you that the defendant had no problem accusing innocent people of the murder he committed.

"Jonathan Nyce thought he was smart enough to fool everyone, especially the police. But he didn't fool them, simply because he could not keep track of his lies."

Then at 11:45 a.m., after almost an hour on her feet, Doris Galuchie sat down and Robin Lord rose from the defense bench and marched towards the jury.

Wearing a smart lime-green jacket and matching shirt, a leopard-spotted scarf loosely tied around her waist, she began addressing the jury in an almost inaudible whisper.

"Jonathan Nyce, you're here for your wife's sexual affairs," she began, parodying the prosecution's opening remarks. "You are seated at that table for a crime you did not commit."

Then, raising her voice as she moved closer to the jury: "Jonathan Nyce did not murder his wife. This was a tragic and unfortunate accident by a woman who was being confronted for having a sexual liaison that Mr. Nyce had complained about in the past to authorities and to her."

Then, in an attempt to show the jury how her client had feared for his life, Lord took out the fax Nyce had sent Detective Dan McKeown in August 2003, complaining that Enyo was stalking him, and he felt threatened.

But as she began to read from it, a furious Judge Mathesius ordered her to stop, calling an immediate sidebar. He then ordered it stricken from the court records, telling the jury to disregard it.

Then Lord continued, telling the jury to focus on what had happened in the garage on the night of January 16, 2004.

"But for the panic of Jonathan Nyce," she told them, "we wouldn't be here today. Because a man found himself in such a horrible, heart-wrenching situation, he panicked. The death of Michelle Nyce was a sad and unfortunate accident, and the misjudgment of Mr. Nyce is why we're here today."

Then at midday, after taking just fifteen-minutes to address the jury, Robin Nyce returned to the defense desk. Judge Mathesius called a lunch break, telling the jury to be back by 1:30 p.m., when the first witnesses would take the stand.

The state first called PSE&G maintenance worker Richard Archer, who had discovered Michelle Nyce's body in the frozen creek. In his direct examination, Assistant Prosecutor Tom Meidt took Archer through the nightmarish circumstances of finding her body.

Archer likened finding Michelle to a "horror flick" or "a concentration camp.

"We see people all the time in car accidents, dead people," he told the jury. "This was real different. [It's been] burned in my mind."

Jonathan Nyce looked detached and composed, listening intently to Archer and taking the occasional note on his yellow legal pad.

The state's next witness was Hopewell Township Police Department Officer Lincoln Karnoff, who had been called out to 1 Keithwood Court at 6:30 a.m. that Friday, when the alarm had gone off. The eighteen-year veteran told Doris Galuchie he had responded to the alarm at 7:03 a.m., seeing tire tracks running down the front lawn by the garage doors.

He'd then walked around the house in a counterclockwise direction, checking doors and windows for any signs of a break-in. When he was satisfied everything was fine, he had left.

"I made no attempt to gain entrance to the house," he said. "I didn't ring the bell."

Then Lord stood up to cross-examine him, asking the prosecution for the original police report, explaining that five thousand pages of discovery was too much to lug into court. She asked Officer Karnoff why he hadn't mentioned seeing the tire tracks in his report.

"I didn't recall seeing tire tracks in the report," the officer explained. "Then I recognized I did. I had seen them, but did not make a mental note."

Lord asked if he had checked to see if there were any windows open. When he said he hadn't, Lord bared her claws to the jury for the first time.

"Do you think that warms the cockles of the hearts of all those who live in Hopewell Township?" she asked sarcastically.

Driving home her point, Lord then asked about his training for responding to alarm calls, and whether he'd been taught to knock on doors and question occupants.

"I responded to a burglar alarm," Karnoff replied. "I checked security."

"Is that how you're trained at the Trenton Police Academy?" she asked, as she returned to the defense table.

Following afternoon break the jury heard from Officer Michael Sherman of the Hopewell Township P.D., who had been one of the first to the crash site and had helped secure it. In his direct examination, Tom Meidt gave the jury their first glimpse of Michelle's dead body in the Land Cruiser, when he projected a police picture on a screen, taken soon after she was discovered.

Sitting at the defense table, Jonathan Nyce was clearly affected by the gruesome photograph of his dead wife, slumped in her own blood across the front seat of the SUV.

"Blood was on the running board," said Officer Sherman, "passenger door, floor, steering wheel and on the back door."

During her cross, Robin Lord began carefully planting the seed of her defense for the jury—that police had mismanaged the crime scene. She got Sherman to admit that when the forensic team had later fingerprinted the vehicle, they had found another officer's print on it.

♦ ♦ ♦

The next witness was Sergeant Thomas Keyes, of the New Jersey State Police CSI Unit. Before she began her direct, Galuchie turned to the jury, telling them to forget anything they might have seen on television about CSI.

Then she asked the ten-year CSI veteran to explain crime scene investigation to the jury.

"CSI is responsible for processing crime scene," said Sergeant Keyes. "Photography, collecting items of evidence, fingerprints, videography and blood pattern analysis."

Sergeant Keyes said he had been assigned to take aerial photographs of the Jacobs Creek crash site on Friday morning. He had flown over it in a helicopter, taking twenty-four photos.

After landing he'd visited the site, using a surveyor's Impulse laser range finder to measure the crime scene, as well as making rough sketches.

At 3:50, after Sergeant Keyes was dismissed, the prosecution had no further witnesses ready, to the obvious annoyance of Judge Mathesius. As he recessed until 9:00 the following Tuesday morning, he told the jury they would not be permitted to smoke in the jury room during breaks.

"I may add a day or two to your lives," he said. "At lunchtime you can roam free."

A few minutes later, a forlorn Jonathan Nyce was waiting by himself outside in the corridor for the elevator, and was asked how he was holding up.

"My spirits are good," he said almost meekly.

The record heat wave raged through the weekend. By 9:00 a.m. Tuesday, when Tom Meidt and Doris Galuchie arrived at the Ceremonial Courtroom, it was already near 90 degrees on South Broad Street. Fifteen minutes later an agitated-looking Robin Lord walked in with Jonathan Nyce, taking their places at the defense table.

Judge Mathesius entered court as Lord was still sorting through her papers, and he admonished her for being late.

"The court is eighteen minutes late," chided the judge. "I'm a little bit irritated you should be as late as you were. It's not the defendant's fault, as he was standing outside your office at 8:30 a.m. when I saw him. I hope this is the last time counsel causes complications for the jury."

"I apologize," replied Robin Lord. "I didn't anticipate a situation with traffic."

At 9:45, after some routine court business, the jury finally took their seats in their box.

"Good morning, ladies and gentlemen of the jury," said the judge. "There were some transportation troubles. I apologize."

The prosecution's next witness was Sergeant Michael Cseremsak, of the Hopewell Township Police Department. Under Doris Galuchie's questioning, Cseremsak told the jury how he had initially gone to the crash site before being sent to 1 Keithwood Court with Officer Sherman to try to identify the dead woman.

When he'd rung the bell, Trevor and Samantha Nyce had answered, saying neither of their parents were at home. On Jonathan Nyce's return, they met him in the driveway, following his Hummer 2 to the front door. But Cseremsak noticed he had closed the garage door with his remote control, as if trying to hide something in there.

The officer described the defendant as looking "disheveled," with messy hair and several fly buttons of his jeans open. Nyce had said Michelle had worked the previous night's shift at Macy's, and was then going out with a friend. She had told him she'd be home by 1:00 a.m., the defendant had said, adding that that usually meant 2:00 a.m., and sometimes she didn't come home at all.

Cseremsak told the jury he was suspicious and called his supervisor, who told him to read Nyce his Miranda rights.

"I went into the dining room and talked with Officer Sherman about the conversation," said Cseremsak. "I asked him to turn on the in-car video camera and microphone."

During her cross-examination, Robin Lord challenged Cseremsak on his assertion that the defendant did not appear to be under the influence of any drugs that morning.

"Did you receive any training at the police academy of how to identify anyone under prescription drugs?" she asked. "Have you ever seen anyone under the influence of Ativan? Did he sound like he was a zombie?"

Immediately Galuchie stood up to object, but was overruled by Judge Mathesius.

"He was very cooperative," said Cseremsak. "He communicated fine."

After the morning break, during Doris Galuchie's re-direct, the poor-quality videotape of Jonathan Nyce's first encounter with police after Michelle's death was played in the courtroom. Against a backdrop of the snow-covered 1 Keithwood Court, with a Stars and Stripes flapping on a flagpole in front, much of the sound was inaudible.

As the jury watched the tape in rapt concentration, Nyce, head in his hands, repeatedly dabbed his eyes, as if close to tears.

The state's next witness was Detective Dan McKeown, the lead detective on the case. The impeccably dressed shaven-headed detective told how he had been called in to identify Michelle's body, due to his previous encounter with the family six months earlier.

After identifying the body, Detective McKeown and Detective Karen Ortman had gone to interview Jonathan Nyce, arriving as Officers Cseremsak and Sherman were leaving.

After an initial talk, Nyce had agreed to accompany them to Hopewell Township Police Department, where they had taken a ten-page statement.

The tape of the defendant's first statement was played to the jury. At one point, while Nyce is discussing Michelle's affair with Enyo, Judge Mathesius rose to his feet, listening in rapt attention.

After lunch Galuchie asked McKeown about driving Nyce to Timberlane School after the statement, to collect his son Alex.

"As we were walking in," said the detective, "he offered, 'We were getting along so well at that time. We argued when she said she was going to get a place of her own.'

"I asked him the last time they had discussed that and he said, 'Last night.'"

But when he saw Alex approaching, McKeown changed the subject, thinking it would be inappropriate to continue in front of the boy.

Then Galuchie questioned the detective about Nyce's July 2003 allegations that Enyo had blackmailed him for half a million dollars. McKeown explained that after interviewing Jonathan and Michelle Nyce, and Enyo, he had then investigated these claims for almost a month.

When pressed by Galuchie as to why he had refused to sign a criminal complaint against Enyo, Detective McKeown told the jury, "I didn't sign the complaint, because I didn't think Mr. Nyce was being completely honest with regard to the circumstances." He had found Nyce's allegations to be "unfounded."

After the afternoon break, Robin Lord cross-examined the lead detective, attempting damage control. The courtroom's air conditioning had broken down and as the afternoon progressed, it became increasingly hot and uncomfortable.

"Did Dr. Nyce ever express a threat regarding his children and family?" asked Lord.

"He never expressed a fear to me," replied the detective.

"This letter says to the contrary," said the defense attorney, pulling out her client's August 2003 fax again and clearly showing it to the jury.

Galuchie rose to her feet to object, questioning the relevance and admissibility of the fax. A visibly angry Judge Mathesius sustained her objection, warning Lord not to pursue this line of questioning any further.

"You've already gotten more in about this than you're entitled," he reprimanded.

Then Lord changed tack, asking the detective, "Do you think Dr. Nyce had reason to fear a man who had at least five aliases, who had three Social Security numbers, and who was having an affair with his wife?"

At 3:30, a visibly irritated Judge Mathesius called both counsels into a heated twenty-minute sidebar, as the jury looked on in amazement. At one point Judge Mathesius could be heard shouting at Lord, "Don't you argue with me!"

When the court reconvened, Lord doggedly continued questioning Detective McKeown over why he had not investigated Enyo further. This immediately brought another round of objections by Galuchie. As Judge Mathesius told the defender that aliases were more appropriate to TV dramas like *Law & Order* than his court, Robin Lord turned towards the jury and, out of the judge's sight, rolled her eyes in apparent disbelief.

Finally Doris Galuchie complained to the judge, saying, "This is a trial within a trial, within a trial!"

At 4:05 p.m., after yet another lengthy and contentious sidebar, Judge Mathesius dismissed the jury for the day.

"Apparently there's a difficulty in communication," he told them. "It's been a long day—one-hundred degrees outside and one hundred and fifty degrees inside."

33

The Ladies' Man

On the third day of the trial—Wednesday, June 15— there was much excitement in the Ceremonial Court- room, in anticipation of the mysterious Enyo, who was due to testify. When Robin Lord arrived with her client at 9:00 a.m. sharp, several camera crews were already setting up equipment. There were twice as many reporters as the previous day, including *The New York Times*, and *The National Enquirer* had sent ace reporter Richard Gooding.

A dozen female court employees lined the public gallery, curious to see what Michelle's lover looked like. Also among the spectators was Miguel deJesus' common-law wife Patricia Abad, and Lauren Metzger, the woman who had once successfully sued him for child support.

That morning the courtroom was like a sauna, as the air conditioning had broken down, and several spectators were fanning themselves with the morning newspaper.

"I can't work in here," said one reporter. "It's going to be one hundred degrees."

The word from the Mercer County Sheriff's Office was

that a belt had broken on the cooling system, and a replacement was on its way.

But perhaps the coolest person in the court was Jonathan Nyce, who looked unflappable, as he shared a joke with his attorney at the defense table. He was dressed in a gray suit, several sizes too big, a white shirt and a red-and-black-striped tie. Up to this point he had been taking copious notes of the proceedings, but Robin Lord had told him to stop, saying it might make the jury think he was too intelligent.

After meeting both counsels in chambers, Judge Mathesius brought in the jury at 9:45, immediately apologizing for the sweltering courtroom.

"We are aware of the heat situation in court," he told the jury. "It has now been fixed and we will soon have cool air in here."

Then Detective Dan McKeown was recalled to the stand and Robin Lord continued her cross-examination. Resisting the temptation to continue chipping away at Enyo's credibility, she began trying to demean McKeown's detective skills.

As she would do with many detectives over the course of the trial, Robin Lord questioned McKeown about specific aspects of the investigation he was not involved in. Zeroing in on Michelle's three cell phones discovered in the Land Cruiser, Lord asked if he had identified who had left the eighteen messages found on them.

"I was not involved in determining who the individuals were," he told her.

"How many homicides have you investigated?" she asked.

"This was the first one," said the detective.

"How many extortions?" came her sarcastic follow-up.

"I don't know," said Detective McKeown, holding his own.

At 11:40 a.m. Miguel deJesus walked slowly into the courtroom, sitting in the witness stand, just fifteen yards away from Jonathan Nyce at the defense table. When their eyes first met, Nyce glared angrily at the man he blamed for all his woes. An uncomfortable-looking Enyo stared down at the floor, and began running his hands over his face.

Wearing a casual green jacket, an open-neck white shirt and gray baggy trousers, the gardener had a single gray streak running through his short brown hair.

Before recalling the jury, the judge interviewed deJesus to determine if an interpreter would be needed.

Speaking in a heavy accent, Michelle Nyce's 35-year-old boyfriend told the judge he'd been in America for fourteen years, working for the Ostrich Nursery for the last five.

"I run a crew of three to five people," he said proudly.

Then, after a ten-minute sidebar where it was agreed Enyo's English was good enough without a translator, the jury was seated.

"Mr. deJesus, you understand English very well," said Judge Mathesius. "If there are complications and you have difficulty expressing yourself, and a translator is needed, we will use one."

Then Tom Meidt began his direct examination, asking Enyo how he had first met Michelle. Enyo replied that he had been sent to 1 Keithwood Court in 2001 to plant trees, but had not gotten to know her until a year later, when he'd returned to plant more.

He claimed Michelle had pursued him, asking for his cell phone number and saying she wanted to be his friend. They had started talking regularly on the phone and meeting in restaurants or bars after work for drinks.

For the first six months, he told the court, it was purely platonic. But then, in January 2003, they had begun a sexual relationship. At that point in his testimony, his tearful wife, Patricia Abad, got up from the public gallery, walking out of the courtroom.

Enyo said that in July 2003, Jonathan Nyce had called him on his cell phone, saying he knew about the affair.

"He said, 'I want you to keep away from my wife,' " he told the jury, as he fidgeted, avoiding all eye contact with the defendant. " 'If you put your hands on my wife, you're going to be a dead man.' "

Two hours later Enyo called Nyce back, asking if he was looking for him. When Nyce said he wanted Alexander Castaneda, he denied being that person. He then called Michelle on her cell phone, saying her husband knew everything and it was a "big problem," and they should stop seeing each other.

According to deJesus, Michelle had refused to take no for an answer, calling him for the next two months to arrange a meeting. Then in August, Nyce had charged him with harassment, resulting in a hearing at Hopewell Township Municipal Court, where the complaint was dismissed on condition he have no contact with Michelle and her family for two years.

As Jonathan Nyce glared angrily at him across the courtroom, deJesus testified that Michelle had begun calling him again after the court hearing. Then a month later he had taken pity on her, as she sounded "sad," agreeing to see her again.

On their next meeting, they'd talked for fifteen minutes and were not intimate. But at the end of September, after several more meetings, they'd resumed having sex, at a seedy motel on Route 130. Over the next three months they met six or seven times, he said, emphasizing that they did not have sex every time, as they were friends.

Tom Meidt asked Enyo about the evening of January 15, 2004, and his last encounter with Michelle. The gardener said he'd been plowing snow when she called at about 5:30 p.m., asking if they could meet that night. He told her he'd call her later and telephoned about 9:00, arranging to meet her in the parking lot in front of Applebee's restaurant.

Then they had gone to Mount's Motel and had sex. As he described renting the room by the hour, Jonathan Nyce's face flushed red with anger, looking like he might get up and attack Enyo at any moment.

"Did you cause any marks on her body, or hurt her?" asked Meidt.

"No," replied deJesus.

Then the assistant prosecutor showed Enyo eighteen pictures of different areas of Michelle's naked body, displaying her injuries. As each came on the screen, he asked if she'd had that injury when he'd last seen her. He said she had not to every one.

"Did Michelle get a phone call while you were in the motel?" asked Meidt.

"[Jonathan] called her on her cell phone," said Enyo. "She didn't answer. Then she turned it off."

He said that after the motel manager had called at midnight, saying their time was up, they had taken a shower together, and Michelle had put on perfume, before leaving to drive home in her Land Cruiser.

"We said goodbye and she left," he told the jury. "We parted at twelve-thirty a.m."

It was late afternoon when Robin Lord began her cross-examination. Another belt had broken on the air conditioner. It was becoming increasingly warm in the courtroom, and would soon get even hotter, as Lord went straight on the attack.

"Did you attempt to extort half a million dollars from Jonathan Nyce in July 2003?" was her first question.

"No," said deJesus, tugging at his shirt collar and looking uncomfortable.

"You had a particular interest in the Nyces' financial situation, did you not, sir?" was her follow-up.

"No."

"You were aware that their house was on the market for one-point-six million dollars. [You knew] about the jewelry Michelle was wearing. You even knew the purchase price of a watch she wore on her wrist, that being eleven hundred dollars."

"No," said Enyo, running his hands over his face and looking even more ill-at-ease.

"Are you Puerto Rican?" Lord asked next.

"Yes."

"Do you admit telling others that you were born in

Guatemala, and you even lied to police about where you come from?"

"I never told people I was from Guatemala," said the landscaper defiantly.

Then Lord cornered him, saying that he had told this to Judge Bonnie Johnson when he had appeared at Hopewell Township Municipal Court.

"I lied, yes," he conceded.

She then began attacking him for his use of several aliases, pointing out that Michelle only knew him as Alexander Castaneda.

"That's not my name," he said.

When prosecutors objected to her line of questioning, an angry Judge Mathesius ordered both counsels to a sidebar, and could be heard telling them he did not want to create "a thousand little trials."

Returning from sidebar, Lord continued questioning Enyo about his use of aliases, further infuriating the judge.

"What do you care why he uses different names?" the judge chastised Lord in front of the jury. "It's not relevant to this case. Was I speaking to myself, Miss Lord? The Supreme Court, the World Court in the Hague might think differently, but that's my rule!"

Lord passionately argued the witnesses' history of aliases was important, as her client believed he posed a real threat to him and his family. She then repeated for the jury's benefit his use of several different Social Security numbers and dates of birth.

"Come to sidebar!" screamed Judge Mathesius, hurling his pen down on his desk in a fit of pique.

The jury looked astonished as Judge Mathesius and Robin Lord continued the argument at sidebar. Finally, when they retook their places, Judge Mathesius turned to the defense counsel, curtly saying, "Next subject, thank you," as if daring her to defy him.

Lord then moved on to the night of Michelle Nyce's death.

"The incident at Mount's Motel," she asked. "You paid for two hours. It's by the hour?"

But she got no further, as her question was punctuated by the sound of a cell phone going off in the courtroom.

"Next time that happens," said the irritated judge, "It's going to cost the person fifty bucks."

"In your statement," continued the defender, "you said you got blood on your penis?"

After he agreed that he had, Lord asked if Michelle had been wearing her wedding ring that night.

"Yes," he said. "We showered together. Michelle was wearing her wedding ring. I remember seeing rings."

On re-direct Tom Meidt asked deJesus whether the blood on his penis had come from Michelle's period, and he said it had.

But then, just as Judge Mathesius was about to dismiss the witness, Robin Lord's partner Pat Whelan had a word in her ear.

"Did you wear a condom?" she asked, rising from her chair.

"No," said deJesus, who was then allowed to step down from his ordeal and leave the courtroom, managing to avoid reporters.

That night the thirteen-day heat wave finally broke, and Thursday morning, the fourth day of the trial, was comfortably cool, in the 70s. Soon after 9:00 a.m., Jonathan Nyce strolled into court with his father and two aunts. He appeared to have had a haircut, and his shortly cropped grayish blonde hair only made his bald spot more pronounced. Then Robin Lord, wearing a black jacket with a silver star-shaped broach, wheeled her large boxes of discovery up to the defense table, apparently recovered from the contentious day before.

That day the prosecution would call three detectives from the New Jersey State Police who had played different roles in the Jonathan Nyce investigation.

First up was Detective Geoffrey Noble of the Major Crimes Unit.

The squat, bald-headed ten-year veteran told Doris

Galuchie how he had been assigned to liaise between all the different agencies, ensuring information was shared.

"I managed the scene," he explained. "I kept up constant communication [with all personnel] and relayed information."

He had also been given the assignment of investigating Miguel deJesus, interviewing him with Detective Dan McKeown late Saturday afternoon. Afterwards he'd gone and re-traced Enyo's route the night of Michelle's death, which all checked out.

After morning break, Robin Lord questioned Detective Noble about his investigative visit to Mount's Motel.

"There was sex on a round table?" she asked, as Tom Meidt immediately objected, prompting Judge Mathesius to call a sidebar, to the amusement of several jurors who began giggling.

After some debate the judge sustained the objection.

"Bruises can occur in hitting a table?" continued Lord, prompting another objection from the prosecution, which was sustained.

Refusing to be diverted from her course of questioning, Lord asked Detective Noble, "Did you establish if there were any round tables?"

Once again Meidt stood up to object, and the judge again refused the question.

Then Lord focused on the crash site, projecting graphic color photographs of Michelle's injuries on a large white screen, across from the jury box. In what would become a pivotal part of the defense, Lord endeavored to show the jury that many of Michelle's bruises might have been caused by something other than Jonathan Nyce. It was a theme she would return to again and again, in an attempt to mitigate the injuries caused by her client in the garage.

She asked the detective about the Land Cruiser's descent down the embankment into the creek, and whether it had struck anything.

"It appeared the vehicle hit objects on its way down," said Noble. "Three green metal chairs . . . one was on its side, and there was green transfer paint on the vehicle."

Then she asked Detective Noble if Enyo had mentioned having sex with Michelle once in her home.

"Yes," said the detective, reading his interview notes. "He said he had sex one time in her home. She said her husband was away. Her father was there. I spoke to her father."

At the end of her cross, Robin Lord relentlessly questioned Noble about Enyo's alleged interest in Jonathan Nyce's finances, to a flurry of successful objections by Tom Meidt. Lord finally threw up her arms in frustration at the judge's repeated rulings against her.

"The jury is seeing pathos appearing on your face, Miss Lord," chided Judge Mathesius. "Be a little more stoic. This is not Drama one-o-one."

Next on the stand was Detective Sergeant Jeffrey Kronenfeld, who told the jury how police had immediately suspected foul play at the crash site, with Jonathan Nyce soon coming under suspicion. He testified that he had been among the first officers in the Nyce garage on Saturday evening, testifying that there had obviously been a clean-up, and the floor had been painted green, to cover up blood evidence.

"Someone had attempted to clean the floor," he testified. "There was some reddish brown smears on the floor, the snow blower, wet-vac and a green recycling bucket. In the laundry area was red-tinged free-standing water in the washing basin."

He had gone back the following day, after Jonathan Nyce's statement telling where he had hidden some of the evidence.

"On entering the basement," he told the jury, "we moved a set of file cabinets in front of a chimney flue, and there was a black metal door. Inside was a plastic bag with paper towels wet with blood."

Two days later, on Tuesday, January 20, he and other detectives had returned to the house, discovering portions of a cut-up shoe sole scattered around the basement.

"[That] was pretty significant," he testified.

* * *

The final witness of the day was Detective John Ryan of the New Jersey State Police CSI Unit, who described to the jury how Michelle's body had looked when she was found frozen in the creek.

"The victim was slumped over to the right on the front driver's seat, her hands in front of her," he testified. "She was wearing black . . . and in her clenched left hand we found hair and fibers."

At 4:10 p.m. Judge Mathesius recessed for the day, telling Detective Sergeant Ryan to resume his testimony the following Tuesday.

"Ladies and gentlemen, you did a fine job, and took lots of notes," Judge Mathesius told the jury before they filed out.

On Friday morning, Robin Lord led her defense team to Jacobs Creek on an exploratory mission, to gauge the depth of the embankment. But first they tipped off the press, and Lisa Coryell of the Trenton *Times* accompanied Lord, John Coy and Tamara Melendez on a walk through the crash site.

It was four days before the official start of summer, and the scene was very different from the sub-zero snow conditions eighteen months earlier.

"I came here to refresh my recollection as to how steep the twenty-foot drop is," Lord told Coryell. "We believe it is significant."

The following week Robin Lord would officially request Judge Mathesius conduct a field trip to the crash site for the jury, so they too could see the scene of the crime first-hand. And that request would dramatically change the whole course of the trial.

34

"Your Stainless Steel Heart"

As the Jonathan Nyce trial moved into its third week, the prosecution called more police officers to the stand to bolster its case. On Tuesday morning Detective John Ryan resumed testifying and Tom Meidt asked him about the incongruity between Michelle Nyce's horrific injuries and the barely scratched Land Cruiser.

For the first time in the trial the jury was shown a graphic close-up of Michelle's bruised and bloody face, her long hair matted behind her in blood. Jonathan Nyce recoiled in horror at the defense table, taking out a handkerchief to dab his eyes, and had to be comforted by Robin Lord.

Then, in one of the most dramatic moments of the trial so far, the assistant prosecutor asked Detective Ryan about a wooden baseball bat found in the garage, attempting to introduce it as evidence.

"We had no idea what caused the injuries to the victim's head," Detective Ryan explained, "and [the bat] had a dark-colored stain on it, so we collected it."

As Ryan removed the bat from a long brown evidence bag and showed it to the jury, Lord stood up to object. After a lengthy sidebar, in a rare victory for the defense, Judge Mathesius ruled that the baseball bat could not be introduced as evidence.

In the morning break, reporters flocked to the prosecution table, asking about the significance of the baseball bat. But, though both prosecutors refused to discuss it, they hinted that its importance would become clearer as the trial progressed.

After a twenty-minute break, Tom Meidt questioned the detective about evidence found at the Nyce house. And he was asked about a poem Jonathan Nyce had penned for his wife two days after he first discovered her affair with Enyo.

Detective Ryan testified that the poem had been found in a desk in the defendant's office.

"We opened the desk drawer in the first-floor office," he told the jury. "There was a handwritten letter dated seven/twelve/zero three."

Then Meidt projected a photograph of the letter onto the screen, asking the detective to read it aloud for the jury.

"*Michelle:*

Your stainless steel heart,
Like a knife, rips open my soul
To bleed, unattended, dying.
With another man's semen
Still warm within your belly,
You call me on the telephone
And tell me not to worry.
When, oh when, will my dying end?"

The detective then told the jury how investigators had also discovered a revolver and three magazines of ammunition on a bookcase nearby. And upstairs in a woman's closet in the master bedroom, they had found Jonathan Nyce's forged birth and marriage certificates, altered to make him appear eight years younger than he really was.

The jury was then shown a picture of the electric scroll

saw found in the basement, used by Nyce to cut up the soles of the shoes he'd been wearing the night of Michelle's death.

"As a result of Mr. Nyce's statement," Ryan told the jury, "we had continued searching for footwear which could have made [the footprints at the crash site]. There were fourteen separate cut-up pieces scattered all over the basement. Two of the sections were found in a toy box also containing Christmas trees and Christmas lights."

Detective Ryan also explained that the soles had apparently been removed from a size 12 pair of Brahma boots, and then glued to a pair of moccasins, also found in the basement. Then the soles had been removed a second time, and cut up and hidden.

After lunch, Robin Lord cross-examined the detective, attempting to pick holes in the police investigation. She asked Ryan about a "white residue" found on the garage floor, which investigators had thought was connected with the clean-up. Lord asked why it had not been analyzed, suggesting it may simply have been street salt.

Then Lord repeatedly asked the detective if the Land Cruiser had been "airborne," during its twenty-foot journey into Jacobs Creek. The detective said he couldn't be certain, but a key point of the defense, that Michelle's injuries could have been caused outside the garage during the drive, was reinforced to the jury.

On Wednesday, June 22, Detective William Scull took the stand, as the prelude to the playing of Jonathan Nyce's controversial confession to the jury. Smartly dressed in a brown suit and blue floral tie, the youthful New Jersey State Trooper was an important witness for the state. During his two days on the witness stand, Detective Scull would often talk directly to the jury, as if taking them into his confidence.

He told Doris Galuchie he had been assigned to interview the defendant soon after he became the prime suspect. In preparation for the interview, Scull had visited the crash site, attended Michelle Nyce's autopsy and spent time at 1 Keithwood Court, during the first Saturday search.

On Sunday, January 18, 2004, he had arrived at Hopewell police station early, speaking with Detectives Ortman and McKeown, and reading Nyce's first statement, which they had taken two days earlier.

At 9:00 a.m. Nyce had arrived with his father and brother Michael, and Detective McKeown, who sat in on the interrogation, had introduced him to Detective Scull. Then Nyce was led into a conference room, where he was read his Miranda rights.

Then the detective had asked him if he had taken medication or consumed any alcohol and Nyce said he had not.

The detective said his main priority at the beginning had been to win Nyce's trust. He did so by being honest with him about the current state of the investigation, and how it would proceed to uncover what had happened to Michelle.

Scull said that several times, the defendant had mulled over getting an attorney, but after Scull had said he couldn't advise him, Nyce decided against it and continued talking.

Eventually, when he'd told him there was probable cause to arrest him for Michelle's murder, Nyce asked if he would be able to go home if he gave a statement, implicating himself in Michelle's death. The detective said no, and that he would have to provide the truth.

Then, when he'd realized his arrest was imminent, Jonathan Nyce had naïvely offered to make a statement, on the condition that he only spent a short time in jail. Scull told him he would not even present that proposition to prosecutors.

At this stage of the interrogation Nyce had looked deflated and insecure, unlike when he had first walked in, brimming with confidence.

When Captain Meyer had knocked on the door, informing him that his attorney, Lee Engleman, had telephoned instructing Nyce not to say anything further, he had first checked with Tom Meidt, and then returned to the interview, placing Engleman's number on the desk. Nyce had pushed it away.

"Were there two factors that led to the confession?" Doris Galuchie asked the detective.

Scull said there were. The effect of Michelle's death on his children, and whether Michelle had been with Enyo that Friday night.

At this point, Detective Scull told the jury, Nyce had broken down in tears, asking how he could be certain he was not being lied to. The detective then told him police knew that his wife had "doused" herself in perfume before returning home, and he believed he had smelled it too.

Detective Scull told the jury that Nyce had then broken down, sobbing, "I didn't mean to kill her."

While the jury was at lunch, the Ceremonial Courtroom was prepared for the playing of the confession. Jonathan Nyce waited nervously in the public gallery with his parents, as court officers distributed wireless headphones and transcriptions of the three tapes to the jury and both counsels. Once again a television crew from ABC's Channel 6 were setting up a camera, and a sound feed from the recorder. The press bench was packed and there was much speculation among reporters about whether or not the defendant would break down during the playing of his confession.

Finally, at 1:05 p.m., as Court Officer James Freeman prepared to bring in the jury, Jonathan Nyce shook his father's hand, saying, "See you in a bit." He then walked over to the defense table, put on his glasses and began reading the transcript.

Fifteen minutes later, the jury filed in, taking their places in their box. As the fluorescent lights were dimmed, so as not to interfere with radio reception, everybody, including the judge and the defendant, donned their radio headphones. Then the first of three tapes of the dramatic confession started playing.

But none of the press had been given transcripts or access to headphones. So the irate reporters immediately marched out of the courtroom to the second floor, where the prosecutor's information officer, Casey DeBlasio, made everyone copies.

Back in court Jonathan Nyce listened to his confession with his hands covering his eyes. As he heard himself describing how Michelle had died, his face turned beet red and he looked to be on the verge of tears.

There was a strange kind of tranquility in the courtroom during the dramatic playing of the tapes. The jury listened intently, as they read the transcript along with it, making notes.

At several points even Judge Bill Mathesius got to his feet, as if that would help him listen better.

Towards the end of the third tape, as he professed his undying love for Michelle, Jonathan Nyce broke down weeping uncontrollably.

When the last tape finished at 3:30, several jurors stared at Nyce as he tried to compose himself by blowing his nose into a handkerchief. But it was impossible to tell if the jurors were sympathetic or disgusted with what they had heard.

A few minutes before 9:00 the next morning, Judge Mathesius was taking the elevator up to his second-floor chambers. It was the seventh day of the trial and there was no end in sight, and the judge was sniffling, as if fighting a cold.

"I think it's going to be a hot day," he told a writer covering the trial. "A contentious day."

A few minutes later in the courtroom, during a hearing before the jury arrived, the judge seemed antsy. He was ruling on a defense motion regarding autopsy photographs to be shown to the jury during the medical examiner's testimony. He was angry with the prosecution for not counting them, and ordered them out to do so immediately.

"Some are disconcerting at the very least," he said when they had returned, describing many as "too graphic," in respect to Michelle's injury.

Then Detective Bill Scull retook the stand to be cross-examined by Robin Lord. As Jonathan Nyce glared at his interrogator, the detective seemed in good spirits, as if eager to cross swords with the defender.

Using Detective Scull's forty-nine-page police report as reference, Robin Lord, wearing a black jacket and white slacks, a black-and-white belt sash hanging from her waist, questioned him on every aspect of his involvement in the case. He took all her questions in his stride, as if he was enjoying himself.

Then, in a *Perry Mason* moment, as she was focusing on the examination of Michelle's Land Cruiser at the state police barracks in Hamilton, Lord asked for Michelle's large black suitcase, weighing approximately 75 pounds, to be wheeled in front of the jury. Up to now there had always been a mystique about the contents of the case found in the back seat of the Land Cruiser. Now, as she asked Detective Scull to open it, most of the jurors were on their feet, trying to get a better look. The only person not amused was the judge.

"Is anyone else concerned about what we're doing here?" snapped Judge Mathesius angrily. "Or is it just, 'Let's go crazy!'?"

Then the judge sent the jury out, instructing the court staff to lay out all the items by the court reporter's bench at the front of the courtroom.

Following a scolding from the judge for not having the contents already prepared, Robin Lord began to carefully catalogue all of Michelle's assorted G-string thongs, lingerie, bras and other apparel.

When they had neatly laid everything out, Judge Mathesius returned to the courtroom, delivering yet another reprimand to Lord.

"I don't want this to happen again!" he shouted. "Outside of turning this courtroom into a yard sale, I'm concerned the jury has to stand by. The jury's time is much more valuable than watching this little dance. We're not going to waste any more time on this."

When the jury had returned to its seats, Judge Mathesius apologized for what had happened.

"Ladies and gentlemen," he said. "I know it seems to be confusing, and you don't see it on *CSI* or *Law & Order*, but this is real life."

Robin Lord then resumed her questioning, asking Detective Scull to read out the complete inventory of clothes found in the suitcase, as the jury took copious notes.

Then she turned her attention to Detective Scull's interrogation of her client. Scull told her he was not the New Jersey State Police's main interrogator.

"I was selected because I was available," he said, adding that he had attended "several interview and interrogation classes," as part of his training.

Lord also asked about so-called false confessions, and Scull conceded it was important not to suggest facts and get them.

"Do they teach that interrogation is a psychology?" she asked him.

"Prior to engaging in an interview with a victim or a suspect," replied the detective, "it is good to know where they are coming from. You would conduct an interview differently with the defendant here, than an eighteen-year-old, selling dope on a street corner."

Then Lord fired a barrage of questions at Detective Scull regarding the message from Attorney Engleman during her client's interrogation. Assistant Prosecutor Doris Galuchie repeatedly objected to the questions, with the judge ruling again and again for the state.

At one point Lord threw up her arms in frustration, accusing Judge Mathesius of being "facetious."

"I'm not facetious," the judge snapped. "A butterfly flapping its wing in Madagascar can affect weather. Detective Scull bent over backwards to explain and re-explain about having an attorney. I have rarely seen such a deference paid to a defendant."

And when Robin Lord once again rolled her eyes in disbelief at the jury, the judge chided: "You can make a face and look unhappy," and recessed for lunch.

• • •

After lunch things became ever more contentious between the judge and the defender. When Robin Lord started grilling Detective Scull about whether he'd known that the defendant had taken anti-anxiety drugs, Judge Mathesius had had enough.

"We've heard fourteen questions about lorazepam," he told her. When Lord attempted to argue her point, he got to his feet, shouting: "Don't interrupt me!"

Then he called both sides into a sidebar, where he could be plainly heard by the jury, screaming at the defender. After the sidebar he warned Lord not to interrupt again, calling her behavior "insulting."

At 3:30 p.m. Robin Lord finally finished her cross-examination and sat down, conceding the floor to Doris Galuchie for her re-direct.

But once again tempers flared when Lord began objecting to her questions and was repeatedly overruled.

"Do you want to take some time to compose yourself?" the judge asked her. "Yes or no?"

Finally Detective Scull stepped down from the witness stand at 4:05 p.m., and the judge recessed for the day, to the relief of many.

35

"The Manner of Death Is Homicide!"

On Tuesday, June 28, the Jonathan Nyce murder trial moved into its fourth week. There was much anticipation today, as Mercer County Medical Examiner Dr. Raafat Ahmad would be taking the stand to tell jurors how Michelle Nyce had died. A small hawkish woman in her fifties, Dr. Ahmad had faced Robin Lord's questioning many times, and it was common knowledge they disliked each other intensely.

At 9:00 a.m., in a closed hearing, the prosecution announced it wished to make a second attempt to introduce the baseball bat into evidence during the medical examiner's testimony. Not surprisingly, Lord opposed this vehemently, and Judge Mathesius ruled that the bat could not be introduced through Dr. Ahmad.

"She will not be able to testify if the bat caused the injuries," he told Tom Meidt. "I don't want you to introduce it through her."

A few minutes later, after the jury filed into its box, the Pakistan-born medical examiner took the witness stand. She was wearing a white suit, sporting a large frilly black brooch, and a pair of glasses dangled on a chain from her neck.

Tom Meidt first asked her to tell the jury what a medical examiner does.

"All violent, unexpected or unnatural deaths are investigated by an M.E.," she replied.

Then the assistant prosecutor asked about Michelle Nyce's injuries, and whether they could have been caused in a car crash.

Dr. Ahmad said that after a cursory examination of Michelle's body, she had determined this was no simple car accident. And then, using autopsy photographs to illustrate her points, the board-certified forensic pathologist took the jury through a gruesome account of Michelle's terrible injuries.

First she said that Michelle had put up a desperate fight to save her life, which could be seen by "defensive wounds" on her hands and wrists.

"She was protecting her vital areas," she explained, "her head and her face, from the assailant. It was a reflex action. When she was attacked, her hands went up to protect her face."

Dr. Ahmad said all the bruising to Michelle's body was antemortem, before death, and had all happened at about the same time.

Assistant Prosecutor Meidt then showed the jury a particularly gruesome close-up photograph of Michelle's battered face, with one eye open and one closed. Several jurors looked away, while at the defense table, Jonathan Nyce shut his eyes and began mumbling to himself, as if he was trying to rein in his emotions.

"What could have caused this?" asked Meidt.

"Blunt force trauma," replied Dr. Ahmad, "the edge of a table or a baseball bat. Somebody beating or punching can cause this. These are all massive injuries."

Then animatedly using her hands to make her points, Dr. Ahmad described the three deep lacerations to the head and a fourth one higher up.

"All three [injuries] are down to the skull," she said.

"There is seepage of blood from the forehead into the right eyeball, which caused the eye to close. [Also] there is one massive injury to the right of the forehead, which actually exposed her skull."

The pathologist also testified that she'd found brain damage, as well as internal injuries to Michelle's spleen, pancreas, adrenal gland and lymph node.

Meidt asked how many blows Michelle had received, and whether she would have died instantly.

"There were at least four major blows to the forehead and one on the top of the head," said Dr. Ahmad. "They were all blunt force trauma injuries."

She revealed that Michelle had lived for about ten minutes after the attack had ended. This was proved, said Dr. Ahmad, by "bloody froth" she'd found in her lungs, indicating that she was alive, breathing in her own blood and gasping for air.

"She was having difficulty breathing," said the doctor. "Her brain was injured, her skull was injured, her heart was still beating."

She said that she had toxicology samples of Michelle's blood, urine, brain and stomach contents analyzed by a laboratory, and there were no traces of caffeine or ecstasy.

Finally, at the end of his four-hour direct examination, Tom Meidt asked Dr. Ahmad what Michelle Nyce's actual cause of death was.

"Massive blunt injuries to head," she replied. "Fracture of the skull, contusion to the brain and intra-cranial bleeding."

Then looking straight at the jury, she declared, "The manner of death is homicide!"

Robin Lord stood up to object and Judge Mathesius called an immediate sidebar. A few minutes later the judge retook his seat to address the jury, in this pivotal moment of the trial.

"Ladies and gentlemen," he began, "a question of the prosecutor called for a conclusion by this witness of the label as to the type of death suffered. Ultimately that's your job. So you should disregard the ultimate conclusion that was announced by the pathologist, because ultimately I'm going to tell you, no matter what anybody says, it is your determination as to what happened in this case."

During the judge's lengthy directive, Dr. Ahmad sat in the witness box, between the judge and the jury box, rolling her eyes and shaking her head in disagreement at the jurors. And this spectacle, which could have led to a mistrial, went unseen by Judge Mathesius.

At 2:55 p.m. after a ten-minute afternoon break, Robin Lord began her cross-examination, in an attempt to demolish Dr. Ahmad's credibility. The obvious animosity between the two strong-willed women was apparent from her first question.

"You were essentially offering your opinions?" declared Lord dismissively.

"I was basing everything on the facts in my report," replied Dr. Ahmad, meeting the defender head-on. "The opinions that I have given are correct. It was based on my experience and all the injuries I found on the body."

Then Lord began picking at the doctor's medical background in Pakistan, intimating to the jury that the medical training there is inferior to America's.

"That's not true," said Dr. Ahmad angrily.

As Lord continued to whittle away at her qualifications for her job, Judge Mathesius stepped in to stop it.

"We're flirting with remoteness," he chided. "I'm calling an end to discussion of her qualifications."

Then the defender asked how she could be so certain Michelle's injuries were caused before death.

"You're aware," she told the forensic pathologist, "that medical journals say you cannot tell the difference between postmortem [after] and antemortem [before] bruises."

Rising to the bait and demonstrably jabbing her forefinger into the air, Dr. Ahmad challenged this view.

"You can differentiate based on examining the bruising," she told Lord. "I look at dead bodies every day. I know when postmortem bruising has happened and when antemortem bruising has occurred. All the injuries in the case of this woman who was murdered were antemortem."

Judge Mathesius then wryly observed to the jury that "the level of sarcasm" between the two women was on the "Beaufort scale," the official measure for hurricanes.

Lord then wanted to know why Dr. Ahmad had only sliced open a quarter of the bruises on Michelle's hand to check for fresh blood, a sign of antemortem.

"The woman has to have a funeral," snapped the medical examiner. "They were all coming up the same. I didn't want to keep cutting her. I was sure. You want me to mutilate her face?"

Then Lord questioned the medical examiner's motives in testifying, suggesting that she was in cahoots with the prosecution. She asked if her descriptions of the injuries were given to help the state prove its theory "in this case."

"No," said Dr. Ahmad vehemently. "You only get those injuries when somebody beats you up, brutally."

Robin Lord finished her cross-examination at 4:00 p.m. On re-direct, Tom Meidt asked the medical examiner about the defensive injuries she had found.

"This woman had trauma injuries which were massive," she said. "She was raising her hand over her forehead to protect herself—that's how she got them."

On her re-cross Robin Lord began asking Dr. Ahmad about the standard textbook called *Forensic Pathology*, by Vincent J. DiMaio and Dominick DiMaio, which she said she had consulted before her testimony.

"You were carrying the book in the courthouse today," observed Lord derisively.

"So were you," snapped Dr. Ahmad.

Then the always well-primed defender drew her attention to a chapter which described postmortem and antemortem bruising as virtually identical.

"I didn't read that chapter," admitted the medical examiner, finally at a loss for words.

Later it was discovered that Dr. Ahmad had been using a 1993 edition of *Forensic Pathology*, while Robin Lord had the latest 2001 one, containing the chapter—a fact not lost on the jury.

When she was finally dismissed from the witness box, the doctor looked visibly relieved.

"Am I finished?" she asked the judge. "I don't have to come here again?"

The next morning—the tenth day of the trial—Michelle's sister Melodia Ragenil and her father, Teodoro, were due to testify. Sparing no expense, the prosecution had spent $1,426 flying Melodia over from the Philippines, as well as putting her up in a nearby hotel and giving her a daily food allowance. The prosecutors had also engaged the services of two interpreters, in case there was any language problem, although Melodia spoke fluent English.

The state viewed Michelle's youngest sister as a key witness. She would testify about a telephone conversation with Jonathan Nyce, several weeks before he'd killed Michelle, when he'd called her in the Philippines, asking if her sister was having an affair. They hoped that would prove premeditation and shoot down the defense argument that it was a spontaneous crime of passion, carrying a far lesser penalty than murder.

But Robin Lord had fervently objected, leading Judge Mathesius to personally determine if a translator was required.

Visibly nervous, Melodia, 28, wearing a smart black suit, was gently questioned by Judge Mathesius in the witness box, out of the presence of the jury.

She told the judge in faltering English, with the help of an interpreter, that she had a college-level education and had been married for seven years. She had occasionally spoken to her brother-in-law Jonathan Nyce on the phone, usually through Michelle.

"Sometimes I'd ask my sister what Jonathan was saying," she said. "Because I don't understand."

"I'm unconvinced of the reliability of the witness's testimony," the judge told Assistant Prosecutor Doris Galuchie.

He then asked Melodia to wait at the back of the court, while he consulted with both counsels, and she went to sit on the press bench.

Then Galuchie asked if she could call her and just ask if she knew that Alexander Castaneda had been her sister's boyfriend.

"She does understand some basic small talk," she said.

"I don't believe it rises to a level of reliability," said the judge. "We're presented with a language barrier."

Galuchie argued that if Melodia was not allowed to testify, it would significantly "lower the legal bar" for Jonathan Nyce from murder to passion/provocation manslaughter.

Then Robin Lord told the judge that her client had supported Melodia and the rest of the Riviera family until July 2003.

"What happened," she said, "was that he cut them off when he found out about Alexander Castaneda. She asked for more money for school and he wouldn't because of Alexander Castaneda."

Judge Mathesius said he felt the witness had "demonstrated a gross incapability with the English language," and that the "bramble bush" that would grow from her testimony would be "far too much."

He then recalled her to the stand, so he could question her further about her December 2003 conversation with her brother-in-law.

"How many times did you speak to Jonathan Nyce on the telephone?" he asked.

"In December 2003 he called me," said Melodia. "He was just asking me if I knew about my sister's boyfriend. I said no."

Melodia said that her brother-in-law then asked if she knew "Alex," and she replied that she only knew he was Michelle's friend and nothing more.

"You know," he had said loudly, before hanging up.

As she told this story more fluently than before, Judge Mathesius realized that Melodia's English was far better than he'd originally believed. And he realized his mistake in allowing her to remain in the courtroom when they'd discussed her, for she had overheard Doris Galuchie present the state's case strategy, involving her evidence. Now, any testimony she might give would be tainted, proving fertile grounds for a later appeal by the defense.

"I'm not going to permit her to testify with or without an interpreter," he ruled. "Much of what was exchanged [in the courtroom] she was present to hear, and it's gone too far. She represented that she did not understand the English language."

Then a visibly angry Doris Galuchie asked the judge for a few minutes to decide with her colleagues if the state would appeal the decision. Judge Mathesius said she could do what she wanted, but he wasn't going to change his mind.

Jonathan Nyce was clearly delighted with the decision not to let Michelle's sister testify. At the mid-morning break, the smiling defendant triumphantly walked back to his family in the public gallery and kissed them.

Later that day Judge Mathesius stopped off at the second-floor press room to read an account of the trial in yesterday's Trenton *Times*.

"Why do you think the prosecution wanted Melodia to testify?" he asked a writer who also happened to be in there.

"Because the December phone call mentioning Alex would show premeditation," said the writer.

"No," replied the judge conspiratorially. "Because she looks like Michelle, and she's going to cry on the stand."

The next witness was Michelle's best friend, Larissa Soos, who told the jury about Jonathan Nyce's strange behavior in the hours after her death. She described how he had come over to her house Friday evening to collect his children, and launched a bitter attack on Michelle.

"The first thing he said was that Michelle had a wild side," she testified. "I was like, 'What do you mean?' He told me Michelle was bi-polar and she likes sex all the time [and that] she was seeing a psychiatrist. I don't know why I'm hearing it. I mean, my friend has just died."

Then she told of reading to Jonathan Nyce over the phone Saturday's morning edition of the Trenton *Times*, with its front page story calling Michelle's death homicide.

"He started to cry," she testified. "I read the whole story out to him."

In her cross, Robin Lord asked if Michelle had ever discussed her sex life with Larissa.

"I don't know anything about that," she replied.

The defender then wanted to know if Soos knew about Michelle's affair, her sexual liaisons in motel rooms, as well as other unsavory details of her life.

Galuchie presented objections to each and every question, which were sustained by the judge.

Finally, Lord asked her about Nyce's Sampaguita perfume company, and whether he'd shared his marketing strategy with her. When Galuchie objected yet again, Judge Mathesius wryly noted, "I think the scent's been allowed to drift."

It was a rare joke from the judge, getting a laugh from several jurors.

The next morning—day eleven of the trial—Robin Lord had come down with the flu. As she walked into court at 9:00 a.m. for a hearing to determine if Teodora Riviera could testify, she looked pale and unwell, continually breaking into coughing fits.

Now that the judge had refused to allow Melodia to testify, her father had become an even more important state witness. They wanted him to testify about the true way his daughter had met Jonathan, and their marriage in the Philippines, as well as the fact that Michelle's sister had not starved to death.

He was the only person with any inside knowledge of Jonathan and Michelle's relationship, having lived with them for months at a time. Lastly the prosecution wanted to let the jury know that Michelle's family had only heard about her death from a friend, and not from Jonathan, as might have been expected.

The state had offered the defendant's statement and now wanted to attack it with one of their witnesses.

"Nothing in past New Jersey history is analogous to this," said the judge.

Putting forward the state's case, Tom Meidt said Nyce had lied to police about how he'd met Michelle in Hawaii, when she was actually "a mail-order bride."

"He has admitted his involvement in his wife's death," explained Meidt. "But lies about how they met . . . trying to make himself appear in a better light. This is a husband killing a wife, and they had marital problems. Even as he's admitting the killing of Michelle, he's minimizing and calling it an accident. This is how far the defendant will go by lying how they even met, and trying to paint himself in a positive light."

Then Lord broke into a fit of coughing and her mother, Janet Kay, sitting in the front row next to Jonathan Nyce Jr. and Emma Nyce, discreetly walked forward to the defense table, handing her daughter some medicine.

"I have a fever and a head cold," Lord huskily told the judge. "Bronchitis."

"Do the best you can," said Judge Mathesius sympathetically.

"I don't think any of us are forgetting he picked up his dead wife, put her in the car and drove her to the creek," she told Mathesius. "How does he paint himself in a favorable light?

"He sent emergency food shipments to the Philippines. He sent the kids to school. He built schools. Maybe Michelle told Dr. Nyce her sister died of starvation to get him to help them some more. Who cares where they met or not? What does it have to do with his knowledge she was out with Enyo?"

"Miss Lord is not unimaginative," noted the judge. "I can see mini-trials emerging, and I'm disinclined to have mini-trials. Who cares if the defendant is embarrassed by saying he had a mail-order bride? How material is that? It puts him in a delusional light."

But Tom Meidt disagreed, saying it went to the very core of Jonathan Nyce's character, and the lengths he'd go to lie for advantage.

"This is a pattern of deception by the defendant," he told the judge. "Michelle didn't even find out how old he was until after they had three children. He lied about the birth certificate and he lied about the marriage certificate. It goes to the defendant's credibility."

Lord then reminded Judge Mathesius about Riviera's command of the English language.

"Remember, he does not speak English," she said. "I have no means of cross-examining him."

Finally the judge ruled that Teodoro Riviera could not testify at the trial, meaning none of Michelle's family would be given the opportunity to take the stand and speak up for her.

"The court declines to permit testimony from the father on three remote issues," he said. "It would invite a mini-trial . . . [Also, the fact that] the father does not speak English creates extra problems."

Then Robin Lord, dabbing her nose with a tissue, asked the judge to allow the jury to go to Jacobs Creek and view the crash site.

"The photos don't do it justice," she said. "It's a very steep cliff, and it's important for the jury to understand it."

Tom Meidt argued against the jury going, pointing out that the site is "extensively different" from the way it was eighteen months earlier.

"To go there more a year after the fact is mere speculation for the defense," he declared.

Judge Mathesius said he reserved his judgment and would review. Then he dismissed the jury, wishing them an enjoyable July Fourth holiday until they returned to the jury box the following Tuesday.

The next morning, Judge Mathesius spent his day off visiting Jacobs Creek, accompanied by several members of the prosecution team. It was a scorching hot day in the 90s when the judge, dressed casually in a dark short-sleeve shirt and loose-fitting white pants, strolled through the densely wooded banks of the creek.

For Judge Mathesius, it might also have been a chance to contemplate his future. A few days earlier, the seasoned jurist had learned he was to be transferred to the civil division in September. Although it wasn't an official demotion, the Trenton *Times* had reported the story citing his running "afoul" of the New Jersey Supreme Court in his heavily criticized 2002 opinion.

Later, after the verdict, when asked if working civil cases would still hold his interest after the excitement of murder trials, Judge Mathesius was candid.

"I don't know," he said. "We're going to find out. The difference is, with the criminal, I had a feeling that I was doing something more societally beneficial."

After they had finished examining the scene, the judge made the mile-long drive to 1 Keithwood Court, so he could see Jonathan Nyce's house. Interestingly, the house, which was still up for sale, had now become 18 Todd Ridge Road.

"Frankly," the judge would later say, "I found the observation of the house, and not the crime scene, to be enlightening."

On Tuesday, July 5, the final two prosecution witnesses were called, with the state expected to rest its case by lunch.

Dr. Theodore Siek, a forensic toxicologist and self-described "expert witness," said his Feasterville, Pennsylvania, laboratory had analyzed Michelle Nyce's stomach contents, brain, liver, spleen and kidney.

He said traces of caffeine had been found, but absolutely no drugs, like amphetamines or ecstasy.

"It is not unusual, as most of us drink coffee," he said.

In her cross-examination, Robin asked Dr. Siek if he had personally tested the substances, and he admitted he had not.

"I was told to expedite the case," he explained. "It was an important case."

While he was testifying, a victims' advocate brought in

Melodia Ragenil, who sat down at the press bench. For the rest of the trial the prosecutors would have Melodia, and occasionally her father, attending the court proceedings, providing the jurors with some sense of Michelle's presence in the courtroom.

The final state witness was New Jersey State Police Forensic Toxicologist Edward Gainsborg. Asked about his job by Tom Meidt, Gainsborg explained that he specialized in trace evidence or "putting the puzzle back together."

On January 23, 2004, he had been asked to reassemble the fourteen boot sole parts found hidden in Nyce's basement.

"There were several pieces of cut-up soles of a boot to be put together," he told the jury. "And once reassembled, to see if they had been put on a pair of moccasins."

Then he demonstrated for the jury how he had done this, taking each of the fourteen pieces of the sole and reconstructing them on a table. A projecting device allowed the jury to see him fitting together the pieces like a jigsaw puzzle, before he dramatically turned it over to reveal the complete sole.

"The analysis was a physical fit," he declared.

He also explained how he had matched up the footprints found in the snow at the Jacobs Creek crash site to Nyce's Brahma boot soles, microscopically by size and manufacturer's design.

"The snow's a very good medium for picking up details of footprints," he said.

The state of New Jersey finally rested its case against Jonathan Nyce at 11:35 a.m. on Tuesday, July 5. It had called a total of nineteen witnesses, taking almost twelve days to present the case.

After the jury filed out for lunch, Judge Mathesius called a hearing to determine if jurors would be able to visit the Jacobs Creek crash site and Jonathan Nyce's house.

"It will be significant for the jury to comprehend the

case," argued Robin Lord. "It screams out for the jury to see for itself."

But Doris Galuchie disagreed, saying it was mid-summer, and as there was snow on the ground at the time the crime had occurred, it would be deceptive.

"Quite frankly," said the judge, "I found it interesting. It took some degree of care to drive. I must agree with Miss Lord. It does bring another extra angle to this case."

Then the judge granted her application for the jury to visit the crash site and then drive by the Nyce home.

"We're going on a field trip," he told the jury after their lunch break. "We're going to the scene of the final resting place of the Land Cruiser and drive by the house Mr. Nyce lived in at that time."

He told them to be ready to be bused out there the next morning, warning them the entire trip would be in silence.

"Just visit both of these scenes without comment," he told them. "Wear casual clothes. Obviously there will be no snow tomorrow. If I wake up and there's snow on the ground, I'm not coming."

Then, after the jury was asked to wait in the jury room, Robin Lord asked Judge Mathesius to dismiss all the charges against Jonathan Nyce, claiming the prosecution had failed to prove its case that Nyce had "knowingly and purposely" murdered his wife.

The judge denied her motion, saying that "purposely and knowingly" were key words to this case.

"There is a wide panorama of conclusions that could be drawn in this case from the defendant's actions," he said. "And they certainly extend to any number of conclusions. It is certainly in the breadth of a reasonable jury to find any one of the conclusions, including that the defendant did purposely and knowingly cause the death of Michelle Nyce.

"But this court is not ready, at this point, to rule a resolution that the jury cannot find murder beyond a reasonable doubt. The motion is denied."

36

The Defense

At 1:45 p.m. Robin Lord called her first witness, as her parents looked on proudly from the public gallery. Originally she had told the media that famed television forensic pathologist Dr. Michael Baden would be on her defense team. But he had been replaced by veteran Baltimore-based forensic pathologist Dr. John Adams. Now the defense was counting on the elderly white-haired doctor to refute Medical Examiner Dr. Ahmad's scathing autopsy report and add credibility to Jonathan Nyce's version of how Michelle had died.

Dr. Adams had graduated from the University of Maryland Medical School almost half a century earlier, and had performed or supervised thousands of autopsies during his long career.

He told the jury he had come to the case three months earlier, when he was sent Dr. Ahmad's autopsy, police reports and forensic lab reports to review.

"I formed an opinion," he told the jury. "Contracoup contusion . . . classic fall injuries."

The contracoup injury to the brain occurs when the brain

strikes the skull on the opposite side of impact, most commonly in a traffic accident, but also as a result of a fall. Once the skull has stopped moving forward, the brain continues moving backward, striking the base of the skull.

"There is very substantial g-force in the brain itself," Dr. Adams explained to the jury, using a color diagram. "The brain rattles around the skull."

Dr. Adams said he had carefully reviewed Dr. Ahmad's autopsy report and that it was important that the injuries were to Michelle's forehead, and there was bruising on both the front and back of her brain.

"There is no evidence at the back of the head," he said, "telling you the injuries were contracoup."

The doctor said that, in his "very considerable experience," Michelle's injuries were the result of a single fall, and her skull fractures were associated with the point of impact.

At this point Robin Lord put up a second presentation board, showing two graphic autopsy pictures of the top of Michelle's shaven head. They clearly showed the deep lacerations down to the skull. Once again, Jonathan Nyce looked away and grimaced.

"Are the injuries consistent with falling out of an SUV," asked Lord, "with the head hitting the running board?"

"Probably possible," replied the veteran forensic pathologist.

He told the jury that Michelle's internal injuries and extensive bruising could be the result of her body bouncing around inside the Land Cruiser during its descent down the embankment into Jacobs Creek.

"The excessive handling that this body was subjected to," he said, "in my experience, would cause some degree of marking, bruising. I would have concerns for a body moved a lot. How was she got in the car? Taken down the bank while unbelted? That would be enough to produce bruising, and freezer burn makes for a very confusing set of circumstances."

Then Lord asked him if it was medically possible to differentiate between antemortem and postmortem bruising.

"You can't tell the difference," he replied resolutely. "They both look the same."

He added that if the bruise happened to be over eight hours old, you could tell, but anything less was impossible.

At this point Lord removed the gruesome photographs and the judge called the afternoon break. Twenty minutes later, when the trial resumed, Melodia Ragenil was in the front row of the public gallery for the rest of the day's testimony.

Lord first asked about Michelle's body being frozen solid in the sub-zero temperatures and whether that could have caused bruising.

"Freezing causes a change in the wounds, and changes to the skin," replied the doctor. "It can produce blemishes of vague discoloration. I think that's the case here. If her knee was resting on the steering wheel, it could cause postmortem bruising. I'm concerned this was freezer burn."

Then Lord put up autopsy pictures of Michelle's bruised and bloodied brain. Melodia burst out crying and had to be comforted by a victim support counselor.

"Is it possible to tell how long she was alive from the outset of the injuries?" asked the defender.

Dr. Adams said he knew of no scientific method of determining if Michelle had lived for ten minutes after the attack, as the M.E. had testified.

"That doesn't make any sense to me," he said. "I've never heard of a way to do it in my forty-odd years as a forensic pathologist."

He maintained that froth in lungs is a "very common postmortem phenomenon," and can be generated for hours after death. It was the result of trapped air in the lungs mixing with blood and mucus, he told the jury.

Then Robin Lord finished her direct examination and the judge told Dr. Adams to be back at 1:30 p.m. tomorrow—after the field trip—when the state would have its opportunity to cross-examine him.

* * *

At precisely 10:00 a.m. the next morning the yellow jurors' bus, driven by Mercer County Sheriff's Officer Pablo Santiago, arrived at Jacobs Creek. Inside were the sixteen jurors and Judge Bill Mathesius, who had traded his robes for a starched white shirt and floral tie. Following behind in a convoy of motley vehicles were the prosecutors, the defense team and a gaggle of reporters, as well as a Channel 6 TV crew.

It was a hot, muggy day in the high 70s, as the jurors walked around the opening where the Land Cruiser had gone into the creek. The more intrepid ones actually went down the steep embankment to explore further.

Although ordered by the judge not to discuss it, several jurors did. One even questioned Judge Mathesius about the steep drop.

"You're not going to get any instructions from me," replied the judge.

"You're not really helping the cause, are you?" the juror snapped back.

In another conversation a reporter heard one juror commenting to another that the police photographs they'd seen during the trial were "somewhat deceiving."

"Yes, it's much steeper," agreed the other.

After about twenty minutes at the scene the jurors got back in the bus to visit Jonathan Nyce's home, so they could get an idea of the distances and see the scene for themselves. Officer Santiago did a slow driveby, stopping for two minutes at the top of the hill, alongside the house. Then he turned around and drove back to the court.

When reporters returned to the Ceremonial Courtroom they discovered a potential defense witness named Paul Everton waiting outside with his attorney and his mother. The 29-year-old aspiring corrections officer, wearing dark glasses and a Kangol hat, said Robin Lord had subpoenaed him as a witness, as he'd had an ongoing flirtation with Michelle Nyce.

"Robin told me they had found my number in [Michelle's] purse, and I told her we had exchanged numbers," he informed the reporters. "I don't know why they want me. We only met once."

And when a reporter asked about his relationship with Michelle Nyce, he was only too eager to tell. The genial shaven-headed trainee corrections officer said he had met Michelle two months before her death, when she'd struck up a conversation with him in Macy's.

He said over the next few weeks they had talked on the telephone, but had never actually met, although they had frequently discussed doing so.

"She told me she had a jealous boyfriend she was worried about," said Everton, who proudly displayed his tongue-piercing for reporters, saying it had intrigued Michelle.

Everton said he had called Michelle twice in January and left messages.

"I thought she had just stopped calling me back," he said. "The first I knew she was dead was two months ago when Robin Lord called me and was very intimidating. I got scared when she told me I could be imprisoned if I didn't turn up, so I got a lawyer because I thought I might be in trouble."

Ultimately Judge Mathesius refused to allow Everton to testify, saying he was irrelevant to the case.

Earlier that day, after returning from the field trip, Judge Mathesius had considered a complaint from the prosecution that Dr. Adams had changed his original findings to be more favorable to the defense case. The judge said he had carefully reviewed "the entire three inches of documents" Dr. Adams had in front of him the day before, including twenty-four pages of notes in a yellow legal pad.

Judge Mathesius said he had "two areas of concern," regarding Dr. Adams' first draft report of May 20, 2005, a second made four days later, and his final report on May 25.

"This is a critical test for the jury," Assistant Prosecutor Tom Meidt told the judge, wanting to question the expert about these changes. "The state has a right to examine how he changes his mind. This goes to the very bias of the witness [and] if his testimony was influenced."

Pondering the situation, Judge Mathesius asked, what if an expert had concluded one thing in his original report, and then, after "discussions," reversed his opinion?

"I'm trying to wend my way through a very complicated thicket of the defendant's rights," he said. "It troubles me that a shift, subtle or dramatic, changes an expert's viewpoint."

Defending her expert, Lord told the judge that Dr. Adams was not "a hired gun" or "a hired whore."

Describing it as a "complex situation" Judge Mathesius said he would mull over the problem at lunch.

About ninety minutes later the judge was back in the courtroom, telling counsels he had spent "substantial time" researching the matter, which raised critical issues in the case.

"[It's] doubly difficult," he said. "It's a complex, devious issue. These reports reflect a back-and-forth exchange between the doctor and counsel. I would say that the court is extremely troubled by the omission of certain observations by Dr. Adams that did not find their way into the final version. It opens up the door to miasma. The mini-trial becomes a maxi-trial.

"The court will try and seek a road. The court will permit cross-examination of Dr. Adams."

He then ordered the jury in, and Tom Meidt began his crucial cross-examination. Right from the start, Dr. Adams refused to back down from his theory that Michelle Nyce's injuries were caused by a fall.

"You have no way to tell if the fall injuries are the result of someone falling to the ground," said the assistant prosecutor, "or being grabbed and pushed to the ground."

"For the fourth time today," snapped back the forensic pathologist, "I said this is a fall injury. I do not know how it occurred. I do not know if she was pushed or not. I have no way of knowing."

"If a victim's forehead is being driven into a concrete floor," asked Meidt, "could it [result in] lacerations?"

"Yes," replied the doctor, "but I know the body was in an SUV and dived over an embankment."

When asked if all Michelle's internal injuries could be the result of someone kneeling on her back, Dr. Adams said no. The prosecutor followed up, asking if they could have been caused by a beating in the abdomen area.

"It could be the result of a blow by a fist," Dr. Adams conceded. "It could also be caused by someone going down an embankment and hitting the steering wheel. It's a typical steering wheel injury."

Then Meidt asked how much he was being paid to testify for the defense.

"Three hundred dollars an hour," he replied. "And I spent probably fifteen or twenty hours [on the case.]"

On her re-direct, Robin Lord asked her expert again and again about the contents of various forensic pathology textbooks, in a further effort to discredit Dr. Ahmad's testimony.

Again and again Tom Meidt objected to her line of questioning, and Judge Mathesius repeatedly sustained him.

"I told you to move on!" shouted the judge, fast losing his temper.

"I'm done," Lord said angrily, storming back to the defense table and hurling her books down hard on the defense table.

"Miss Lord," said Judge Mathesius, "if you feel like you want to throw some books around, please don't. You got a little hissy fit? That's unbecoming."

Then turning to the jury, he endeavored to explain what was going on.

"I'm supposed to be a referee," he said sarcastically. "I hope you don't think my comments to Miss Lord in any way relate to her ability. They're personally all lovely people. They're just part of the stress of a very complicated trial."

On Thursday, July 7—day 14 of the trial—there was much anticipation that Jonathan Nyce would take the stand in his own defense. Although Robin Lord refused to confirm or deny anything, there were many rumors flying around as to whether he would or not. The inside scoop was that he wanted to testify, but his counsel refused to let him, as she'd have no control over what he might say. There was also the question of how well he'd hold up under the state's cross-examination.

In the end Nyce didn't take the stand, and the defense's second and final witness was Hopewell Township Police Sergeant Thomas Puskas. Although Lord had wanted to call her predecessor Lee Engleman and Detective Karen Ortman as witnesses, the judge refused to allow it.

In an effort to show that investigators had not properly searched for the stiletto-like knife, the weapon Nyce claimed Michelle had attacked him with, Lord asked Sergeant Puskas about his search of storm drains.

"I was assigned to the storm drains," he said, "to check for any articles that might have been discarded. But it was difficult to do. There was snow and ice and the grates were frozen."

Sergeant Puskas told the jury he had to "visualize" what was in the drains, as they were all frozen shut. But the search was fruitless and they found nothing.

In his cross-examination, Tom Meidt asked if Puskas had been able to open any of the drains, and he said there had been one opened on Jacobs Creek Road.

"We got down on our hands and knees and looked into them," he said. "If there was anything with shape and dimension, we'd poke around inside. I mean, it was storm drains."

At 10:15 a.m. Robin Lord rested the defense case, and, after sending the jury back to their room until he could brief them about summations, Judge Mathesius asked Jonathan Nyce to stand up.

"Did Miss Lord discuss your opportunity to testify?" he asked the defendant, who towered over his lawyer.

"Yes," replied Nyce softly.

"And that if you testified, you'd be subjected to cross-examination by the state?"

"Yes."

Then Judge Mathesius told him that he would instruct the

jury not to infer any guilt from the fact that he had chosen
not to testify, as he was perfectly within his legal rights not
to do so.

After the judge left, the court reporters converged on the
defense table, asking Lord about Nyce's decision not to testify.

"The state has not met its burden of proof," she told them.

Later that afternoon, after dismissing the jury for the day and
telling them to be back in court the following Monday for
closing arguments, Judge Mathesius held a special hearing to
rule if the jury could consider lesser charges against Nyce.

In a pivotal motion that would transform the entire trial,
Lord asked the judge to instruct jurors to consider convicting
her client of passion/provocation manslaughter, which carried a 5-to-10-year prison sentence, instead of murder, 30
years to life.

The judge indicated that he was prepared to do so, but
would make a final ruling on Friday.

"I am deeply concerned about the charges offered to the
jury," said the judge. "It's a two-count indictment, [but]
much more complex."

It was a stunning victory for the defense and the next
morning there was even better news for Jonathan Nyce. Cap-
italizing on her momentum, Lord asked the judge to add the
example of the extra-marital affair when instructing the jury
on what could provoke someone to commit murder in the
heat of passion.

She argued that standard examples of provocation are
usually threats with a weapon.

"This case is not about a gun or a knife," she told him.
"This case is about an extra-marital affair."

Then, to the abject dismay of the prosecution, Judge
Mathesius agreed to add an affair to his list of possible
provocations when he instructed the jury next Monday, before they retired to consider their verdict.

37

"Justice for Michelle"

On Monday, July 11, the fifteenth day of the Jonathan Nyce trial, the Ceremonial Courtroom was packed to hear closing arguments. On the left of the center aisle, behind the defense table, sat the entire Nyce family, including the defendant's grandmother Ellen, his parents, three brothers and various aunts, uncles and cousins. Sitting with them were Robin Lord's parents, who had hardly missed a day of their daughter's most high-profile trial yet.

Across the courtroom, behind the prosecution in the second row of the public gallery, sat many of the detectives who had worked the case. Dan McKeown, Geoffrey Noble, William Scull and Jeffrey Kronenfeld all felt personally involved, and there had been several lasting friendships made between them during the investigation.

Directly in front of them sat Michelle's sister Melodia, wearing a mauve top and jeans, sitting next to a victim counselor named Alisha. She explained her father, Teodoro would be late, as he was working.

The press were there in force with several reporters from each of the two Trenton newspapers, Jonathan Miller of *The*

New York Times, and producers from *Dateline NBC* and the tabloid TV show *A Current Affair*.

But all eyes were on the well-groomed defendant Jonathan Nyce, who appeared relaxed in his usual baggy gray business suit. Looking confident, he leaned on the top rail of the public gallery, chatting with his family and shaking hands with his relatives as they arrived.

At the defense table Robin Lord supervised the setting up of a blackboard in front of the jury box, with a large flip chart that she would use for her presentation. Dressed in a red suit and black polka-dot blouse, Lord was as focused as a laser beam, knowing she would have to deliver the speech of her life to win her case.

At 9:40, with Judge Mathesius and the sixteen men and women of the jury in their places, Lord strolled up to the blackboard and opened the flip chart, to reveal the words in large type, "Speculation, Conjecture and all Forms of Guessing Play no Role in the Performance of Your Duty."

"It was seven weeks ago," she began, talking directly to the jury, "that the prosecution told you a story about a woman, who they characterized as a normal sweet woman, who was lonely because her hard-working husband was away a lot on business. Except that he was at home, out of work and taking care of their three children.

"She became increasingly lonely, so she turned to the loving, caring gardener for comfort. And one night she returned home from a comfort visit in her red thong, her red panties and her red bra. And she told [her husband] she was going to leave him, and he pulled her down and she hit her head on the ground. The only problem is that [the prosecution] are not playwrights, they're not screenwriters.

"It is a promise by them as to how they are going to convince you beyond a reasonable doubt.

"The only problem with that story was that it wasn't even remotely supported by them. Michelle Nyce was hardly a normal sweet woman. A normal sweet woman does not have an affair while her husband is working. A normal sweet woman does not have unprotected sex in a rent-by-the-hour motel room, with a man who has many different aliases while her husband is supporting her family in the Philippines, building schools, duck farms and playgrounds. A normal sweet woman doesn't do that.

"The state has the burden of proof. They have to prove to you beyond a reasonable doubt that Jonathan Nyce is guilty."

Then pointing at the words on the blackboard with her long white square-tip manicured nails, Lord told the jury that "speculation and guessing" play no role in their deliberations. They would have to return a verdict of not guilty.

Lord then identified twenty-two "areas of reasonable doubt" for the jury, putting each up on her presentation flip chart as she discussed them.

Getting into her stride, the defender argued that the prosecution motive, that Michelle was walking out on Jonathan, was wrong. She claimed the suitcase was nothing more than one she used when sneaking away for sexual escapades.

"What was in the suitcase is very important, as is what was not," declared Lord, pointing out that right at the top had been an empty packet of Victoria's Secret thigh-highs. "Some underwear is dirty, as if just used. Shirts were inside out, as if just taken off. You know the suitcase was not packed by Michelle that night. It was her comfort bag."

Then Lord launched a bitter attack on Michelle Nyce and her family, reducing her younger sister Melodia to tears.

"Where exactly was she going?" Lord asked. "This woman wasn't about to move out. She lived a single life while he stayed in the house, bringing up their three children.

"She's from starving Philippines. He supports her family. She had it made. She had it absolutely made. She wasn't going anywhere, and I think you know that. It's a fiction, a rush to judgment by the police."

Lord told the jury that Jonathan Nyce never had any intention of killing Michelle, and if he'd wanted to, he could have done a far better job.

"There was a gun right there in his office," she told the jurors, many of whom were making notes. "Right next to three magazines of ammunition. He's a research scientist. He in-

vents drugs. If he had wanted, I suggest, he could have created a drug that could have gone undetected, if he wanted to
kill her. But he kills her in his pajamas. In his socks. And
there in the kitchen is a coffee jug and two cups."

In July 2003, when he discovered Michelle was having an
affair, he was "devastated.

"That 'stainless steel heart' [the poem] is a perfect document of how much pain and anguish this poor man was in,"
she said, adding that psychologically, if he had wanted to
murder Michelle, he would have done it then.

She then showed the court graphic photographs of
Michelle's head injuries. The victims' services person asked
Melodia and her father, who had now arrived, if they wished
to remain in court, and they said they did.

"Jonathan Nyce told in his statement that she fell from
the SUV onto the running board, and it was a 'sickening
thud,' " she continued. "From that moment on he was in severe emotional stress. He *truly* adored her."

Then she calmly walked over to the prosecutor's table,
picked up a glass of water and drank it, smiling at Tom Meidt.

"Let's talk about Dr. Ahmad," she then declared. "This
woman is self-taught. She has no residency in forensic pathology."

Launching a scathing attack on the Mercer County Medical Examiner, Lord ridiculed her testimony that it was medically impossible to tell the difference between antemortem
and postmortem bruises.

"[She used] the slice test," laughed the defender. "She
only sliced a few. How dare she come here and tell you with
one hundred percent certainty that all the bruises were antemortem by her own test, when she doesn't even perform it?

"Dr. Adams has forty years of experience. He has never
heard of the slice test. He tells you that you just can't tell the
difference."

She told the jury there was "excessive postmortem bruising" on Michelle's body, that could have been caused by any
number of things, including "rough sex" with Enyo.

"After she fell, he lifts her up," she said. "He has difficulty.

Then he takes her to the creek. Then the body was taken from the medical examiner's office for X-rays and then back. There was excessive handling of the body. You just can't tell the difference. How dare they tell you any differently?"

Lord dismissed Dr. Ahmad's assertion that Michelle was alive for ten minutes, because of the existence of "a red froth substance."

"She's making this stuff up as she goes along," she declared.

The defender then turned her attention to the investigation, claiming police had made no effort to look for the sharp object that Nyce claimed Michelle had used to attack him.

"They ignored him," she said loudly. "They laughed at him. They never looked in the car. He says she took the object out of a Chanel bag—there was a plastic see-through bag.

No one even looked in it, or [on] her person."

Then she dramatically pulled three long plastic hairpins out of the bag, one of which was broken.

"[This] is most important," she said, displaying the broken hairpin to the jury. "It's in two pieces. Plastic does not disintegrate. Plastic does not fall apart. It does if it's fractured by falling to the ground with an object in your hand.

"What did he say? She took it from the Chanel bag, it could have been a hairpin. It happened in split seconds. She lunged. He reacted and she fell. It is more than a coincidence."

Lord continued, telling the jury that after Michelle had died, Jonathan Nyce, under the influence of antidepressants, had "panicked." And the reason he had not called the police was that they had not believed him six months earlier with the extortion attempt.

"I suggest the actions from then on," she said, "are the actions of a distressed man, who's not thinking straight. None of us have ever been in that situation. It's difficult to put ourselves in his shoes. And he's under the influence of Ativan.

"The clean-up attempt is absolutely laughable. The cut-up boots really makes no sense at all. He's alleged to have cut the boots and glued the soles to a second pair of shoes. Cut them up and then leaves them out to be seen. Drives his car with an ice scraper. These are not the actions of a man intending to murder his wife.

"It's a rush to judgment. The police made it, and they want you to make it."

Then Robin Lord told the jury that although the defense firmly believed Jonathan Nyce had not been proven guilty beyond a reasonable doubt, if they disagreed, they could consider passion/provocation manslaughter.

"This was not just any old affair," she said. "This was an affair with Enyo, who had many different names, many different Social Security numbers. There was a no-contact order.

"He planted the trees that Jonathan Nyce looked at. He had unprotected sex with Michelle Nyce, with no regard to his family. And all the time [Jonathan's] supporting her family. She had sex in the house. He's sending money to the Philippines to support her family.

"In conclusion, I'd like to leave you with this."

And at that point Robin Lord slowly walked over to a tape recorder, turning it on to the final part of Jonathan Nyce's confession to Detective Scull for the jury to hear again.

> *Detective Scull: Okay, was there anything else . . . you feel is relevant to what happened in the garage that night between you and Michelle?*

> *Nyce: All I can say is that I love my wife completely. I, I took the marriage vows very seriously, in sickness and in health, and I felt that she was in sickness and I was going to stand by her.*

At this point Jonathan Nyce broke down at the defense table, weeping uncontrollably.

> *In practical terms, I mean, she had this lover. I felt that if she would only stop and come back to the family, I would put this behind me. I'm sorry for this accident. I didn't mean for it to happen. I love her still. I*

wish I could spend my life with her, because I know
she was gonna pull through this eventually.

Then Robin Lord pointed straight at Jonathan Nyce, still
sobbing with his head in his hands, leaving these parting
words with the jury:

"If there is a simple, reasonable doubt existing in your
mind," she intoned, "as to the guilt of the defendant, you
must acquit."

After two hours and forty minutes on her feet, Lord sat
down and Judge Mathesius dismissed the jury for lunch.

At 1:40 p.m. Tom Meidt stood up for his summation of the
state's case. And not unexpectedly he presented a starkly
different portrait of the Nyce family situation. Meidt told the
jury that Jonathan Nyce had said a lot of bad things about his
wife in his statements to police.

"It's easy to do," he said. "The dead don't talk back."

He then urged the jury to use its "common sense," to dis-
cern the real truth of the matter.

"There are always two sides to the story," he said. "In this
case you're not going to hear Michelle's side, because he
murdered her.

"Let's look at the facts of the case. Michelle was having
an affair. That's undisputed. The motive for the defendant to
kill his wife is the *oldest* motive—infidelity. And in this
case, that's a clear motive."

But the assistant prosecutor told the jury that infidelity is
not an excuse for murder, and was what divorce courts were
designed for.

"[Michelle] was a human being, despite the fact she's
been bad-mouthed, besmirched. She was a human being that
has the right to life, just like anyone else. She was a mother.
She was a daughter. She was a wife."

Then Meidt led the jury through the night of Michelle's
death, pointing out various inconsistencies in Nyce's statements to police. When Michelle arrived home, Meidt told

the jury, her husband did not meet her at the car door to help her out.

First he had told police he had heard "crunching tires" on the driveway, but then realized it would not have given him time to get downstairs to the garage to assist Michelle out of the Land Cruiser.

"He realized he made a mistake," said Meidt. "Then the baby—five-year-old Samantha—needed a bottle. That places him in the kitchen."

Then the prosecutor led the jury through the state's version of events, leading up to Michelle Nyce's death.

"What really happened," Meidt explained, "is that she was out of the car and went into the house. They got into an argument about her coming home late. Her pattern of behavior is repeating itself."

The proof she had come into the house, said Meidt, was that she'd taken off her snow boots, and would never have been barefoot in the car on such a cold winter's night.

And, he told the jury, the packed suitcase was clear evidence that Michelle was walking out of the marriage.

"There were sweaters, pants, underwear," he said. "And in another bag was a toothbrush and toothpaste."

Meidt cited further evidence that the argument did not occur by the car door, as Nyce claimed. To prove his point, he showed the jury a photograph of Michelle's left arm, clearly revealing two rows of five little bruises, each of which had been marked with a circle.

"Look at the bruising on her left arm," he urged the jury. "Look at the finger marks. Grab and squeeze. The defendant grabbed her. This is a man six foot, four inches and two hundred forty pounds and Michelle is five foot, two inches and one hundred and forty pounds."

He told them that the suitcase was outside the Land Cruiser when Michelle had been killed, which was proved by it having blood all around it, and that after Nyce had murdered her, he had picked it up, placing it in the back seat.

But Jonathan Nyce had "slipped up" on several occasions, said the prosecutor, and his lies had finally caught up with him. One of his biggest mistakes was telling Detective Dan McKeown they had last argued about her leaving last night.

He said Nyce had known Michelle had restarted her affair with Enyo, and he had stewed on it for more than a week.

"The defendant's mindset," he told the jury. "This is probably a very intelligent man, who thought he was losing his wife to a gardener. He just couldn't believe that Michelle was going to leave him for someone like Miguel deJesus. He wasn't going to let her leave. And that, ladies and gentlemen, is why he killed her."

Meidt concluded his summation by reminding the jury of PSE&G worker Richard Archer's testimony on the first day of the trial, describing how he had discovered Michelle's frozen body in lonely Jacobs Creek.

"He looked in that window and it was like something out of a horror show," said the assistant prosecutor. "Well, the last minutes of Michelle Nyce's life were a horror show. Imagine her last thoughts.

"Michelle's not here to speak and tell her side of the story. So I would ask you to do justice on behalf of Michelle, by returning a guilty verdict."

On Wednesday morning Judge Bill Mathesius instructed the sixteen-member jury panel on the law before the random selection of the twelve who would deliberate and the four alternates, who would stand by in case of emergency.

"You've heard all the testimony," the judge told them. "You've heard very competent counsels offer their opinion and notions."

He then outlined what he called the "panorama of charges" they could consider. The judge told them that although Jonathan Nyce was charged with the murder of Michelle Nyce and tampering with evidence, they could also find him guilty of the lesser charges of aggravated manslaughter, reckless manslaughter and passion/provocation manslaughter.

He informed them that marital infidelity is one example

of a reasonable provocation that could drive someone to kill in the heat of passion. But in order for jurors to find the defendant guilty of this least serious charge, the state had to prove adequate provocation to have impassioned the defendant, and that he had not had reasonable time to cool off and calm down from before killing Michelle.

Then, after the court clerk drew straws, selecting the final eight men and four women who would decide the fate of Jonathan Nyce, Judge Mathesius addressed the panel for the last time, before dismissing them to the jury room to start deliberations.

"You are the judges of the facts," he told them. "You, and you alone, are the sole and executive judges of the evidence and the credibility of the witnesses."

And finally, Judge Mathesius told them to disregard Jonathan Nyce's not taking the stand in his own defense.

"It is his constitutional right to remain silent," he said. "You must not consider for any purpose or in any manner in arriving at your verdict, the fact that Jonathan Nyce did not testify."

At 11:00 a.m. the jury went to their room to begin deciding whether Jonathan Nyce had cold-bloodedly murdered his wife, or if it had been a tragic accident.

For the next two days—from 8:30 a.m. to 4:00 p.m.—the jury pored over the voluminous case, which had generated thousands of pages of discovery. Four Mercer County sheriff's officers were permanently stationed outside the jury room, along the corridor from the Ceremonial Court, at all times, in case the jurors wanted to question the judge on a point of law, or anything else connected with the case.

Inside the well-guarded jury room, jurors started their deliberations with sharply contrasting views of whether Jonathan Nyce was guilty of murder. At the beginning, one juror even wanted to acquit him of all charges.

"[It was] rocky at first," said juror Rob Thomson, a safety research assistant from Hamilton, New Jersey.

But then another juror, Martin Rexroad, applied people skills from his job in human resources to organize the jury and get everyone on the same page.

"This was a very intellectual jury," said Rexroad, who lives in West Windsor. "We all wanted to be able to reflect on the facts, be respectful of instructions."

Early Wednesday morning the jury requested a transcript of the entire trial, as well as a copy of the medical examiner's autopsy report. Judge Mathesius told them an entire transcript of the lengthy trial was unavailable and that Dr. Ahmad's report was not part of the evidence.

Princeton physicist Harlan Robins, 32, said he and the other jurors were unimpressed with the testimony of Mercer County Medical Examiner Dr. Ahmad. Later he would say she was "unconvincing," and apparently "confused" herself.

"By the end of the trial," he told Jonathan Miller of *The New York Times*, "no one had a clear idea of what happened in the garage that night."

As the delegated jury leader, Rexroad requested Post-it notes to be sent into the jury room, and the members spent the rest of the day developing flow-charts, making it easier to see the facts of the case now laid out in front of them. When they went home that night, they were getting closer to a unanimous decision.

During the long hours while the jury was deliberating, both counsels remained in their offices.

On Wednesday afternoon, a highly nervous Robin Lord met with a *Dateline NBC* producer to discuss a possible television interview with Jonathan Nyce. She showed the producer photographs of her client and his children, explaining that just six days before "the incident," he and Michelle had had a "lovey-dovey" night out in Philadelphia.

Every time the phone rang, Lord jumped, convinced that the jury would deliver a quick verdict.

At 4:00 p.m. Wednesday, after a total of twelve hours' deliberation, still not having reached a verdict, the jury asked Judge Mathesius to clarify his written instructions on aggravated manslaughter, and explain the difference between the words "possibility" and "probability."

After consulting with both counsels, the judge told them that "Possibility is an event that may or may not have happened," while "probability is an effect or a result that is more likely to follow its supposed course than not follow."

Then the judge dismissed them for the day, and left the courtroom. Jonathan Nyce and his parents remained behind in the public gallery.

Then suddenly, apparently at Robin Lord's behest, Emma Nyce, 77, gave an impromptu interview, breaking her silence for the first time since the trial had started. As she told reporters how devoted her son Jonathan had been to his wife, he sat nervously in the back of the court listening to every word.

"He wouldn't hurt a soul," she declared. "[Michelle] got everything she ever wanted. She never got a dozen roses, she got three dozen. He felt so sorry for people. The kids got pianos, music, drums. They got everything."

Jonathan Jr., who had attended every day of the trial, said he was sure it was "an accident" that had killed his daughter-in-law.

"It's been awfully hard," he said. "It was very painful to have my son accused of murder."

Then Emma Nyce was asked how her three grandchildren were, and she said that Jonathan and his family were "engulfed in a circle of love.

"The kids are good. They say, 'I love my dad. When can I have my dad?' I don't know what happened to [Michelle] that she did what she did, cheated on him."

Then out of nowhere Nyce's 80-year-old father began telling reporters how his son was always interested in medicine as a teenager.

"He did a lot of experiments," Jonathan Jr. said wistfully. "One day I came home and smelt something awful. He had a raccoon in a pot on the stove in Clorox, and was cooking it, because he wanted to see its skeleton . . ."

Then, before he could say any more, Robin Lord abruptly finished the interview. The following day, although the Trenton *Times* and the *Trentonian* carried the parents' press conference on their respective front pages, neither mentioned Jonathan Jr.'s raccoon anecdote.

38

Verdict

Just after 10:00 the next morning, there was a knock on the jury room door, and foreman Thomas Cooper handed Sheriff's Officer Pablo Santiago a brown envelope. Inside was a handwritten message, telling the judge that they had reached a unanimous verdict after nearly fourteen hours' deliberations, spread over three days. Officer Santiago was so excited that, after giving Judge Mathesius the envelope in his second-floor chambers, he rushed next door into the pressroom with the news.

"Verdict!" he said excitedly. "They've given the envelope!"

A few minutes later, the Ceremonial Courtroom began to fill up as news of the verdict spread like wildfire through the courthouse. There was extra security in the courtroom and everyone had to go through a metal detector at the door.

Jonathan Nyce, wearing his usual baggy gray suit, walked in with his attorney Robin Lord, and hugged his mother, waiting on the front row of the public gallery. Then, after shaking hands with his father, the apprehensive-looking defendant went up to the defense table. sat down and donned his spectacles.

Directly behind him, Mercer County Sheriff Kevin Larkin and one of his officers took up positions, ready to slap handcuffs on Nyce if he was found guilty.

Robin Lord, dressed in a pink suit, appeared jittery and less confident than usual, refusing to chat with reporters as she usually did before court. And then the poker-faced Assistant Prosecutor Tom Meidt and Doris Galuchie walked in, taking their places at the prosecution table, where they were joined by Detective Dan McKeown, his sister, Sergeant Karen Ortman and Detective Matt Norton.

The courtroom was a hive of activity as three television crews set up cameras to broadcast the eagerly awaited verdict, and reporters, notebooks at the ready, lined the three front rows of the public gallery.

Then Michelle's sister Melodia was escorted to her usual position next to the jury box by two victims' support workers, explaining that her father was working and could not attend.

At about 10:35 a.m. Judge Mathesius came into court and summoned the jury, who filed into their box a few minutes later, looking drained and exhausted from their long deliberations.

"Have you all reached a verdict?" asked Judge Mathesius.

"Yes," replied jury foreman Cooper.

"How do you find the defendant—guilty or not guilty of count one, murder?"

"Not guilty," said Cooper.

"Less aggravated manslaughter?" asked the judge.

"Not guilty."

"Reckless manslaughter?"

"Not Guilty."

"Passion/provocation manslaughter?"

"Guilty," said the foreman.

"How do you find the defendant on count two, tampering with physical evidence?" asked the judge.

"Guilty," said Cooper.

Then, as a stunned-looking Jonathan Nyce turned to Robin Lord for consolation, the judge polled each member of the jury to see if this was their decision, and one by one they said it was.

"Your dedication and perseverance and your extended effort over all these days must be appreciated by all," Judge Mathesius told the twelve jury members and the four alternates, who had watched the verdict from the public gallery.

Then Tom Meidt stood up, asking Judge Mathesius to revoke Nyce's $750,000 bail.

Overcome with emotion, a tearful Robin Lord dabbed her eyes with a handkerchief, as she pleaded with the judge to allow her client to remain free until his sentencing.

"He has children at home," she said. "He wants to properly say goodbye for a short period of time."

And she asked Judge Mathesius to lower Nyce's bail to $100,000, on condition he was electronically monitored.

"Allow him to put his affairs in order," she implored. "And say goodbye to his children."

But the judge disagreed.

"I've considered the circumstances," he told Lord. "The presumption of innocence no longer prevails. I'm going to revoke bond. Sentencing will be September ninth."

Then the white walrus-mustached Sheriff Larkin, wearing full uniform for the first time court-watchers could remember, handcuffed Jonathan Nyce's wrists to take him into custody. Looking lost and stunned by the verdict, he slowly turned around to where his parents were sitting, as Robin Lord hugged him.

"Hi, Mom," he said, making eye contact with Emma Nyce, as she broke down sobbing.

He then nodded forlornly at his father, saying he was OK.

On the way out of court, *Trentonian* reporter Scott Frost asked Nyce about the verdict.

"I did nothing intentional," he replied, as he was escorted into the elevator, to be placed in a basement holding cell until he could be transported to Mercer County Correction Center.

Inside the courtroom, Michelle's sister Melodia tearfully

complained to reporters that her sister had not been given justice.

"He killed my sister!" she sobbed. "I wanted murder—no passion/provocation. I wanted life in prison—it's only five to ten years."

A few minutes later Mercer County Prosecutor Joseph Bocchini and his team held a press conference in the basement, across the corridor from where Nyce was being held.

"The jury verdict is in," declared Bocchini, who had come from his father's deathbed to see the verdict. "Our office is satisfied that the jury decision is final. The case is over."

Both Tom Meidt and his prosecution partner Doris Galuchie expressed disappointment in the jury's decision to convict on the lesser passion/provocation manslaughter charge.

"We thought we had the elements for a murder verdict," said Meidt. "We respect their decision, but we're disappointed for the family of Michelle. The jurors didn't hear her story as much as the defendant's. But we can understand why the jury arrived at the decision they did."

Galuchie said the jury had not been able to learn about all the friction between Nyce and Michelle leading up to her death.

"We know there were some heated arguments," she said. "I wouldn't want to set his temper off."

And while her client languished in the holding cell below court, contemplating the possibility of spending the next decade of his life behind bars, Robin Lord and her team toasted the verdict with Mumm's champagne in plastic foam cups.

Later she told reporters that she had mixed feelings about the jury's decision, forecasting that her client would be out in five years.

"Obviously I'm disappointed," she said. "I was hoping they would find him not guilty of all the homicide charges.

However, if they have to find him guilty, this is the best we could hope for."

"She's world-class," chimed in Lord's legal partner Pat Whelan.

A few blocks away, after the yellow Mercer County jury bus had dropped them off in a parking lot, several jurors discussed how they'd reached their decision with *New York Times* reporter Jonathan Miller.

"I think actually, he overheated . . . [in an] angry moment of excessive force," said 51-year-old juror pharmacologist Kip Dresdner. "He used excessive force, and she hit the ground, and that's a cement floor."

His jury colleague, Lynn Michaels, a 35-year-old offshore fund marketer from East Windsor, said she didn't believe Nyce had planned to murder Michelle.

"I got the impression," she said, "that he was one of those men with these intellectual abilities, he was not very proficient in dealing with people, especially the opposite sex."

"We wavered on all the charges," juror Harlan Robins said. "But the higher charges were dropped almost immediately," focusing not on the murder charge but on passion/provocation manslaughter instead.

Most jurors spoken to cited M.E. Dr. Raafat Ahmad as the weakest link in the state's case.

"We had a hard time giving credibility to the medical examiner's reports," explained juror Robins.

The following day Teodoro Riviera announced his intention to continue his fight to gain joint custody of his three grandchildren. More than a year earlier, a family court judge had quietly granted full custody to their Uncle Michael, who was looking after them with his wife in Pennsylvania.

When Melodia Ragenil arrived in New Jersey to attend the trial, she had contacted Michael Nyce, asking to see her two nephews and niece for the first time. Initially he said she would have to meet them at his house, but Melodia refused, saying she would not have any privacy there.

Eventually Nyce agreed to allow her to meet the children at the food hall in the King of Prussia Mall in Pennsylvania.

"They're great," said Melodia. "They said, 'Auntie, you look just like my mom.' Samantha hugged me and was always holding my hand. She said she really missed her mom, and so did the two boys.

"I was asking them if they wanted to visit the Philippines, and they said, 'Yes, Auntie, we want to go.'"

Melodia said she'd talked to them sensitively about Michelle and what had happened.

"They did talk about my sister," she said. "I don't know if they know everything, but they really miss their mom."

39

"It's All About Jonathan"

For the next two months, Jonathan Nyce remained in protective custody at the Mercer County Correction Center, off Route 29 just north of Titusville. He had sunk into a deep depression, asking his family not to visit him until he sent for them. Every day he sent letters and cards to his children, writing them poems and stories. They appeared to be his only reason for living.

"He's pretty hurt," said his mother. "He doesn't want us to see him in there. I don't know how he feels."

His parents, still protesting his innocence, said the trial had been very hard on the family.

"I wouldn't want our worst enemy to go through what we went through," said Emma Nyce. "It was tough on all of us, and I actually lost forty-five pounds, but I'm starting to get it back now."

Emma said she felt terrible for her oldest son and the "horrible" injustice he'd had to endure.

"He's such a kind, gentle man," she said. "Such an intelligent man. And he worked so hard to get where he was."

On Thursday, September 22, when two officers led him

back into the Ceremonial Courtroom for sentencing, Jonathan Nyce looked a broken man. His usual business suit had been replaced by a bright orange inmate jumpsuit, with heavy chains hanging down from his shackled wrists and ankles.

The prosecution had flown Melodia Ragenil back from the Philippines to address the court on behalf of Michelle, along with her father and Larissa Soos. And Nyce's parents, brothers and other family members were there in force to show their support.

At 10:00 a.m. Judge Bill Mathesius entered the court to deliver the sentencing, in what would be the last criminal trial he would preside over. He had already started his new job in the civil division. Today he and his long-time antagonist Robin Lord even appeared to be going out of their way to be cordial to each other.

"This is the day of sentencing for Dr. Nyce," the judge told the packed court, "who was found guilty by a jury of passion/provocation manslaughter, which operates to excuse culpability for the more serious manslaughter sentence."

After thanking Robin Lord for the "excellent arguments" in her submission, requesting a minimal custodial sentence, he said he had read letters received from the defendant and his family, as well as a photograph of him and his children.

"The main theme of the letters is the accidental nature of the events that took the life of Michelle," he told the court. "These documents emphasize that Jonathan Nyce was a kind and gentle person, and they all express concern for his children. I believe their comments are heartfelt."

Then Doris Galuchie stood up to ask the judge to impose the maximum sentence of 11 years for both counts.

"If this court was to impose minimal sentence for the offenses," she said, "that sends a message that proves that if you are impassioned and kill your wife, you're going to do four years' jail time. That is ludicrous."

The assistant prosecutor argued that Nyce's achievements were entirely irrelevant to the sentence, as under New Jersey law, it was the nature of the offense and not the offender that should be taken into account.

"The fact that he's a Ph.D. and is a pharmaceutical exec-utive, has nothing to do with him killing his wife," she said.

But Judge Mathesius disagreed, saying he felt it certainly was a mitigating factor, and the defendant's character was not something to be totally ignored. Then Galuchie asked the judge if Nyce's having a Ph.D. meant he should be sentenced more leniently than a "high school dropout?"

"Is a defendant whose life is largely devoted to eleemosy-nary concerns [to] be considered differently from a person who's a ne'er-do-well, bum, a person who goes [to] prison?"

"The answer to that is yes," said the judge, raising his voice in answer to his own question. "So move on. I understand you."

"Judge," replied the assistant prosecutor. "We received no evidence that this defendant is solely responsible for any life-saving drugs. At the time of the offense he wasn't saving lives. He was an unemployed father, who was, quite frankly, taking an interest in his children for the first time."

"That's too much!" erupted Jonathan Nyce from the defense table, moving forward in his seat and glaring at Galuchie, as Robin Lord clasped his shoulder to restrain him. "That's too much, Your Honor," he repeated.

Infuriated by the outburst, the judge turned on Galuchie, as if she were responsible.

"I don't need such a psychological profile of the defendant," he thundered. "I don't need the psychoanalysis. I don't need the in-depth Rorschach tests. Give me a little credit."

Then, when the judge warned he had already read all the statements from the Riviera family and did not want repetition when they were delivered in court, Galuchie said that someone had to speak up for the victim in this case.

"Judge," she said, "she has to be heard. The jury was not allowed to hear anything about Michelle Nyce. [She] did care for her children. She was not out partying with people every night, as the defense said. Michelle Nyce was a good mother, she took care of her kids.

"This man didn't even bother to pay for his wife's funeral . . ."

"I was in jail!" screamed Jonathan Nyce across the court at the assistant prosecutor. "Jesus!"

"These kinds of outbursts are unnecessary," snapped the judge. "It's a disgrace."

Then Larissa Soos stood up to talk about her best friend.

"Honorable Judge Mathesius," she began, close to tears. "On January sixteenth, 2004, I lost a very dear friend, Michelle Nyce, whom I laughed with, shared stories with, made future plans with. Not only did I realize that my dear friend was gone forever, I also have to deal with an awful fact that she was brutally killed by her husband, whom I thought adored her."

She then told of the "heavy burden" she had undertaken in making Michelle's funeral arrangements, after the Nyce family "abruptly" decided not to. She spoke about being the lone custodian of preserving her friend's memories, which had been "tarnished" by the media during the trial.

"Her children were her life," she told the judge. "She was an active mom. She drove them everywhere—karate, soccer, baseball, swimming, piano, saxophone lessons, ballet lessons and numerous play dates. She planned all the children's parties, as well as Jonathan's company parties."

Finally she turned around to address her one-time friend Jonathan Nyce, who sat stoically at the defense table, without a trace of emotion on his face.

"Jonathan," she told him, "I know that you loved Michelle and your three kids. However, my questions to you now are: One) Are your kids really better off without their mom and dad? Two) Did you ever think there were better options that night? There is counseling and divorce. You and Michelle could still be part of your children's lives today."

Then she asked Judge Mathesius to sentence Nyce to the maximum penalty for killing Michelle.

"Unlike Jonathan," she said, "Michelle did not and will never have the chance to see her children grow, graduate from high school, go to college, get married and see her grandchildren.

"She died so young and so tragically and did not even

have a chance to say goodbye! Most importantly, Michelle can never have a chance to explain to her children her version of events, unlike Jonathan, who is alive and will still get that chance."

Then Melodia Ragenil walked to the front of the court to speak about her sister publicly, for the first time since the trial had begun.

"We have a simple and humble life in the Philippines," she started, sounding composed. "But we never told Jonathan or my sister that we were starving. The one thing that was never mentioned is the fact that Jonathan is a jealous and possessive man. My sister was not able to do what she wants. She was offered a number of modeling jobs, but she knew Jonathan will never approve. Also, she was never able to use her personal trainer's certification, since Jonathan does not allow her to train men."

Then, breaking into tears on the stand, Melodia eloquently petitioned the judge to "preserve the honor and dignity" of her big sister.

"My sister or any other women in this world do not deserve to be brutally killed by their husbands," she sobbed, "just because they no longer want to be married. There is counseling, divorce therapy sessions—but not murder. Murder is not the answer. I ask that you sentence Jonathan to the full extent of the law and I wish and pray that Alex, Trevor and Samantha will be guided by the love we all have for my beautiful and loving sister, Michelle."

Then Michelle's father Teodoro Riviera's statement was read out by a victims' advocate, as he stared at his son-in-law from the front row of the public gallery.

"Jonathan," he wrote, "I went home to the Philippines for only one week, then you hurt and killed my daughter. I trusted you with my dear daughter, I would have done everything to protect Michelle from you. I would have sacrificed my life instead of hers."

He said that his daughter's life "revolved around your lies," and that he had even lied about his age at their wedding.

"Michelle put up with all your lies and rules for the sake of the children," he wrote. "You never even allowed Michelle to bring her children to meet their relatives in the Philippines."

He too asked Judge Mathesius to send Nyce to jail for the maximum time permitted.

"No amount of time spent in prison will ever bring back my dear daughter," he wrote. "However, Your Honor, please give me some peace of mind that Michelle did not die in vain."

Then Jonathan Nyce's cousin Barbara Walko stood up on behalf of the family, pleading for the judge to be merciful. As she told the court that she had been born the same year as he was and how close they had always been, Jonathan Nyce burst into tears.

"We were raised in an environment," she told the judge, "where our entire family would get together every Sunday at my grandparents'. We grew up with a strong respect for our family."

Walko said Jonathan's parents wanted the judge to know that Jonathan was "a very good boy, very gentle," who never caused any trouble.

"They also wanted you to know that he and Michelle were very very happy. That Michelle was loved and accepted in our family. Everyone was devoted to Michelle."

She said her cousin Jonathan had always been there for any member of the family in trouble, or whenever he was needed.

"This trial has hurt us all," she said. "It's been very difficult for those of us who know him very well. This trial has been really long and has spoken to just a moment in Jonathan's life. Those of us who know him best know this was an aberration of Jonathan's life. Please consider all his life and please show mercy, so Jonathan and his children can begin to heal."

Finally, after a rallying pat on the back from Lord, Jonathan Nyce stood up at the defense table, to address Judge Mathesius and make his first public comments since his arrest.

"I love Michelle," he began in a soft, harrowing voice, straining his wrists in the shackles to make the point. "I still love her."

Then after a long silence to compose himself, he continued.

"I helped her with everything. I supported her in every way. I helped her with her citizenship. I helped build her family homes."

Then in a rambling stream-of-consciousness oration, he told the judge what he claimed to have done over the years for Michelle and her family. Portraying himself as their savior, he said he had moved the entire family fifty miles inland, probably saving their lives when a typhoon hit Manila Bay eighteen months earlier.

"And I did all this because I love Michelle so much."

As Melodia broke down in tears and began shaking her head in dismay in the public gallery, Nyce painted a picture of her family as starving squatters, living in squalor on stilted shacks over Manila Bay. He told the judge that he single-handedly had been their selfless champion and benefactor.

"I remember in February 2003," he told the court, "I went to the Philippines for the first time in thirteen years. Michelle and I wanted to see the things that we had built there. And being a professor, I'd brought my telescope, which—I set it up in the playground. And I felt wonderful showing all these children the rings of Saturn through the telescope. And we had a clear view of Jupiter."

But at no time did he address the circumstances of Michelle's death, his involvement in it, or show the least bit of remorse for what he had done.

"I wanted to be her hero," he sobbed to the judge. "These are all expressions of my love for Michelle. I loved her beyond any words I can say."

Finally as the tearful defendant sat down, Judge Mathesius prepared to pass sentence on him.

"Rarely has there been a peer judged by a peer jury," said the judge. "The verdict was . . . perfect in accordance with what this court saw the circumstances were. The defendant, in the simplest circumstances, flew into a rage and got into a bitter tussle with Michelle and killed her right where she'd been on the floor. His conclusion, which as it turned out was appropriate, was that his wife was having an affair with a man he was aware of."

wish I could spend my life with her, because I know
she was gonna pull through this eventually.

Then Robin Lord pointed straight at Jonathan Nyce, still
sobbing with his head in his hands, leaving these parting
words with the jury:

"If there is a simple, reasonable doubt existing in your
mind," she intoned, "as to the guilt of the defendant, you
must acquit."

After two hours and forty minutes on her feet, Lord sat
down and Judge Mathesius dismissed the jury for lunch.

At 1:40 p.m. Tom Meidt stood up for his summation of the
state's case. And not unexpectedly he presented a starkly
different portrait of the Nyce family situation. Meidt told the
jury that Jonathan Nyce had said a lot of bad things about his
wife in his statements to police.

"It's easy to do," he said. "The dead don't talk back."

He then urged the jury to use its "common sense," to dis-
cern the real truth of the matter.

"There are always two sides to the story," he said. "In this
case you're not going to hear Michelle's side, because he
murdered her.

"Let's look at the facts of the case. Michelle was having
an affair. That's undisputed. The motive for the defendant to
kill his wife is the *oldest* motive—infidelity. And in this
case, that's a clear motive."

But the assistant prosecutor told the jury that infidelity is
not an excuse for murder, and was what divorce courts were
designed for.

"[Michelle] was a human being, despite the fact she's
been bad-mouthed, besmirched. She was a human being that
has the right to life, just like anyone else. She was a mother.
She was a daughter. She was a wife."

Then Meidt led the jury through the night of Michelle's
death, pointing out various inconsistencies in Nyce's statements to police. When Michelle arrived home, Meidt told

As Nyce swayed back and forth, looking unsteady, the judge told him he would be credited with 274 days for time served in custody, and that he had forty-five days to appeal.

"Miss Lord, I'm sure, will advise you about this aspect," he said.

Then Judge Mathesius concluded the sentencing and Jonathan Nyce was led out of the courtroom, to start serving his jail sentence.

After watching the sentencing from the prosecution table, Mercer County Prosecutor Joseph Bocchini was outraged, telling reporters, "That guy's the luckiest SOB in the world! Mathesius is a good judge, but I just think he totally missed it on this one."

His two assistant prosecutors, Tom Meidt and Doris Galuchie, were also angry about the judge's light sentence, which meant that Nyce could be freed on parole in less than five years.

"It was all about Jonathan Nyce and the good things he's done," said Galuchie. "Maybe he's bucking for an Oscar."

And Tom Meidt said Nyce's self-serving speech was yet another indication of his cold-bloodedness.

"I've never seen such a lack of remorse," he said. "I've never seen a defendant not say they were sorry for causing the death in some manner."

Across the courtroom Robin Lord said she didn't believe her client deserved to go to jail at all, but conceded that things could be far worse.

"I am extremely pleased that he's not doing life in prison," she said. "But am I happy he's going to jail for the next five years? No."

EPILOGUE

Less than two hours after his sentencing, Jonathan Nyce was escorted into Robin Lord's office across the street, to give his first-ever interview to *Dateline NBC* and this author. His orange jumpsuit had been replaced by a business suit, and he wore a bulletproof waistcoat for his own protection, as he was led into Lord's office by three sheriff's officers.

Over the next hour-and-a-quarter, Nyce would face some difficult questions. As part of the ground rules, in an arrangement negotiated by Lord, her client could not be questioned about the night of Michelle's death. But for the first time, Nyce would face hardball questions about his version of their marriage and the alleged extortion attempt by Enyo.

First he was asked how he was going to serve a minimum five years in jail, probably in general population.

"It's going to be difficult," he conceded. "I've been torn away from my children, who I love with my own heart, and love me, for something I didn't do."

He was asked what his three children knew about their mother's death.

"I've told them the truth and they know me very well," he said. "They know that I would never harm their mother."

Then he was asked to clarify exactly how he'd met Michelle, and whether she was a mail-order bride. For the first time he admitted concocting the story of tripping over her on a Hawaiian beach, but claimed it had been her idea to do so, not wanting the fact that she had worked in Olongapo City to be misinterpreted.

"She wanted to make it very clear," he claimed, "that there wasn't any chance that she'd be mistaken for a [prostitute]. And that mail-order bride thing is outrageous and untrue." Later, Teodoro Riviera would confirm that Michelle had worked in Olongapo, selling dresses, at about the time she had started writing to Jonathan. He stressed that not all jobs in Olongapo were bad.

Time and again during the interview Nyce spoke of his love for his dead wife, repeatedly boasting about everything he claimed to have done for her and her family. He lit up with confidence as he described starting EpiGenesis and building it into a multi-million-dollar company, before getting fired in a board takeover.

In hindsight, he conceded, maybe he had loved Michelle too much, and been too generous, after moving to New Jersey.

"But I loved her," he said sadly. "And I felt that this is what a wife should be able to do—to go into her house and buy the furniture and put chandeliers in every room."

He kept harping back to his hatred of Enyo, and how he was a victim of a miscarriage of justice by the Hopewell Township Police Department, something he planned to put right at his appeal.

Once again he told of his alleged half-a-million-dollar extortion attempt by Enyo.

"You know the police kissed off your complaint," stated *Dateline NBC*'s reporter Dennis Murphy. "They thought it was maybe made up."

"Absolutely not," snapped Nyce. "That's a ridiculous statement, and the reason that they're saying that is to protect themselves. But that's a question for my appeal."

According to Nyce, Michelle had told him that Enyo had attempted to recruit her in a murder plot against him, so they could collect on his life insurance.

"I told the police everything," said Nyce.

"They continued to not believe you," Murphy pointed out.

"It's even more bizarre," said Nyce, warming to the subject. "After Michelle broke up with Enyo, he began to stalk her. She complained to me about it, and I even caught him parked outside my house."

Towards the end of the interview, he was asked why he now refused to discuss what had happened inside the garage the night of Michelle's death.

"It's our point of appeal," said Nyce, as Robin Lord stepped in, saying he could not comment further on the advice of his counsel.

"In the appeal you will learn the facts which did not become at all evident in this trial," he explained.

Finally he was asked if there would be another untold story of how Michelle Nyce had met her death.

"Absolutely," he declared. "There's no question. I do not expect to be in jail for that period of time. I expect to win my appeal, and actually I expect to put other people in jail, who lied to put me here. You can mark my words on that."

The following day there was an outcry that Mercer County Sheriff Kevin Larkin had allowed Jonathan Nyce to give the interview. The Mercer County Prosecutor's Office, who had known nothing about the interview, launched an immediate investigation.

Accusations flew that Nyce was receiving special V.I.P. treatment, by being allowed to don a business suit straight after being sentenced for killing his wife, and then give a national television and book interview.

"That's just outrageous," said Judge Mathesius, when he was told. "When I left that courtroom he was in the hands of the sheriff's department."

But on Friday, Sheriff Larkin apologized, saying he was wrong to have allowed the interview.

"In retrospect," he told the Trenton *Times*, "it was probably an error in judgment, and it's my responsibility, and I take the hit for it."

Meanwhile Jonathan Nyce was back in Mercer County Correction Center awaiting transfer to the intermediate Central Reception and Assignment Facility, near the grounds of the Trenton Psychiatric Hospital, where it will be decided where he should serve his sentence.

Made in the USA
Las Vegas, NV
23 June 2023